The Case for Rural America

RURAL STUDIES

Conner Bailey and Jennifer Sherman, editors

Rural Studies publishes books on a wide range of social issues with the goal of advancing the scholarly, political, and public discourse on rural spaces and the people in them. The titles in this series seek to foreground important experiences and processes concerning rural life, communities, and the environment in an effort to improve the lives of rural people at the local and global levels.

A complete list of books published in Rural Studies is available at https://uncpress.org/series/rural-studies/.

The Case for Rural America

J. Tom Mueller

The University of North Carolina Press CHAPEL HILL

Set in Merope Basic by Westchester Publishing Services
Manufactured in the United States of America

Library of Congress Cataloging-in-Publication Data
Names: Mueller, J. Tom author
Title: The case for rural America / J. Tom Mueller, PhD.
Other titles: Rural studies series (Chapel Hill, NC)
Description: Chapel Hill : The University of North Carolina Press, [2025] |
Series: Rural studies series | Includes bibliographical references and index.
Identifiers: LCCN 2025015419 | ISBN 9781469691510 cloth |
ISBN 9781469691527 paperback | ISBN 9781469683126 epub | ISBN 9781469691534 pdf
Subjects: LCSH: Rural development—United States | United States—Rural conditions | BISAC:
SOCIAL SCIENCE / Sociology / Rural | POLITICAL SCIENCE / Public Policy / Economic Policy
Classification: LCC HN90.C6 M84 2025 | DDC 307.1/40973—dc23/eng/20250613
LC record available at https://lccn.loc.gov/2025015419

Cover art ©smolskyevgeny/Adobe Stock.

This book will be made open access within three years of publication thanks to Path to Open, a program developed in partnership between JSTOR, the American Council of Learned Societies (ACLS), the University of Michigan Press, and the University of North Carolina Press to bring about equitable access and impact for the entire scholarly community, including authors, researchers, libraries, and university presses around the world. Learn more at https://about.jstor.org/path-to-open/.

For product safety concerns under the European Union's General Product Safety Regulation (EU GPSR), please contact gpsr@mare-nostrum.co.uk or write to the University of North Carolina Press and Mare Nostrum Group B.V., Mauritskade 21D, 1091 GC Amsterdam, The Netherlands.

Contents

Illustrations

Acknowledgments

This book represents the culmination of years spent living in, traveling through, and studying rural America. While I was born and raised in a city, my father and his family had rural origins, and I spent my teenage summers working at a camp in northwest Missouri, where I stood out as "the city kid." The culture shock of this new environment for a fourteen-year-old was intense, but it opened my eyes to the realities of rural life at a formative time. These experiences led to my migration to Montana for college—where I spent much of my time out in rural areas and was fortunate to take a field semester focused on rural livelihoods and working landscapes. In turn, I spent my time working, traveling, and living in the rural American West as an outdoor educator and itinerant rock climber. After moving to Penn State for graduate school, I had the opportunity to experience a new kind of rural America in the ridges and valleys of central Pennsylvania. My time in central Pennsylvania consisted of fieldwork in the state forests, an education in rural sociology, and a growing interest in rural development or the lack thereof. I convey this brief personal history to show that this book has been the product of innumerable influences and people across rural and urban America, many of whom I cannot thank adequately in the limited space here. That said, some specific thanks and acknowledgments are in order.

Although the ideas and arguments in this book had been building over the course of my years in graduate school and my initial time as a new assistant professor, it was not until I chatted with my dear friend and research collaborator Matt Brooks at the 2022 Population Association of America meeting that I actually thought seriously about writing any of it down. It was Matt who told me to take the arguments I was making and do something with them. While that initially meant another theory paper, it quickly became clear that a longer treatment was necessary. I am forever grateful to Matt, for his encouragement initially and his continued support throughout this process.

This work is heavily indebted to the Department of Rural Sociology at Penn State. I cannot thank them enough for allowing me to transition my PhD to rural sociology while also exposing me to the ideas and concepts that are found throughout this work. I want to thank Kathryn Brasier for lighting the spark of sociology for me, Leif Jensen for exposing me to critical perspectives on development, and Brian Thiede for his role in helping me become the kind of rural demographer I wanted to be. Most importantly, I want to thank Ann Tickamyer for taking me under her wing when I was a somewhat lost graduate student who just wanted to try and understand natural resource development in rural America. It is hard to overstate how much our weekly chats about sociology, theory, and academia shaped this work and myself.

I am also indebted to the departments I have worked in during this process. The sociology faculty at Utah State University provided me with a truly welcoming experience as a new professor during the COVID-19 pandemic; the Department of Geography and Environmental Sustainability at the University of Oklahoma provided me with the freedom to pursue this effort; and the Department of Population Health at the University of Kansas Medical Center welcomed me back to my hometown and immediately showed me that making the move was the right decision. Finally, I must also acknowledge the support of my department chairs — Scott Greene at the University of Oklahoma and Simon Craddock Lee at the University of Kansas Medical Center — who gave me the essential support I needed to pursue a more long-term unfunded project such as this.

Getting a book published is not easy. As an academic who had only ever written articles, this endeavor was new to me. It is only because Conner Bailey and Jennifer Sherman, editors of the Rural Studies Series, believed in me and this book that it is seeing the light of day. Further, I am immensely grateful to Lucas Church, my editor at the University of North Carolina Press, for both his support and role in guiding this book along the publication process. I also would like to thank my two anonymous reviewers for strengthening this work considerably. Although we did not necessarily agree on many points, their comments, feedback, and suggestions pushed me to strengthen and improve the book you now hold.

This project was a labor of love and was written during the most tumultuous time in my personal life to date. I am forever grateful to those who were there through everything. Without their support, this work would never have been published. Lizz, Geronimo, Beulah, Matt, The Greatfellas, the fantasy football crew, friends from the climbing gym, you matter more than you know.

Lastly, I must thank my parents, Anne and David, both gone far too soon. Their support of my many pursuits was unconditional and has helped me so much in my life. I miss them dearly.

The Case for Rural America

Introduction

Rural America, what remains of it in the 2020s, is at a crossroads. Down one path, it will continue to dwindle away through urbanization and out-migration, and down the other, it will find a way to stabilize and persist. As rural areas either become urban or are incorporated into nearby metropolitan areas, we have seen a dramatic reduction in the portion of the country still counted as rural since 1980.[1] At the same time, we have also seen persistent rural out-migration, a decrease in births in rural areas, a transition away from traditional rural industries, and an increase in mortality due to the aging rural population and rising midlife mortality rates—stemming from the opioid crisis, economic insecurity, and other factors.[2] When this decline is considered alongside persistently high levels of poverty, inequality, and limited economic mobility in many rural parts of the United States, it is unsurprising that there have been increasing calls to "save" rural America through sustainable rural economic development. This call—although certainly well-intentioned—has layered within it numerous contextual and conceptual factors that complicate what seems like an otherwise straightforward goal. In fact, it is likely these calls would not send us down the path toward stabilization but would instead lead us to an even quicker loss of what remains of rural America.

Although a noble goal, the very idea of sustainable rural economic development carries with it two fundamental issues that, alongside broader issues of contemporary capitalism in the United States, will be critiqued and explored in this book. First, the concept of sustainable rural economic development represents a fallacy. When an area is developed from an economic standpoint—meaning conventional approaches to economic development anchored in linear models of growth—it moves from a lower level to a higher level of development. In general, this means a rural place becomes more urban. This transition from rural to urban is characterized by increasing population density, the expansion of infrastructure, increases in the number and diversity of industrial activities, integration into other labor markets, and increasing access to urban amenities. While this transition may be viewed by some as a positive outcome, the rural area we were trying to sustain has now been fundamentally altered and lost. The long-run outcome of this push for development is the overall urbanization of rural places. This means, by definition, that we cannot have long-term sustainable rural economic development because this form of development actively removes the rural qualities we are trying to preserve in the first place. Thus, the whole idea that sustainable rural economic development can save rural places *as they currently are or used to be* is likely wrongheaded and may lead to outcomes not actually desired by those pushing for development to begin with.

The second core issue baked into contemporary rural economic development research and practice is the assumption made by many scholars, practitioners, and policymakers that rural places *should* be saved. Although many people may share this assumption, its justification is not obvious on its face, and it is a belief that fundamentally rests upon values and political priorities. Once we consider the nature of this assumption, we have to face the questions: What is lost if rural towns disappear? What is gained if rural towns are no longer incorporated? Should rural places becoming urban be viewed as the ultimate rural success story? Additionally, there is the question of which rural places should receive resources to foster development. Often, it is clear that the intent is not to save all of rural America but a certain kind of rural America. This is a fraught and complex issue because what we think of as "rural America," while full of many valuable social, cultural, economic, and environmental characteristics, is a social construction that has been shaped through history. Thus, our social construction of rural America is shaped not only by positive elements of history and the strength of rural communities but also by elements of white supremacy, Indigenous genocide, forced migration, slavery, classism, and environmental destruction, among other social forces. As such, regardless of their intent, sustainable rural economic development efforts that do not grapple with these questions are likely to exacerbate existing injustices throughout the United States.

While the points made above offer a stark overview of the factors motivating this book, readers familiar with rural America and rural development writ large will note that lying underneath these arguments is a bed of nuance. For example, the focus here is on foundational issues with rural *economic* development as typically practiced—an approach largely tied to linear models of economic growth. But development can take many forms. Community development, for example, eschews a focus on economic growth and instead focuses on developing community capacities and social and cultural capital.[3] Further, the term "rural" is not as straightforward as it seems. How do we decide what counts, and what does it mean for a place to no longer be rural?

It is this very nuance and complexity that will be explored throughout this work. While these complicated issues of rurality, development, capitalism, and policy will be addressed in detail in the following chapters, in what remains of this introduction we will see the broad contours of rural America today, as well as an outline of the larger argument to come.

Rural America in the 2020s

As noted, the geographic extent of rural America is far less today than it was forty years ago. This loss from 1980 to today is illustrated by the maps of the contiguous United States in map 0.1, where the shaded counties reflect the extent of rural America in each time period. Using the metropolitan (i.e., urban) and nonmetropolitan (i.e., rural) definitions of the Office of Management and Budget, we can see that in 1980, of the roughly 3,140 US counties, 2,402 were classified as rural or nonmetropolitan.[4] By the 2020s, that number declined to 1,956. Visually, we can see that this loss of rural counties has occurred in pockets nationwide, with an increase in the unshaded metropolitan counties found in all regions. That said, the clearest visual impact has been on the eastern half of the United States. This nationwide decline in areas classified as rural highlights the uneven patterns of urbanization and stagnation found across the United States over the past forty years. Rural places that have prospered have tended to be reclassified as urban, or metropolitan, while less economically successful rural areas have maintained their rural status—even if not a high level of well-being.[5]

Although certainly a nationwide trend, it is not as if there has been a singular rural experience over the past forty years. Instead, what we find across rural America is dramatic variation in patterns of urbanization, population growth, and well-being. To further illustrate the complexities at play, consider four counties, all classified as rural in 1980, that have followed remarkably different trajectories:

• *Washington County, Utah*—Located in the southwestern corner of Utah and home to the city of St. George, Washington County is an emergent county that developed from a rural county into an urban county absent the influence of an immediately neighboring metropolitan area. Rising from a population of just 26,065 in 1980 to 180,279 in 2020, the county has seen a decline in poverty over time, with the rate dropping from 15.8 percent in 1980

1980

2020

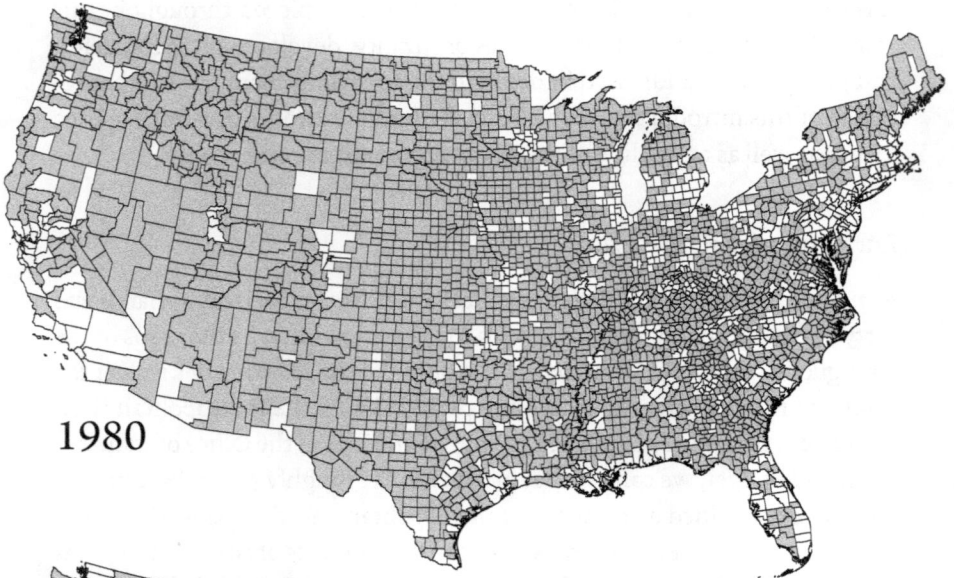

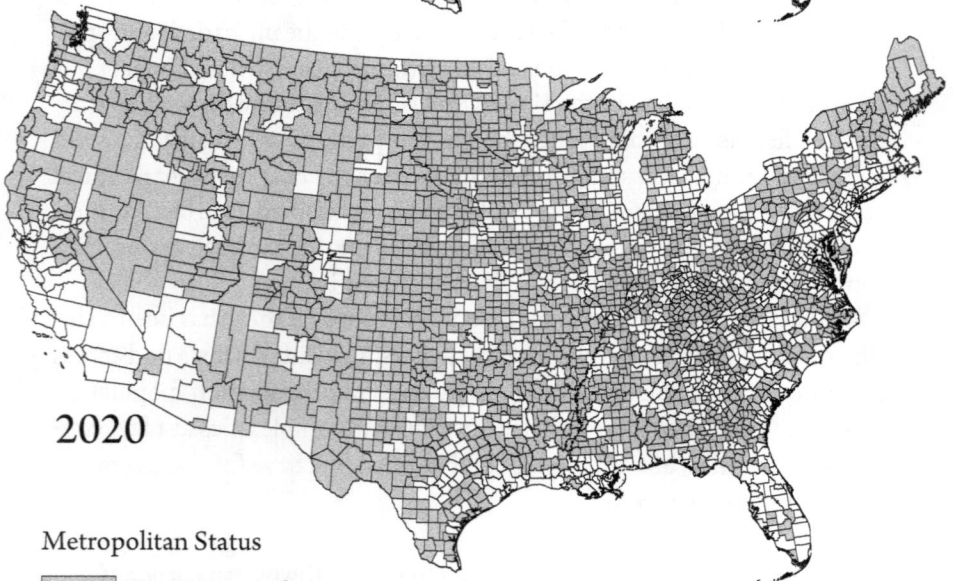

Metropolitan Status

Non-Metropolitan

Metropolitan

MAP 0.1 Map of metropolitan and nonmetropolitan America, 1980 and 2020 (national rate = 13.0 percent) to 8.8 percent in 2020 (national rate = 12.5 percent).[6] As the county has urbanized, the health of residents has improved, with the age-adjusted all-cause mortality rate dropping from 794.0 per hundred thousand in 1980 (national rate = 1,038.7) to 606.8 in 2020 (national rate = 775.3).[7] Similar to much of rural America, the population in Washington County has grown older over time, with the median age rising from 24.8 in 1980 to 37.6 in 2020. The county has also grown in ethnic diversity over the past forty years. While the county was 97.5 percent non-Latino white in 1980, in 2020, it was 81.8 percent non-Latino white and 11.4 percent Latino.

- *Butler County, Pennsylvania* — This county in western Pennsylvania grew from a population of 147,912 in 1980 to 193,763 in 2020. Although it is already a neighboring county to the Pittsburgh area, it was not considered as part of the Pittsburgh metropolitan area until 1990. Poverty in Butler County was just 7.2 percent in 1980 and only rose to 7.9 percent by 2020. Health in the county has improved over time, with the age-adjusted all-cause mortality rate dropping from 993.7 per hundred thousand in 1980 to 787.2 in 2020. Butler County has also aged over time, moving from a median age of 29.7 in 1980 to 43.6 in 2020. The county has only diversified slightly, dropping from 98.8 percent non-Latino white in 1980 to 92 percent in 2020.

- *Dillon County, South Carolina* — This relatively small county in eastern South Carolina has experienced some of the lowest relative population change since 1980. The population of Dillon County was 31,083 in 1980 and 28,292 in 2020. Dillon County has faced persistent struggles, with a very high poverty rate of 30.0 percent in 1980, which rose to 31.6 percent by 2020. In step with this trend, mortality rates remain high in Dillon County. All-cause age-adjusted mortality was 1,191.3 per hundred thousand in 1980, and it only fell to 1,091.6 by 2020. Population aging in Dillon County has been pronounced, with a rise in median age from 26 to 41 between 1980 and 2020. Unlike the other counties considered here, Dillon County has long had a strong non-Latino Black population that represented 41.2 percent of the county in 1980 and has increased over time. As of 2020, the white and Black populations were 45.9 percent and 44.9 percent, respectively.

- *Sheridan County, North Dakota* — Now one of the least populated counties in the United States, Sheridan County is situated in central

North Dakota. The county's population shrank from 2,819 in 1980 to 1,265 in 2020—one of the largest relative population reductions observed in any county over this forty-year period. As the county has shrunk, poverty has declined. Poverty in Sheridan County was 23.1 percent in 1980 and declined to 6.9 percent by 2020. Similarly, all-cause age-adjusted mortality declined during this period, dropping from 822.6 per hundred thousand in 1980 to 475.9 in 2020. Already older than many other counties in 1980, with a median age of 37.6, aging in Sheridan County has continued, with a median age of 51.8 in 2020. The county remains racially homogeneous in 2020, with the non-Latino white population share standing at 94.2 percent. Although this is lower than the 99.8 percent reported in 1980, it is still more homogeneous than many other rural counties.

Each of these counties represents a different form of rural economic development—or lack thereof. Washington County represents what many may argue is the goal of long-term rural economic development. The county has a large and growing population with access to many amenities. Further, there are still parts of the county that one may consider rural upon sight—but the benefits a metropolitan area can provide are never far away. Counter to this, Butler County represents a different form of idealized rural development. With its full integration into the greater Pittsburgh area, residents of Butler County can commute throughout the city for work, live in an area with slightly less density than the inner city, and still have access to much of what makes living in a bedroom community ideal. However, because of their population density and connectivity to metropolitan amenities, one thing we could not argue is that either of these places remains truly rural.

The two counties that do remain rural reflect two sides of persistent rurality. The first, Dillon County, arguably reflects a truly sustainable rural county. The population is largely the same as it was forty years ago. It has not grown, but it also has not withered away. The second, Sheridan County, is a direct contrast. Although Sheridan County was already small in 1980, it lost 55.2 percent of its population between 1980 and 2020. Certainly, no one who wishes to see rural America preserved would describe this as a favorable outcome. That said, the persistently high levels of poverty and mortality in Dillon County relative to Sheridan County—which are inescapably tied to its history as a county in a former slave state with the legacy of Jim Crow—raise the question: Is this the kind of sustainability we want to be pursuing?

These distinct cases point to the core questions considered throughout this book. Are the outcomes of Washington County and Butler County desirable for those interested in sustaining the rural way of life? If not, is the trajectory of Dillon County, even with its persistently low levels of well-being, closer to what proponents of rural renewal are really hoping for? And finally, is population loss and the disappearance of areas like Sheridan County something we should avoid or promote?

Beyond these questions about the entire premise of sustainable rural economic development, a number of persistent myths about rural America will be addressed and countered throughout this book. Influenced by the media, romanticized narratives, and stereotypes, many (although certainly not all) Americans carry assumptions about rural people and places that do not hold up to scrutiny. These myths may hinder the future success of rural places in the United States because they mask many of the best qualities of rural America while also standing in the way of effective policy development. Let us look at a few of these myths.

Rural America Is a Region Populated by Just White People

Counter to what you may believe, rural America has significant Black, Latino, and American Indian populations that are regionally clustered. These populations are long-standing communities with rich cultures that have historically endured and, in many cases, continue to endure some of the highest levels of marginalization and racism found in the United States.

Everyone Living in Rural Areas Works in Agriculture

Although agriculture remains a dominant industry in many regions, the vast majority of rural workers are employed in the service sector—just like in urban America. However, rural service-sector work tends to provide fewer opportunities for advancement than in urban areas while also being far more likely to be low paying, seasonal, and precarious. Even areas that still have a strong agricultural presence do not employ nearly as many rural residents as you may expect due to mechanization, economies of scale, and a lack of interest from rural Americans in many forms of agricultural labor. For example, just 5.4 percent of rural employment in 2022 was classified as farm labor.[8]

All of Rural America Is in Decline

The real story of rural America in the 2020s is one of highly uneven growth and development. Many rural areas have been successful over the past forty years; however, those successful places have often been reclassified as urban, which means they should no longer be considered rural. Beyond this, a relatively small number of rural areas have achieved population growth/stability and economic vibrance while still retaining their rural status. These rural counties are often centered around natural amenity tourism and retirement migration, bringing with them a host of social and economic issues related to inequality, culture clash, and poor economic outcomes for longtime residents.

Rural Areas Are a Lost Cause and Not Worthy of Investment
Given Their Low Population

As will be discussed at the end of this book, we have the ability to sustain rural and urban America in tandem through universalist policies. There is no need to pit rural against urban. The further loss of what remains of rural America would result in the erasure of important history, the loss of many diverse cultures, and the further destabilization of the US political system. Not only are rural places worthy of investment, but that investment does not need to come at the expense of urban needs.

WE NOW FIND OURSELVES in a position where the actual path forward is unclear. If, as will be shown in this book, rural economic development is not the path forward for a sustainable rural America, what is? Thankfully, there is a path for us to take. Although, to get there, we have to first understand the driving force behind rural America's decline by looking deeply within the mechanisms of capitalism and uneven development. As we will see, the reason we are continuing to see the bifurcation of rural America into either metropolitan areas or depopulated zones stems from the constrained freedom we all experience under capitalism. We are all free to move, but only to where capital is willing to pay us. The implications of this false freedom for rural America are many and will become apparent throughout this book.

Overview of the Book

In what follows, you will find a critique of rural economic development in the United States that also makes the case for saving rural America. The core argument is that the decline and ultimate elimination of the vast majority of rural America is exactly what we should expect under our contemporary American capitalist system. Yet the matter of whether or not we should save rural America, and which parts we should save, is a complicated, racially coded, and class-based conversation. This conversation is tied to our social construction of rurality and popular imaginings of the American way of life. When weighing what we stand to lose, we will see that stabilizing and sustaining rural America is necessary due to cultural, social, and political considerations. Finally, we will uncover that the only equitable way to prevent rural America's long-term decline is through a radical decoupling of where we live from how we make our money. The argument proceeds through the following chapters.

Chapter 1 contains a discussion of what is meant by "rural." There exist many definitions of rurality, and it is vital to establish from the outset which definitions are being used. This chapter broadly describes the two primary ways rurality is defined within contemporary scholarship. The first positions rurality as a place-based phenomenon characterized by low population density and a lack of access to metropolitan amenities. In the second, rurality is viewed as a social construct that is characterized by the symbols and meanings we attach to rural life—also known as the rural idyll. The chapter concludes by discussing the benefits and drawbacks of each and why we should ultimately rely upon the place-based approach for the bulk of this book.

Chapter 2 presents a brief and partial history of rural America to provide necessary context for the arguments made in later chapters. Beginning with an overview of colonization, Indigenous removal, genocide, and slavery, it highlights the fact that rural America was established through the mistreatment of Native, Black, Latino, and Asian people. The chapter also makes clear that rural America is not monolithic and is instead full of diversity along many dimensions, including ethnicity, race, income, and economic profile. From this, the remainder of the chapter is spent focusing on the trajectory of rural America from 1980 onward. Considering economic, demographic, and social dimensions, we will see how rural parts of the United States have changed since 1980 and how those rural areas that were already faring the best on many indicators of economic, social, and physical well-being have been the most likely to develop into urban areas—thus being excluded from what we think of as rural America in the 2020s. The chapter concludes with a discussion of our contemporary context, with a focus on rural America during the COVID-19 pandemic.

Chapter 3 provides necessary theoretical background on the various academic conceptualizations of "development." Through a presentation and comparison of linear and critical theories of economic development, the chapter draws out the strengths and weaknesses of each viewpoint as they relate to rural America. The chapter broadly compares two schools of development thinking: (1) the Rostow-inspired view of linear development and modernization and (2) critical frameworks advanced by the dependency school and Marxism. Within the linear economic development model, the frameworks that have been tailor-made for subnational rural economic development efforts are discussed, including the Community Capitals Framework; industrial organization theory; innovation and entrepreneurship; the Tailored, Resilient, Inclusive, and Collaborative (TRIC) approach; and Rural Rising. The chapter then moves beyond these two schools to discuss the relevant work on uneven development from Karl Marx, David Harvey, and Neil Smith. In doing so, there is a focus on the theoretical concepts of both the spatial fix and the seesaw of uneven development. Importantly, this discussion explains how these many frameworks do (or do not) apply to a subnational understanding of rural economic development in the United States.

In Chapter 4, the core theoretical argument of the book begins with a presentation of the fallacy found within the narratives and frameworks of contemporary rural economic development. In brief, the fallacy is that all frameworks focused on economic development position the urbanization of rural America as the end goal. Thus, rural economic development seeks to make rural areas urban. This means sustainable rural economic development is an inherently contradictory concept that seeks to transform and erase the places it purports to assist and preserve. This argument is reinforced by critical development theory and locates the false freedom of labor under capitalism—wherein we are only free to move to places where we could plausibly make a living—as the mechanism driving the ongoing patterns of out-migration in rural America. The chapter then works outward to a broader analysis of constrained labor mobility through the continued dominance of the United States in globalized markets. In doing so, the chapter unearths how capital in the contemporary United States no longer requires internal peripheries and their labor for the production of goods. When this reality is combined with the false freedom of labor, the decline of rural America is to be expected.

Chapter 5 takes a step back and interrogates the question underlying any actions taken to alter the course for rural America: Why should we care if rural America, at least as we know it, goes away? Further, which rural areas are people trying to save when they set out to conduct rural economic development efforts? The chapter begins with a discussion of just what is actually lost when rural America disappears, making the important point that a loss of rural America does not constitute a loss of all pastoral areas or small towns. The chapter then revisits the rural idyll and draws on the diversity of rural places to critique the contemporary narrative surrounding rural America and the monolithic treatment of the rural United States as being white, working class, and tied to agriculture. Following this, we will examine, from cultural, social, and political angles, just what we stand to lose if rural America goes away. We will then consider the strengths and weaknesses of relevant arguments for why we may actually decide to let rural America continue to wither. In doing so, we will consider utilitarian concerns of how to balance the few with the many when confronting the notion of "saving" rural America. Finally, after considering the various arguments, we will see that we should save rural America—as we stand to lose far more than we would gain if rural America disappears.

Chapter 6 turns toward the future and offers several paths for rural America in the coming decades while discussing the merits and drawbacks of each. The first path offered is business as usual, or the Status Quo Path, which would accept an inevitable loss of much of rural America through the dual modes of depopulation and urbanization. The second path is termed the Accelerated Path of Rural Destruction, and it is a path where we would actively discourage rural living and adopt a political model where we encourage the out-migration of populations from our rural spaces. The third is called the Soft Path for Rural Sustainability, and it is focused on decoupling income from residence without radically altering our political economic system. The soft path is anchored in a new kind of rural labor model tied to remote work, infrastructure investments, incentive programs for certain types of labor, and student loan forgiveness.

The final path is presented in Chapter 7 and represents a more radical approach, termed the Hard Path for Rural Sustainability. This path more fully severs the link between where we live and how we earn our money and is anchored in the implementation of a universal basic income, the creation of a single-payer health care system, the payment of reparations to Black Americans, and the establishment of a federal program of tribal restitution. We will then see how the hard path and the soft path would likely need to be implemented in tandem if we are to truly incentivize rural residence across the United States. Ultimately, we will see that adopting the hard path is the only equitable way to sustain rural America. This view is supported by detailing how it is the only path that addresses the core issue driving rural depopulation—the false freedom of labor under capitalism—while also explicitly acknowledging the linked fates of rural and urban America *and* addressing issues of both social injustice and utilitarian concerns over resource allocation.

The book's conclusion presents a more forceful argument for the adoption of the hard path while also discussing how this path is related to two important initiatives focused on improving societal well-being but largely absent from the arguments made here: (1) labor organization and unions and (2) the increasingly popular yet controversial environmentally grounded economic model of degrowth. In discussing these initiatives, the compatibility of the hard path with these movements is highlighted and the need to turn onto the hard path is stressed. Rural America is a diverse region with much to offer. However, without direct attention to its current trajectory, it will be a very hard road ahead.

CHAPTER ONE

What Is Rurality?

This book is focused on rural America. However, there are many meanings of "rural" and many misunderstandings. Thus, it is necessary to detail the definition employed in this book, as well as the other meanings that exist. To begin, it should be known that the term and definition of rural are hotly contested and unlikely to ever be agreed upon. There are considerable differences in interpretation between scholars, countries, and continents. For many early sociologists, who generally held a linear view of modernization, including Karl Marx, Max Weber, Émile Durkheim, and Ferdinand Tönnies, rural society was something that was to be left behind on the forward march of progress.[1] Rural society was viewed as a natural, ancient, and archaic way of life and not a social phenomenon in need of serious study. Marx, for his part, generally considered the destruction of feudalism and the peasant way of life by capitalism as an essential step toward a grand socialist future.[2] Others, including Durkheim and Tönnies, described the transition from a romanticized rural society to a detached urban society during the industrial revolution. This was expected to result in anomie, alienation, and social disorganization. Thus, as industrialization occurred, the loss of communal social ties, or the move from Gemeinschaft (community) to Gesellschaft (society), would follow.

While early leading sociologists were developing a linear urban-oriented view of society and development, rural-focused scholars were simultaneously developing a very different view of rurality. Their position was that rurality should not be viewed as a residual or ancient way of living but as a modern lifestyle with issues distinct from those issues occurring in urban society.[3] As industrialization and modernization have continued, this perspective of rurality as a modern form of social arrangement has endured. Rural life, at least in some form, is here to stay, and in many ways is essential to the continuation of urban society. Indeed, the linear view of development, still popular among many practitioners and mainstream economists and fully described in chapter 3, has received increasing criticism from scholars of all stripes for its sidelining of the importance of contemporary rurality. However, while the discussion of whether or not rural spaces reflect a modern condition or a way of the past is valuable for understanding how researchers view rural society, it does not address what exactly is meant by the term to begin with. It is not clear what it means for a location or a person to be *rural*. Romantic notions of community, solidarity, conservatism, isolation, and remoteness abound, but romantic notions are hardly satisfying. Further, these romantic notions do not answer the fundamental question: What makes someone or someplace rural?

I follow the lead of David Brown and Kai Schafft (2019) — to whom this chapter is heavily indebted — and argue there are two main ways of thinking about rurality: (1) a place-based approach and (2) a social constructivist approach. The place-based approach is the approach most often seen in the North American tradition of rural scholarship, and it is also the approach generally adopted by federal, state, and county governments in the United States. It is vital to acknowledge from the beginning that even the existence of the polarizing terms "rural" and "urban" presents a false dichotomy that makes any frank discussion of rurality oversimplified. Despite the functional need for those interested in rural people and places to describe things as they are in "rural areas," all working rural scholars would likely admit that rurality is really a spectrum. There is not some magical threshold where an area suddenly and obviously shifts from rural to urban. That said, there is some agreement under the place-based model as to how we can measure and categorize this spectrum.

The place-based approach is ultimately materialist — a place can be considered rural if it shares a set of material conditions with other rural places along dimensions that we believe characterize rurality. These dimensions can vary based upon the preferences of specific scholars and can include things such as population settlement structure, access to urban amenities, landscape, economic factors, institutions, and sociocultural characteristics. In practice, however, only two dimensions are often used: (1) population density and (2) connectivity/remoteness.[4] As such, a rural place is defined not just by its low population density but also by its limited connectivity to major metropolitan centers or urban amenities. Importantly, connectivity/remoteness does not refer to simple distance or geographic isolation; instead, it refers to economic connectivity through employment and access to goods and services found in urban areas. It is for this reason that an area like Washington County, Utah, one of the counties described in the introduction, can have large swaths of land with low population density and still be considered urban due to its high connectivity and access to metropolitan amenities.

Importantly, within a place-based framework, rurality has rarely been defined outright. Rather, rurality tends to represent anything that is left over after all of the non-rural places are accounted for.[5] When classifying areas as rural or urban, researchers generally face two choices: (1) determining what scale or boundaries to use and (2) how many categories to use. John Cromartie and Shawn Bucholtz note there are three main concepts available for deciding what boundary to use when determining whether an area is rural or urban. These concepts are the administrative concept, the land-use concept, and the economic concept.[6] The administrative concept uses administrative boundaries such as municipal city limits to classify urban areas; the land-use concept identifies urban areas based upon density of settlement as it would be viewed from the sky; and the economic concept—the one most commonly used in rural scholarship—tracks the influence of urban cores on surrounding areas to establish larger commuting zones.[7] In addition to having to define boundaries, researchers must decide the appropriate population thresholds to mark an area as rural or urban. Thresholds for rural as low as 2,500 people and as high as 50,000 have been used. All told, if a geographic area defined using either the administrative, land-use, or economic boundary conception has a population cluster over the set threshold, it is classified as urban. All other geographic areas not classified as urban are considered rural.[8]

Various versions of the previously described approaches are used and regularly released but will not be detailed here for the sake of brevity. That said, because it is relevant for discussions in subsequent chapters, it is important to detail the classification scheme that is arguably the most common—the metropolitan and nonmetropolitan categories created by the United States Office of Management and Budget (OMB).[9] According to the OMB formula, counties in the United States are classified as metropolitan if they are a core county with one or more urban areas with at least 50,000 people, or if they are an outlying county tied to the metro core by 25 percent of employed commuters. Any county not classified as metropolitan is classified as nonmetropolitan and is often termed rural. Under the current classification, which was released in July 2023, there are a total of 1,187 metropolitan counties and 1,956 nonmetropolitan counties.[10] Many scholars use a more detailed version of this categorization—known as the Rural-Urban Continuum Codes. This classification scheme further separates counties into nine categories. Metropolitan counties are divided into three levels of population, and nonmetropolitan counties are divided into six categories broken up by population and whether or not a county is adjacent to a metropolitan area.[11]

It should be noted that relying on counties as the scale of analysis when determining rural or urban status is not without its limitations—counties vary in size and are often quite heterogeneous. The size variation is not random, either. As one moves westward across the United States, counties tend to become larger. In fact, relying on counties has often created some humorous cases in the American West. For example, the Grand Canyon is located within the same county as Flagstaff, Arizona. This means that the Grand Canyon—a famously desolate region—is in an "urban" area. Although counties are imperfect, they are still the best choice for rural demographic scholarship and longitudinal research for several reasons.

First, the average size of counties best facilitates the two-dimensional conception of rurality. This is because subcounty units in many areas are too small to properly capture the remoteness necessary for an area to be rural. Even if something like a census tract has a low population density, we need a clear way to capture whether or not there is a broader metropolitan area to which that census tract belongs. This inattention to the second dimension of connectivity has rendered the US Census Bureau's historic definition of rurality insufficient. Historically, the Census Bureau defined urban areas based upon whether or not at least 2,500 people lived in tracts or blocks with either 500 or 1,000 people per square mile. While this definition was changed to focus on housing units instead of people, it still does not take the dimension of connectivity into account.[12] Thus, while the largest weakness of using counties is that they vary in size, if they did not, they would likely accomplish our goals quite well.

It is, of course, possible that we could create larger metropolitan areas out of census tracts instead of counties. In fact, both the tract-level Rural-Urban Commuting Area codes used by the US Department of Agriculture (USDA) and the block-level work by Katherine Nelson and Tuan Nguyen attempt to do this and are worth exploring.[13] However, for reasons to be discussed below, using these smaller units still works against the benefits of counties.

The second reason that counties are ideal is because they are political units. Because of this, research at the county level can rely on much more grounded assumptions regarding possible solutions to problems. For example, in my work on rural water quality, we had to make an assumption regarding which populations were likely being served by community water systems. The public dataset told us where a community water system's address was located but not who that water system served. Since community water systems are regulated at the county level, we felt comfortable assuming that if a community water system was in a county, then the residents of that county were being served by that system. However, if we were to use census tracts, that assumption would have been far less tenable because we had no idea which census tracts in a county were specifically served by a given system.[14] This political nature of counties ultimately makes applied solution-oriented research more feasible. Making policy recommendations at the county level is fairly reasonable and has the potential for real action.[15] If we instead work at something like the census tract level, realistic recommendations are difficult to generate, and it is unclear who the recommendations are intended for in rural areas.

The third reason counties are valuable is because they are relatively stable over time. Although they have changed boundaries over the years, it is not terribly difficult to establish a database of counties with stable geographic units from 1980 to today. Doing something like this with subcounty units such as towns or census tracts would be nearly impossible. Towns and cities constantly annex new territory, and tracking those patterns on a national scale is infeasible. Similarly, census tracts generally change with each new census. Given the need to track long-term impacts, counties quickly become the only realistic unit available.

The fourth and final reason that counties are ultimately the best scale for determining rurality and conducting research is data quality and availability. Because both privacy and sample size are concerns, data on rural America is always a struggle for researchers. In many federal datasets, rural data below the county level is simply suppressed. If it is available, the statistics are often unreliable. For example, the margins of error on statistical estimates from the American Community Survey—our primary survey on the detailed demographics of the United States—are so extreme for subcounty units in rural areas that using the data is dubious at best. For these reasons, counties are the unit used in most US rural scholarship and what is generally referred to when discussing rural areas throughout this book.[16]

It must be stressed that these classifications are dynamic in two important ways. First, the rurality of counties—that is, whether they are considered metropolitan or nonmetropolitan—changes over time and is updated with each round of the decennial US Census. Thus, as the United States has urbanized, the number of counties actually considered rural has shrunk. Although many academic researchers will hold rurality constant for various analyses, statistics reported by the government and many other research groups do not. This means that many of our impressions of the decline of rural America can often be influenced by which counties happened to remain rural, as opposed to objective declines in health or other factors within a consistent set of rural counties. In the discussion of rural America from 1980 to the present in chapter 2, this misunderstanding will be addressed directly.

Given that this dynamism reflects either the direct urbanization of rural counties or the annexing of rural areas into existing metropolitan areas, this dynamic and shrinking pool of rural counties is a vital piece of many of the arguments made going forward.

Another way these categories of rurality and urbanity are dynamic is less relevant to the case made here for rural America but quite relevant for policy. This is the dynamism introduced through changes to the metropolitan definition over time. Procedurally, the Census Bureau classifies the urban tracts and blocks (i.e., core urban areas) that are then used by the OMB to actually construct the corresponding metropolitan statistical areas. However, since 1970, the OMB, as well as the Census Bureau, have made changes to both the definition of an urban area and a metropolitan area. For example, in earlier iterations of the metropolitan classification, subjective opinions regarding connectivity were allowed to influence which counties were included if the level of commuting was below the established threshold.[17] In the current iteration, this kind of subjectivity is not allowed. Obviously, allowing these classifications to change over time carries significant weight for any longitudinal understanding of rural areas in the United States.

Unfortunately, changes continue to be made. At time of writing, the Census Bureau enacted changes to how it counts an area as "urban." As the OMB builds its metropolitan definition upon census-defined urban areas, this has created significant issues not only for scholarship but also for rural policy and well-being. This is because a variety of federal programs make eligibility determinations based upon the metropolitan/nonmetropolitan classifications—despite the OMB asking them not to. The vast majority of the public comments from both academic and policy groups on the proposed changes were negative and unsupportive, but the Census Bureau still ultimately changed how it defines urban areas.

The Rural Idyll

While American scholars have often adopted a materialist and descriptive view of what it means for a place to be rural, rural sociologists in the United Kingdom have placed more emphasis on imaginative geographies and rurality as a social construct. The key distinction between rurality as a social construct and a place-based view of rurality hinges on materialism or dematerialism.[18] Keith Halfacree makes the distinction between "rural as space, and rural as representing space" and argues that rurality is increasingly being detached from space and should be considered as a dematerialized concept of the imagination.[19] Whereas place-based definitions of rurality attempt to classify locations as rural based upon relatively objective dimensions such as population or commuting patterns, this approach does not attempt to define rural as a descriptive or material entity. In this model, rurality should instead be identified through the signs and symbols associated with rurality, which is often termed the rural idyll. Thus, the rural idyll perspective argues that there is something symbolic and intangible about being a rural person or being in a rural place. This perspective is less about the material conditions of living in a rural location and more about the construction of the self as a rural person or the place as a rural place. Further, Paul Cloke and Paul Milbourne argue that the cultural component of rurality, which is analogous to the symbolic definition yielded by Halfacree, has emerged due to the erosion of the distinction between rural and urban in the modern era.[20] This perspective is tied to the rural idyll and encourages academics to not define rural on their own terms but in the terms of those living in these locales.[21]

Within the frame of the rural idyll, space is manufactured, and a distinction must be made between rural as space — meaning the descriptive material properties of space — and rural as representing space, which denotes the social representation of rurality that exists both at an ideological level and through the exercising of that ideology on rural spaces. In this view, how society imagines the rural idyll (e.g., quaint townhomes and country lanes in the United Kingdom) drives how rural spaces are physically created, which then feeds back into the local conception of rurality.[22] Because this framework allows for personal interpretations of rurality, it is more flexible to specific representations held by various genders, classes, and ethnicities. The rural idyll can be leveraged to demonstrate the way that the gap between social representations of the rural and the physical characteristics of the rural locality are linked. For example, when the European Union equated rurality with small family farms, it led to an increase in the number of small family farms and government support for them. However, once the European Union viewed agriculture as less essential to rural life, rural localities became decentered from agriculture and alternative forms of "being rural" evolved.[23] Within the view of the rural idyll, there is a network comprised of the rural locality, the representations of the rural, the lives of the rural, and the lay discourses of the rural. As the social representation held by the rural universe shifts, the network *practices* the rural as the social representation warrants and pushes the rural area in a way that reduces the gap between the social representation and the current characteristics of the place.[24] As a result, this perspective is both imaginative and material within a dialectical tradition.

As will be seen throughout this book, invoking the rural idyll is essential at times for understanding why (or why not) society values some kinds of rural places and not others. However, there are some conceptual and practical issues with the model of the rural idyll worth noting. Conceptually, this perspective conflates, as Cloke and Milbourne state directly, rurality with culture.[25] By reducing rurality to a generally fluid set of symbols held by people living in a location, rurality is reduced to local or regional culture as it relates to the countryside. From a materialist perspective—which is the perspective broadly adopted throughout this book—there are several difficulties with this reduction. First, rurality can easily be shown to be a social construct, but that does not mean it is not a real type of location that is consistent over time and can and should be studied and classified.

Second, there are very real and material consequences of living in areas that we descriptively classify as rural. Saying that what is rural should be specific to class, gender, ethnicity, and time reduces our ability to understand and resolve these material consequences of rurality. It is true that the experience of living in a rural area will vary by these social dimensions, as all experiences do. But reducing rurality to a flexible social construct removes much of the utility of the concept. Further, if rurality is discursive and dialectic, then attention to hegemony is crucial—as the dominant view of rurality, and which kinds of rural places matter, is likely to be informed by those currently in power.[26] Thus, an uncritical usage of the rural idyll could easily lead to the erasure of marginalized people and places by handing a flexible definition to the power elite, which they could bend to their will.

Third, space is fundamental to an understanding of the relationship between rural and urban areas.[27] While the rural idyll perspective agrees on this point, the postmodern emphasis risks downplaying the importance that space and place play in shaping rural livelihoods. Halfacree argues that space is both produced by society through social representation and is also used to create other spaces, thus being a resource for future creation.[28] This dialectic and circular logic, while an incredibly clever and insightful analytic tool for understanding how social representations shape material conditions, presents remarkable difficulties for following places over time and appears more appropriate for understanding change within specific rural places than changes across rural areas generally. A region's geographic location and characteristics have enormous implications for that same region's structural location within the global economy. The view of rurality as a social construct pushes against spatial determinism—meaning against the notion that elements of space have causal impacts on human behavior. However, it pushes so forcefully that it ultimately ignores the very real difficulties imposed by the remoteness associated with rural spaces.

Finally, on a practical and methodological note, to redefine rurality as a social construct limits its analytic power to such a degree that many existing research questions become impossible to answer or monitor. Any definitions of rurality that are not place-based will pose unwieldy methodological issues for social scientists interested in longitudinal research. To be a useful analytic category or tool, rurality must represent a set of material conditions shared by a set of locations. If we rely on imaginative formulations, we are fundamentally assessing something else. For example, we know that persistent poverty is more prevalent in counties with lower population density and more remoteness (i.e., rural) than in counties with higher population density and less remoteness (i.e., urban).[29] How do we follow up on this finding or track it over time if we begin to describe rural as a set of symbols and perceptions that will vary by class, gender, and ethnicity? The distinctions between rural and urban America can often be located in class divides; by reducing rurality to a fluid concept that varies by class, we risk losing the essential components of rurality that create the analytic tool.

Conclusion

Although they have been presented as two distinct approaches, these two ways of viewing rurality are not necessarily competing. In fact, they are often complementary and interactive.[30] For example, even though the current presentation of a rural area is produced using the dominant conceptions of modern rurality, each rural area is also a direct product of the natural physical geography of that region. Although we may not wish to lean fully into spatial determinism, it is a simple fact that the specific physical properties of an area will shape the local culture and rural idyll. Areas with rich timber endowments are likely to develop a culture distinct from a rural area defined by fishing or ranching. Indeed, the physical geography of an area has been shown to shape specific rural idylls, cultural boundaries, and identity. One example can be found in Dwight Billings and Kathleen Blee's *The Road to Poverty*, where the presence of salt-producing waters within a remote Appalachian county in the early 1800s led to the genesis of a rural culture defined by salt-making and fierce competition between wealthy rural families over resources. This initial cultural formation carried into the present day and fostered the resource-dependent and high-poverty nature of the area.[31]

Another example can be found in Giulia Urso's work in Italy, which found that the physical topography of a region limited interaction across watersheds and fostered the formation of separate, as opposed to unified, local identities within a rural region.[32] Beyond industry and identity, values and priorities of rural cultures can easily be seen as a direct outflow of the material conditions unique to the rural experience. The importance of self-sufficiency, the tolerance for remoteness and isolation, and a strong sense of individuality—all hallmark traits of rural culture in the United States—can be viewed as socially constructed cultural elements that are directly informed by the experience of living in areas with low population density and a lack of urban amenities.

Ultimately, it may be best to view the two schools of thought presented here as coexisting and mutually reinforcing. This view is in line with how Jones and Woods describe localities as simultaneously having material coherence—the "social, economic and political structure and practices that are uniquely configured around a place"—as well as an imagined coherence where residents "have a sense of identity with the place and with each other, such that they constitute a perceived community with shared patterns of behavior and shared geographical reference points."[33] Thus, even if we elect to define rural areas based upon material factors alone, within each rural place there exist rural idylls that are grounded in those material factors and are both related to, and distinct from, the rural idylls held throughout the rest of the country. The salience of those rural idylls to the current research, policy, or program will be dependent on the specific objective at hand.

Another way to think about these two formulations of rurality is that they are simply addressing different questions. Place-based views of rurality ask, What are the shared conditions of those who live in remote and sparsely populated areas? By contrast, the social constructivist approach asks, How do people view what it means to live in a place they define as "rural"? Although questions from pure versions of either approach may be different, there is no reason these perspectives cannot be situated within one another. For example, one might ask how the dominant rural idyll has changed as rural areas across the United States have developed and become urban. Key to addressing this question would be to first define what we mean by a rural area using some form of material classification. From that, we could then use a variety of data collection tools to determine the rural idyll and its trends over time within the populace. Thus, the social constructivist approach is well suited for analyzing changes within specific rural places as well as understanding why certain kinds of rural spaces seem to be privileged over others in the popular imagination. Comparatively, the place-based definitions are clearly more useful for broadly defining rural places and tracking them over time. This means that just about all research and policy focused on rural areas will have to engage with the place-based definitions when selecting study sites or determining eligibility criteria. Comparatively, the social constructivist model is more likely to be invoked when research or policy is focused on specific places, cultural preservation and analysis, or local and regional planning efforts.

The remainder of this book primarily follows the North American tradition and relies upon the material formulation of rural as place. In particular, the statistics you see will generally rely upon the widely used OMB definitions of metropolitan and nonmetropolitan, categorizing metropolitan areas as urban and nonmetropolitan areas as rural. As such, the default spatial unit being discussed is the county. This choice is essential for the largely conceptual focus of this book. As will be made clear in the following chapter, it is vital that we be able to consider broad trends and changes across a clearly defined "rural America." Although this work does not heavily rely upon the social constructivist view of rurality, the framework is revisited in chapter 5 when discussing what it means to lose rural places and why the American people seem to (1) care about some rural places more than others and (2) continue to imagine rural America as steadfastly agrarian, white, conservative, and working class.

CHAPTER TWO

Rural America

A Brief and Partial History

What we think of as rural America is shrinking and has been for a long time. Of the roughly 3,140 counties in the United States, there were 2,406 classified as rural, or nonmetropolitan, in 1980. By 2023, there were only 1,956. Since this process has unfolded slowly over decades, attention to this issue has been long-standing. For example, Arthur Vidich and Joseph Bensman were already arguing in 1958 that rural America had been infiltrated by mass society, and in 1986, William Friedland argued that rural America had disappeared and thus rural sociology was irrelevant.[1] Although we may or may not be inclined to agree with Friedland's position, his claims highlight the long duration of concern for rural America from the scholarly community. That said, while many have been paying attention to the dwindling of rural America since at least the 1950s, what constitutes rural America was dynamic long before then.

Based upon our contemporary understanding of rurality as a combination of the two dimensions of population density and remoteness (see chapter 1), one could argue the vast majority of the United States was rural prior to colonization. In fact, based just upon square mileage, the same argument holds true today. There were certainly settlements and permanent towns inhabited by the Indigenous peoples of North America—and even Indigenous cities as impressive as the large city of Cahokia near present-day St. Louis, Missouri—that rivaled European cities such as London during the thirteenth century.[2] Yet the majority of the United States remained largely "rural" until the arrival of European colonists.

Through the process of colonization, the urbanization of the United States began in earnest and was characterized by plague, genocide, and the forced removal of Indigenous peoples from their homeland.[3] From the 1600s onward, native peoples were forced to assimilate to European religions, give up their land, and fight for their very existence.[4] Included in this mistreatment was the famous Trail of Tears, where the federal government forced tribes from the Southeastern United States to the Indian Territory now known as Oklahoma. In addition to forced migration and ethnic cleansing, the Homestead Act of 1862 allowed settlers to claim up to 160 acres of public land as their own as long as they paid a small fee, lived on the land, and "improved" it.[5] In many ways, homesteading mirrored the privatization of the commons in England—now known as the enclosure acts. Importantly, much of the land open to homesteading was either traditional or treaty lands of existing tribes. All told, war, genocide, homesteading, and forced migration resulted in native tribes losing access to much of their land. To this day, many treaties are not honored. From the arrival of colonists to the present day, there has been a 98.9 percent reduction in land for tribes in the United States. If a tribe does still have land, it is often far away from ancestral homelands and shared with tribes with whom they were not historically affiliated.[6]

The outcome of this mistreatment in the present day is reflected by the largely rural and underdeveloped nature of tribal reservations.[7] Although the majority of American Indian populations do not reside on reservations, the majority of rural American Indian populations do.[8] These populations often live on marginal land and experience high levels of poverty and negative health outcomes, where poor infrastructure and a bureaucratic patchwork make improving well-being difficult.[9] Further, although tribes remain sovereign entities, states continue to resist their sovereignty and have a long history of bullying tribes in order to get land, resources, or policies that they want, with mixed success. As a result, tribes have had to fight tooth and nail for the basic rights and security supposedly guaranteed to them by their treaties with the federal government. On a positive note, in the twenty-first century, there have been some favorable court rulings for tribes that have corrected and pushed back against state aggression. For example, in 2001, the state of Idaho was required to give back the portion of Lake Coeur d'Alene it stole from the Coeur d'Alene Tribe, and a 2020 Supreme Court ruling upheld that much of eastern Oklahoma was still tribal land.

At the same time that native peoples were being forced off their ancestral lands, the slave trade was forcibly moving Africans to the United States for agricultural and other forms of labor. Slavery in the United States, known as chattel slavery, was an exceptionally brutal form of slavery which equated human beings to livestock. Beginning in 1619, Africans were transported in inhumane conditions across the Atlantic. The population of slaves was large, ultimately accounting for 4 million of the 12.2 million people living in active slave states in 1860.[10] Although slavery existed across the entire United States, it remained legal the longest and was most concentrated in the Southern states—where many slaves were forced to work hard labor on rural southern cotton plantations.

Following the Civil War, it initially appeared that reconstruction would usher in a period of prosperity for the formerly enslaved through the

Freedmen's Bureau and the occupation of the Confederate states by union soldiers. Reconstruction policies were designed to both rebuild the war-torn South while also ensuring the fair treatment of newly freed slaves. However, just twelve years after the Civil War, the Freedmen's Bureau had been dissolved, and the military was pulled out of the South with the Compromise of 1877. This compromise, which remains contentious to this day, settled the disputed 1876 presidential election. Southern states would accept Rutherford B. Hayes as president contingent on the removal of the remaining federal troops from formerly Confederate states. As such, reconstruction was ultimately unsuccessful. Former slaves generally found themselves without land or capital, and they were forced into tenant farming—an agricultural system where families pay rent to landlords with either cash or a share of their yield for the ability to farm and live on the land—on many of the same plantations where they were formerly slaves.[11]

Tragically, the abuse of rural Black farmers continued through the twentieth century and continues today. Many Black farmers had to work as tenant farmers. Yet by saving money over years of work, adapting to changes in the Southern economy, and participating in notable instances of collective action, many of them ultimately purchased and worked their own land in the period following the failure of reconstruction.[12] By 1920, estimates suggest Black farmers owned over 16 million acres and represented 14 percent of all farmers.[13] However, as of 2019, Black farmers only owned 1.1 million acres and were part owners of another 1.07 million acres. Black farmers now only represent less than one percent of all farmers in the United States—although in the South, this proportion is higher. Importantly, while one may be inclined to think this mass dispossession happened during the early twentieth century, the reality is that most of the dispossession of Black farmland happened from 1950 onward.[14]

The extreme volume of Black land dispossession since 1950 has occurred through a "war of deed and title."[15] The tactics used in this war have generally centered on three mechanisms. The first, heir property, stems from the fact that many Black farmers did not have formal wills because they lacked access to the legal system. Thus, their property was equally split among descendants. As this property continued to pass through generations—who also did not have wills—many, many individuals had claims to the same plots of land. This generated confusion and made it easy for developers to convince just one family member to sell while preying on family miscommunication. The second tactic was based on annual property taxes. Many Black residents on a fixed income could not afford to pay their rising annual property taxes, so they would default on said taxes, and their land or home would be sold by the county. Third, the Torrens Acts—which were laws passed by states to implement the Torrens system of managing land titles—were often abused to dispossess Black landowners. Torrens Acts were supposed to simplify title registry in the United States. However, they created a loophole that allowed developers to secure a partial sale from one heir property owner without notifying the other owners. Once the developer owned that portion of the land, the other owners had limited or no recourse to fight back against a full sale of the property through a partition sale.[16] This legalistic appropriation of Black land has directly contributed to the racial wealth gap in the United States, with estimates of the land lost between 1950 to 1964 in just Mississippi amounting to between $3.7 billion and $6.6 billion in 2019.[17]

The failure of reconstruction, the rise in tenant farming, Black land loss, and the continued mistreatment of Black populations through discriminatory policies have resulted in many rural areas of the South still being primarily inhabited by Black Americans descended from former slaves. These descendants have never received reparations and have had to endure continuing intergenerational trauma throughout their lives. These predominately Black rural areas of the South, although often rich in culture and community, face some of the harshest material conditions in the country.[18] Poverty and mortality are incredibly high, access to basic services remains sparse, and economic opportunity and mobility are often limited. These negative outcomes stem from the highly unequal nature of the rural South, wherein the white power elite withheld rights and resources from rural Black populations well past the time many outside the rural South would imagine. For example, Cynthia Duncan documented the existence of a clear racial hierarchy upholding Jim Crow in the Mississippi Delta well into the 1990s.[19] Although progress has been made in many areas since the 1990s, continuing patterns of white supremacy and structural racism have suppressed many opportunities, withheld rights, and continue to re-create the patterns of poverty and hardship rural Black populations have now faced for centuries.[20]

Beyond American Indian and Black populations, Latinos also experienced significant mistreatment and hardship through the creation of what we now consider rural America. Two important factors to note are the Mexican-American War and the bracero program. The Mexican-American War was a conflict that started when the United States annexed the Republic of Texas against the will of the Mexican government. Unhappy with Mexican rule because of the abolishment of slavery, the demand to pledge loyalty to Mexico, and the requirement that they convert to Catholicism, a growing number of colonists led Texas to declare independence in 1836. The ensuing battle with Mexico and uneasy tension between Mexico and the Republic of Texas lasted until the United States formally annexed Texas in 1845.[21] The contested nature of the independence of Texas caused the Mexican-American War.

This war ultimately resulted in Mexico losing 50 percent of its territory to the United States. As such, many Mexicans living in Mexico suddenly found they were living in the United States and considered US citizens—although the actual conferment of citizenship was delayed due to racism until 1898.[22] This delayed citizenship, combined with broad patterns of hostility and racism from white settlers, facilitated a large-scale dispossession of land from Mexicans by white settler-colonists.[23] Through this dispossession, many rural areas occupied by Mexicans who were supposed to have become US citizens became occupied instead by primarily white settlers, a pattern that has shaped rural America to the present.

A second important historical element of rural Latino populations is the bracero program and its legacy through the Immigration Reform and Control Act of 1986 (IRCA). The bracero program was a labor program that began in the 1940s and facilitated the temporary migration—up to six months at a time—of Mexican farmworkers to the United States.[24] Initially designed to address wartime labor shortages, this program created strong and enduring migration networks between Mexico and rural America. Ultimately, labor demand outstripped the number of formal braceros, leading to a rise in undocumented immigrants from Mexico. When the program was ended in 1964, seasonal migration continued to occur through largely undocumented channels and generally increased up until the implementation of the IRCA.[25]

A policy signed by President Ronald Reagan stemming from conservative fears of undocumented migrants taking American jobs, the IRCA resulted in the hardening of the US-Mexico border while also criminalizing the hiring of undocumented labor and legalizing the status of existing undocumented migrants within the United States. In addition, the IRCA was responsible for establishing the H-2A visa program, which continues to serve as the primary legal means of temporary farm labor immigration into the United States. Although the IRCA initially resulted in a reduction of undocumented labor, this trend quickly reversed. Unexpectedly, the lawmakers who enacted the legislation discovered that while the IRCA did reduce seasonal migration due to the new difficulties in crossing the border, the law actually increased permanent undocumented migration.[26] Once people managed to get past the hardened border, they were less likely to leave. Thus, the bracero program and the IRCA created strong migration networks and fostered a permanent increase in rural Latino populations in the decades that followed.

The impact of these dynamics on the well-being and settlement patterns of rural Latinos is evidenced by the state of current border colonias—informal housing developments that began developing around seventy years ago in rural areas along the US-Mexican border in Texas, New Mexico, Arizona, and California—where some of the most abject conditions in rural America are found. Although the majority of colonia residents are US citizens, the communities remain isolated and ignored by state and federal governments.[27] Colonias often lack basic infrastructure such as paved roads, water treatment, or electricity.[28] As such, residents of colonias often experience food, housing, and water insecurity.[29] The state of border colonias today broadly reflects a myriad of social forces stemming from the annexation of Texas and a lack of care shown by developers, states, and the federal government for residents of these unincorporated towns. For example, ethnographic work has shown that many residents purchased and moved onto lots where developers promised to install paved roads, water, sewage, and electricity. However, after purchasing the properties, the developers vanished, and the residents were left with incredibly high levels of insecurity.[30]

Although current representation in rural America is low, Asian people also played a significant role, and endured significant abuse, in establishing what we now think of as rural America. Sadly, this history is rarely discussed and often forgotten. Beginning with immigration to Hawaii in the 1850s, Asian workers, particularly Chinese laborers, were brought in to "set an 'example' for the Hawaiian workers" on sugar plantations, where they suffered regular abuse and discrimination.[31] In North America, the first large wave of Asian immigrants arrived from China in 1848 at the start of the California gold rush.[32] They worked in mining and construction and served as the primary source of labor on the intercontinental railroad.[33] Following the gold rush, California experienced a significant economic decline, and white residents developed increasingly anti-Chinese sentiments because they believed Chinese laborers were taking their jobs and undercutting their ability to organize labor unions.[34] This anti-Chinese sentiment grew across the country and ultimately led to Congress passing the Chinese Exclusion Act of 1882. This act barred immigration of Chinese people for ten years and prevented the 110,000 current Chinese residents of the United States from becoming citizens. This act was renewed in 1892 and ultimately made permanent in 1902. The ban was later expanded in the Immigration Act of 1917, which barred immigrant labor from nearly all of Asia, the Middle East, and India. Although this ban was lifted partially in 1943 and more fully in 1952, it directly created the rural America we know today—which is largely absent of Asian Americans— through direct and legalized discrimination of Asian people.

It goes without saying that while American Indian, Black, Latino, and Asian populations were mistreated, killed, and forced to migrate to new areas through the establishment of what we now call the rural United States, white settlers from Europe were expanding ever westward through the Homestead Act and other drivers of migration. Notably, this expansion into recently "opened" land was spurred in part by the Jeffersonian democratic view that "those who labor in the earth are the chosen people of god."[35] This view posited that the yeoman farmer best represented the foundation of democratic society and civic virtue and served as a motivating factor in the expansion of agriculture westward through the cultural belief of manifest destiny—the belief that European settlers were destined to expand across North America. Manifest destiny was rooted in the concept of American exceptionalism—a still-popular belief structure that posits America holds a special status relative to other nations and cultures around the world—and was used to justify much of the abuse of non-Europeans just described. These still-present paternalistic values of Jeffersonian democracy, manifest destiny, and American exceptionalism led to the establishment of the family farm model of US agriculture and have an enduring legacy in rural America.

The Industrial Restructuring of Rural America

One of the most vital factors to discuss when considering the state of rural America in the 2020s is the fundamental reorganization of rural industry and labor demand that happened from 1900 onward. A hallmark of this period of industrial restructuring was the dramatic decrease in the share of Americans working in agriculture. Compared to 50 percent of employed persons in the United States working in agriculture in 1870, just 4 percent worked in agriculture by 1980, and only around 0.5 percent worked in agriculture in 2022.[36] Looking at only the rural counties, just 5.4 percent of employed individuals worked in farming in 2022.[37] Thus, despite what you may think, agriculture has played a relatively small role in most rural labor markets since as early as the 1960s. This dramatic change was primarily due to the adoption of labor-saving technologies such as tractors, combines, harvesters, and irrigation systems, which resulted in a large decline in the share of the US population living on active farms.[38] While there were 31 million farm residents in the United States in 1920, this declined to 2.1 million by 2007 and has only decreased further. When compared to the overall population, that equates to a drop from 30 percent of the population in 1920 to less than one percent in 2007.[39]

The decline in agricultural labor demand was paired with significant improvements in rural infrastructure, with rural electric, water, and transportation infrastructure all experiencing significant investment during this period. For example, between 1930 and 1960, the share of rural households with electric services increased from 10 percent to nearly 100 percent because of the Rural Electrification Administration.[40] The broad improvements in rural infrastructure—much of which was supported by the public works job creation programs during the Great Depression—led to increased quality of life while also facilitating more profitable farming and other industrial activities.[41] Importantly, electrification occurred alongside vast improvements in both rail and highway transport infrastructure. This facilitated rural-urban commuting while also decreasing shipping costs and fostering the growth of urban companies. For example, the advent of cheaper transportation costs and the ability to leverage economies of scale fostered the concentration of meatpacking and processing among four or five key urban outfits for much of the 1900s.[42] This continued until innovation in transportation and refrigeration technology displaced the need for large stockyards, facilitating the transition of meatpacking to rural areas from 1980 onward.[43]

Although we witnessed a steep decline in agricultural labor from 1900 to today, the ownership structure of farming in the United States has remained fairly stable. Family farms—those farms "in which the majority of the business is owned by an operator and/or any individuals related by blood, marriage, or adoption, including relatives who do not live in the operators household"—have continued to dominate rural America by absolute numbers.[44] That said, while the majority of farms in the United States are owned and operated by a family, the romantic narrative surrounding family farms as small, self-sustaining family businesses has been largely misleading since at least the 1980s.[45] This is because while the vast majority of farms in the United States *are* family owned and operated, the vast majority of them do not generate sufficient income to sustain the family in question—and it has been this way for a long time. Instead, most family farms are supplemented by off-farm income. In 2019, 96 percent of farm households derived some income off-farm, and this income contributed an average of 82 percent of total household income.[46] Further, the US Department of Agriculture (USDA) reported that 84 percent of farm households in the United States earned the majority of their income off-farm in 2022.[47] Off-farm income, which is disproportionately earned by women, is most common among smaller producers.[48]

Since 1900, the demand for agricultural labor has decreased while the largest producers have grown in farm size and concentration. Although small family farms accounted for 88 percent of all US farms in 2023, they only accounted for 18.7 percent of agricultural products sold. Comparatively, large family farms and nonfamily farms accounted for 6.1 percent of farms and 62.2 percent of total agricultural sales.[49] This relatively weak contribution of small family farms has been ongoing, with the largest 5 percent of producers accounting for 38 percent of sales in 1939 and accounting for as much as 55 percent by 1987.[50]

A major turning point in the profitability of small family farming in the United States, as well as the landscape of farm labor, was the 1980s farm crisis. This crisis was brought about by a confluence of factors stemming from agricultural bull markets of the 1970s—wherein global macroeconomic conditions facilitated the massive expansion of US agricultural exports and rampant speculation of agricultural land.[51] Throughout the 1970s, persistently high inflation generated heightened investment in land as a hedge against future inflation. This was particularly the case in agriculture where changes to the structure of the US exchange rate combined with global food scarcity made demand for agricultural exports, as well as corresponding prices, skyrocket. As such, both farm and nonfarm entities invested heavily in agricultural land and agricultural production. By the end of the 1970s, global food scarcity needs were being met by the massive expansion of agriculture in the United States and abroad, and prices began to level off. As farm income subsequently fell, banks allowed refinancing based on the incorrect assumption that farmland would continue to appreciate.[52]

In the early 1980s, Reagan-era supply-side economics reduced taxes and generated massive debt for the federal government—increasing interest rates as federal borrowing soared. This occurred in tandem with aggressive anti-inflationary measures taken by the Federal Reserve, which restricted the flow of money and significantly raised the exchange value of the dollar. These forces resulted in a dramatic drop of domestic farm income due to the high cost of US agricultural exports in global markets, with export value experiencing a 50 percent reduction in real dollars from 1981 to 1986.[53] As such, a great number of overextended farmers, old and young, found themselves unable to make monthly payments or get refinancing, and agricultural banks began to experience incredible losses. This resulted in a 30 percent devaluation of farmland nationwide between 1981 and 1987, as well as the failure of 126 agricultural banks between 1985 and 1987. All told, there was a 14 percent reduction in the number of farms nationwide from 1982 to 1992, with significant regional variation in the impact of this loss.[54] Importantly, these impacts also varied by farm size, with small and large farms experiencing less stress and greater resilience than medium-sized operations, which tended to be more overleveraged than small operators and less able to weather the storm than larger farms.

The crisis was not solved overnight, but it was instead tempered by changes in Federal Reserve monetary policy, as well as massive increases in direct payments to farm operators from the federal government.[55] For example, with the Food Security Act of 1985, the federal government paid more than $50 billion to farmers from 1985 to 1988, reflecting 31 percent of net farm income during this period.[56] This crisis not only led to the loss of many farms across the United States, but because of the extreme stress placed on medium-sized farms, it also exacerbated the ongoing trend of US farms bifurcating into either small operations or large mega-operations. All told, the farm crisis, alongside continuing patterns of mechanization in agriculture, ultimately resulted in the further reduction of an already dwindling agricultural labor sector in rural America. As such, Brian Thiede and Tim Slack argued in 2017 that "the share of rural workers employed on farms or working as unpaid laborers on family farms has declined to just slightly more than a rounding error over the past five to six decades."[57]

The reduction of farm labor was not the only pattern of industrial restructuring that shaped rural America during the twentieth century. Rural America was also shaped by the migration of manufacturing. Beginning as early as 1970, rural areas had a larger share of employees in manufacturing than urban areas.[58] This represented a shift from the dominance of urban manufacturing in the first half of the twentieth century and was mostly focused on manufacturing related to agriculture and natural resources.

The reasons for the migration of manufacturing from urban to rural America were both technology and profit driven. In some cases, new technology related to communication and transport—as previously discussed with meatpacking—made it more profitable to manufacture goods closer to raw materials.[59] That said, arguably the largest factors in the migration of manufacturing from urban to rural areas were dynamics in land, labor cost, and power. The longer manufacturing remained in urban areas, the more labor became organized, supported unions, and demanded better wages and treatment. To avoid this, capital relocated much of their production to rural and suburban areas where land was inexpensive and labor power was weaker, cheaper, and less unionized.[60] Unfortunately, the same reasons manufacturing left urban America ultimately led to the exit of manufacturing from rural America. With the turn toward further neoliberal globalization, a large portion of manufacturing in the United States has relocated overseas in pursuit of even cheaper production costs.[61]

While a sizable portion of rural manufacturing was and is related to natural resources, natural resource development was a major contributor to the rural American economy long before the rural manufacturing boom in the late twentieth century.[62] Natural resource extraction such as mining, oil and gas development, and timber logging has long been a hallmark of the rural economy, and the pursuit of these resources directed much of the rural settlement patterns we still see today. That said, the actual presence of these activities in 2023 is far less than people normally imagine. With the exception of region- or resource-specific booms, extraction in rural America has largely been on the decline since the 1920s and mostly flat since 2000.[63] For example, the share of rural (i.e., nonmetropolitan) employment in extractive activities was 2.6 percent in 2001 and 2.0 percent in 2022.[64] While nationally the presence is lower than often assumed, it should be noted that these patterns are highly regional. Thus, although natural resource extraction plays a smaller role in rural employment nationally than it did historically, there are still many areas in the United States with very high levels of specialization in the extraction of natural resources. This specialization has often been termed natural resource dependence because of the tendency for areas with high levels of specialization in natural resources to have negative social and economic outcomes. Sometimes termed the "resource curse," these negative outcomes have often been tied to exploitation and the extreme booms and busts of the extractive sectors, among other factors.[65]

This phenomenon of natural resource dependence has experienced a vast amount of attention from the scholarly community over the past fifty years, with findings consistently showing that rural areas in the United States with high levels of natural resource extraction tend to also have elevated levels of poverty. Although many explanations for natural resource dependence and its associated negative outcomes have been advanced for decades, a more recent framework is one termed the framework of dual dependency.[66] The model of dual dependency, which was developed through my own dissertation work, argues that natural resource dependence is a result of the contradiction between the need for investors to be able to keep capital in motion and the simple fact that natural resources are geographically fixed in space. It is much more difficult to relocate investment in logging and mining than it is in something like manufacturing, where you can truly relocate all of production. This contradiction creates friction for the movement of capital and perverse incentives for corporations. This friction leads them to seek out exploitive strategies to keep profit high in resource-rich communities, often to the detriment of local rural people.[67] Ultimately, this dependence is characterized by many factors, including high poverty, low labor market diversity, high inequality, high levels of external corporate influence, gendered labor markets, corruption, and low levels of educational attainment, among others.[68]

Although employment in natural resource extraction in the United States has long been on the decline due to a mixture of environmental regulations, shifting demand, globalization, and mechanization, another form of natural resource development has been growing.[69] This form of development, which we can call nonextractive natural resource development, is a largely service-sector form of natural resource development and includes activities such as nature-based tourism, real estate, recreation and amusement, and other forms of natural amenity development. This sector has grown substantially over the past several decades and represented 13 percent of rural employment in 2022.[70] Unlike natural resource extraction, where decades of research have reached a tentative consensus regarding negative impacts when specialization is high, the economic ramifications of this growth in nonextractive activity remain unclear.

Some scholars, including myself, have argued that nonextractive development shares the same exploitive characteristics as extraction—meaning it is a fraught path forward for rural America.[71] In support of this, others have found the emergence of rural gentrification processes and a remarkable growth in inequality in rural tourism destinations.[72] Although gentrification is arguably an even larger problem in urban areas, rural gentrification is unique because the smaller community leads to elevated levels of direct conflict and animosity; in addition, there are often very few options to relocate within the same labor market. Thus, people are not just priced out of their neighborhood but priced out of the entire economy in which they live and work. That said, not all scholars have found negative results, with a number of economic analyses citing either positive impacts or no impact in either direction.[73] Regardless of long-term economic outcomes, the growth of this form of development reflects the broader trend of a shift in rural America

toward service-sector employment.[74] This sector now represents a significant majority of rural labor, with roughly 74 percent of rural employees working in the service sector in 2022.[75] Although there are service-sector
positions that provide high wages and good job conditions, such as accoun-
tants, doctors, and lawyers, these professional services are much more common in urban areas. Instead, the service-sector shift in rural areas has been
to the arm of the service sector associated with low-wage jobs and limited
opportunities for career advancement—which have been frequently termed
"bad jobs."[76]

Population Dynamics in Rural America

Across rural America, the processes of industrial reorganization occurred
alongside important changes in population dynamics. To those unfamiliar,
population change in an area can only happen through four processes: births,
deaths, in-migration, and out-migration. At a population level, each of these
factors influence and respond to economic context. Beginning with migration, the general trend in the twentieth century was persistent rural out-
migration. Many individuals, particularly those who were young, left rural
areas for opportunities elsewhere over the past four decades. Although the
long-term outcome has been a dramatic decrease in those living in rural areas, it is important to note that there were three significant periods of rural
rebound from 1970 to today.[77] During these rebound periods, the trend of
increasing rural out-migration briefly reversed and resulted in higher in-
migration to rural areas, causing rural America to grow faster than its urban counterpart. These rebound periods occurred in the early 1970s, early
1990s, and early 2000s and generally lasted around five years.[78] More recently,
there is some evidence that the COVID-19 pandemic likely served as a fourth
yet very brief period of rural rebound.[79] Even with these rebounds, estimates
from the Current Population Survey show that from 1986 to 2022, only seven
years of the thirty-two reported showed positive domestic net migration—
meaning in-migration minus out-migration—for rural America. Five of
those years occurred during the rural rebound in the 1990s.[80]

The reasons for these turnarounds were varied and included the electrification of rural America, the growth in rural manufacturing, a generational
preference for rural living, and population aging. Although certainly against
the hopes of many invested in the future of rural America, all of the rebounds
were ultimately short-lived, with rural out-migration quickly returning as the
norm in all cases. That said, migration networks among key populations

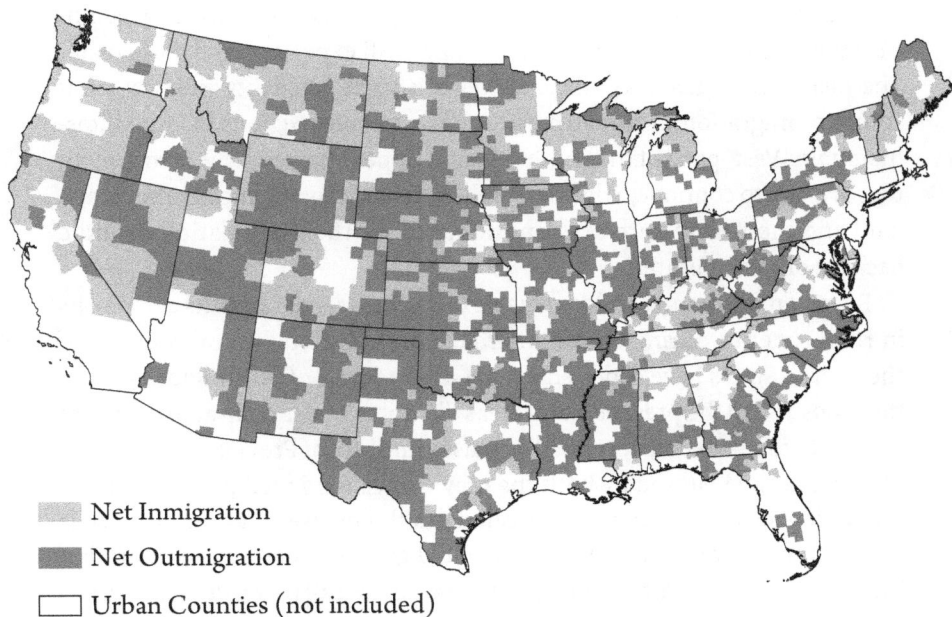

MAP 2.1 Map of rural county-level net migration from 2010 to 2020

established during these rural booms—particularly Latino migration to rural areas—did persist and in many cases grew.[81] In a number of areas, in-
migration and growth of Latino families has actually offset population declines that would have otherwise occurred—with communities that have
embraced new residents thriving and those that have been unwelcoming to
newcomers continuing to decline.[82] Finally, it is important to remember that
migration and industrial restructuring are related. For example, there is a
joint-migration flow of retirees and Latino families who are employed in construction and services to support those aging individuals in specific rural
retirement destinations.[83]

  Although many discuss the overall out-migration of rural America as a major issue, as they should, an equally important factor is the diversity of migration patterns affecting rural communities. It is vital we remember that
even though out-migration is a persistent issue, it is not as if out-migration
is the universal experience across the rural reaches of the United States.
Map 2.1 presents a simplified map of net migration for rural counties in the
United States over the time period of 2010 to 2020. Here we can see that between 2010 and 2020, 76 percent (1,171) of the counties considered rural in

2020 experienced net out-migration. However, we also can see that a signifi-cant number of rural counties, 24 percent (378) experienced the opposite. The takeaway is that a significant level of spatial inequality exists when it comes to migration in rural America. High amenity regions like the inter-mountain West, parts of the Southeast, and Upper Midwest have seen growth that is likely to continue, while less well-endowed regions such as the Heart-land and the Deep South are continuing to see their population dwindle because of out-migration.

Beyond migration, it is also valuable to discuss trends in births and deaths in rural America during the twentieth century. Although rural counties of the United States have experienced persistent levels of out-migration from the 1900s and to the present, rural areas did not experience an actual net loss in population between decennial censuses until 2020. Previously, true pop-ulation loss was buoyed by both the previously mentioned periods of rural rebound and what demographers call natural increase. Natural increase is the term for how much a population would grow if there was no migration (i.e., births minus deaths). When it is negative, we call that natural decrease. Historically, natural increase was the norm in the United States, and natu-ral decrease was rare but more common in rural counties. However, natural decrease has been increasingly dramatically from 1980 onward.

In the 1990s, only 29 percent of rural counties experienced a natural de-crease, but from 2010 to 2020, that number was 55 percent.[84] There are sev-eral explanations for this, but two related reasons are arguably the most vital. First, the rural population of the United States is, and has been, aging. Population aging means that the average age of the population is increasing. When there is a large cohort entering late life and a relatively smaller cohort at earlier life stages, the absolute number of deaths increases. Second, the persistent out-migration of young people from rural America is pulling away those who would otherwise have children in rural areas. This reduces the relative number of births to deaths and fosters natural decrease. This persis-tent out-migration of young people, often termed "brain drain," is the prod-uct of limited real opportunities for young people in rural areas, as well as the ever-increasing importance of college for social mobility. Unfortunately, once young people do obtain college degrees, there is little to pull them back to the rural places where they grew up.[85] Natural decrease and population aging have unfortunately led to a vicious cycle for many rural areas. As popu-lations age, the tax base dwindles, and there are fewer children. This can then lead to the closure of schools, which leads to even less in-migration of young families and ultimately the complete collapse of the rural area.

Rural America in the Contemporary Era

Up to now we have largely explored the factors that shaped rural America from colonization to around 1980. However, this book is largely concerned with rural America in the 2020s, and so a richer description of the current status and recent history of rural America is needed. Here, the focus will be largely on the social, economic, and health-related dimensions of well-being in rural areas from 1980 to today.

You need not look far before finding a paper, report, or news story discussing rural decline in the United States. Long before the 2016 presidential election put this topic in the spotlight, there was a strong discourse on rural disadvantage and rural people in the United States being "left behind." However, the reality of this decline is not as straightforward as it appears on its face. The reason is that since 1980, many of the rural counties faring best on indicators of well-being have been reclassified as urban. In total, there are now 450 fewer rural counties than there were in 1980. These counties have transitioned from rural to urban over this period either due to incorporation into existing metropolitan areas or because of internal urbanization. This reclassification effect has been termed by Daniel Lichter and Kenneth Johnson as "the paradox of rural population decline."[86] The implications of this paradox cannot be overstated, and the recent work exploring how rural-to-urban reclassification affects our perspective on rural decline stands, in many ways, as the technical counterpart to some of the conceptual arguments that will be made in chapter 4.

Since 1980, many would argue that we have seen a decline in rural population overall, with a reduction from 54 million in 1980 to 46 million in 2020. However, this is only true if we reassess rurality every decade. Suppose we instead ask, "How much have counties *that were rural in 1980* grown since 1980?" If we ask this question, we would find that rural American has actually increased from 54 million to around 70 million people.[87] This effect is similar for many other indicators of rural well-being. For example, it is well documented that mortality rates are higher in rural America than urban America. However, Matthew Brooks and colleagues showed that more than 25 percent of the mortality disparity between rural and urban America is attributable to this decadal reclassification since 1980.[88] In fact, in each successive decade of reclassification, it was the rural counties with the lowest mortality rates that were reclassified as urban. You will note that if reclassification only accounts for around 25 percent of the gap, this still leaves a sizable disparity between rural and urban Americans.

This is because although the paradox of rural decline does influence our interpretation of rural-urban trends over the past forty years, it does not fully explain or account for the very real and growing difficulties still faced by those living in counties either currently or formerly classified as rural. For example, holding rurality constant, mortality rates between rural and urban America were largely at parity in 1980. However, by 2018 this disparity had grown to 14 percent. This disparity can be attributed to concurrent patterns of population aging and rising midlife mortality stemming from the opioid crisis and other social factors.[89]

Other indicators of well-being also reflect persistent difficulties faced by rural counties in the United States, even when accounting for this paradox of decline. For example, poverty, when measured by the official poverty measure of the United States, is, on average, higher in rural counties than urban counties in every decade—even when holding rurality constant in 1980. Further, the average poverty rate in counties considered rural in 1980 has stayed more stable than one would like—declining from 17.1 percent to 15.1 percent from 1980 to 2020.[90] The poverty disadvantage in rural America is well documented. In fact, of the 318 persistent poverty counties in the United States—defined as counties with poverty rates greater than 20 percent in 1990, 2000, 2010, and 2020—270 of them were rural.[91]

Although the official poverty rates paint a story of rural stagnation and disadvantage, even this narrative is open to question. The reason is that the official poverty measure of the United States does not adequately capture hardship in contemporary America. The official measure uses artificially low thresholds, does not have a cost-of-living adjustment, and relies upon gross pre-tax income as the measure of household resources.[92] Acknowledging these limitations, the US Census now produces the Supplemental Poverty Measure, which addresses many of these issues. When this supplemental measure is used, we actually find rural poverty is slightly lower than urban poverty (12.2 percent rural versus 12.4 percent urban in 2022)—largely due to a geographic adjustment for cost of living.[93] In fact, when comparing these two measures of hardship, we find that rural poverty was higher by both metrics in 1980, but the supplemental measure flipped in the 1990s, with rural areas having lower poverty rates from then on. That said, there is currently an ongoing and dynamic academic discourse surrounding the validity of the current geographic adjustment, which means that the Supplemental Poverty Measure may not yet accurately capture rural poverty in the United States, either.[94]

Beyond poverty, other outcomes in rural America highlight the vast differences felt between rural and urban areas. For example, in 1980, 15 percent of adults in urban counties had at least a bachelor's degree, on average, and in rural counties, this number was only 10 percent. If we hold rural classification constant, then we find that the disparity is even greater in 2020, with 32 percent of urban adults and only 21 percent of rural adults having at least a bachelor's degree, on average.[95] Similarly, we also find that population aging has disproportionately affected rural America, even when holding rurality constant. When holding rurality constant in 1980, the average median age of rural counties in 2020 was 42.5 compared to the urban average of 39.9, and the percentage over the age of 65 was 20.6 percent in rural counties, on average, relative to only 16.8 percent in urban counties. Finally, even when accounting for inflation, per capita income in rural counties has, on average, been lower than urban counties in every decade, although the gap has been relatively constant.

The COVID-19 pandemic highlighted many enduring differences between rural and urban parts of the country, and it would be negligent to not acknowledge this important recent history. Although COVID-19 began in largely urban areas, it quickly became a problem for rural areas as well. Importantly, the high likelihood of deleterious rural outcomes was voiced early on in the pandemic by those working on rural health.[96] Because of a lack of COVID-19 public and personal prevention protocols, cases ultimately spiked in rural areas and remained high—with a greater share of rural residents contracting and dying from COVID-19 than their urban counterparts by the end of 2020 and through 2021.[97] Aligned with this finding, vaccination rates were far lower in rural counties than urban counties.[98]

Beyond the health impacts, COVID-19 also had dramatic yet nuanced impacts on rural economic well-being. Both early and later work during the pandemic found notable levels of economic disruption reported by rural residents in primary data collected through surveys.[99] However, federal statistics showed a paradoxical effect, wherein rural residents were far less likely than urban residents to report they went unpaid for missed hours, were unable to work (or look for work) because of COVID-19, or transitioned to remote work.[100] The picture is further complicated by research showing high levels of moderate and serious mental distress among residents of the rural West and other parts of the country.[101] Ultimately, these complicated differences are a result of the interaction between economic and public health policy along the rural-urban continuum. Thus, the economic "advantage" felt by rural Americans is a product of the laissez-faire approach rural governments took to pandemic precautions, meaning that the economic advantage found in rural counties co-occurred with a public health disadvantage. Thus, while the picture for COVID-19 mortality clearly shows worse outcomes in rural areas than urban areas, other outcomes remain more nuanced because of the interaction between economic and public health policy.

An important topic of interest in rural America during the COVID-19 pandemic has been the perceived increase in rural in-migration as a result of the pandemic, with some referring to rural growth areas as "Zoom towns." Some point to wealthy in-migrants as the cause of dramatic property value increases and housing shortages, and others look to pandemic migration as a possible mechanism for stalling rural out-migration.[102] Emergent research remains uncertain when it comes to the long-term consequences of pandemic migration for rural areas.

Work from Julia Petersen and colleagues in 2024 showed that net migration did, in fact, increase across rural America during and after the pandemic.[103] This was predominately driven by a decline in out-migration—meaning the pandemic prevented people from moving who likely would have otherwise— and in many cases this increase was not enough to push net migration positive (i.e., overall net in-migration). That said, in the rural counties dominated by recreation amenities, there was positive net migration during the first year of the pandemic. In subsequent years, these counties maintained elevated levels of net migration but largely transitioned back to an overall pattern of net out-migration. According to the analysis by Petersen and colleagues, the overall picture of pandemic migration and rural America is one of less population loss due to net out-migration as opposed to population growth from net in-migration. For example, of the 2,231 counties they classified as rural, only 495 (22.2 percent) reported positive net migration from the last study year (i.e., April 2022 to March 2023). This is a slight improvement from the 392 counties (17.5 percent) that reported net in-migration in the year immediately preceding the pandemic. Although this means that the majority of rural counties are continuing to experience net out-migration, 1,442 (64.4 percent) of rural counties still had greater net migration in 2023 relative to the year before the pandemic. Thus, although it appears the impact of COVID-19 on rural migration is waning, the decline in out-migration endured through at least 2023.

A supplemental view was provided by Kenneth Johnson in a paper highlighting the fact that the intercensal estimates for 2021 suggest a net population growth in rural America for the first time in fifty years.[104] As almost all of this growth can be attributed to the 489 recreation and retirement counties, this growth, even if it holds, is highly clustered on rural counties that were already faring better than the rest of rural America pre-pandemic. This potentially rosy view is further hamstrung by the fact that amid this overall rural population growth, the 2022 population estimates from the US

TABLE 2.1 Average levels of county well-being indicators between rural and urban America, 2018–2022

	Rural (N = 1,956)	Urban (N = 1,188)
Poverty rate	15.5	12.5
Percent over age 65	20.9	17.7
Percent of adults with bachelor's degree or more	20.3	28.8
Civilian unemployment rate	5.0	4.9
Percent with a disability	17.2	14.5
Median age	42.6	40.0
Gini index of inequality	44.8	44.5
Income per capita	$31,061.29	$37,521.71
All-cause age-adjusted mortality (per hundred thousand)	881.1	818.7
All-cause crude death rate (per hundred thousand)	1,275.5	1,030.2
Net migration rate, 2010–2020 (per hundred people)	−1.07	4.17

Note: All data except for mortality and migration comes from the 2018–2022 American Community Survey estimates provided by the US Census Bureau. Mortality data is extracted from the CDC WONDER Underlying Cause of Death file for 2018–2020. Net migration estimates from 2010 to 2020 come from the Net Migration Patterns for US Counties. N values vary slightly between data sources due to availability and agency decisions on consistent boundaries. Rural = nonmetropolitan counties. Urban = metropolitan counties according to 2023 Office of Management and Budget classifications.

Census Bureau showed that 56 percent of rural counties lost population between April 2021 and July 2022.[105] Thus, although it is possible that there may be persistent growth in some rural counties as a result of the pandemic, particularly in recreation and retirement destinations, the results remain mixed, and data suggests a return to pre-pandemic trends where persistent levels of net out-migration are the norm.

As is hopefully clear, rural America generally has worse outcomes on indicators of well-being, even once we account for the paradox of rural decline. Thus, even though this paradox may lead us to overstate trends in rural hardship over the past forty years, there remain very real gaps between rural and urban America, and some of them—particularly related to mortality and population aging—are growing. These gaps, as they stand in 2023, are presented as key indicators of well-being in table 2.1. Although it is important to keep rural-to-urban transitions in mind, these statistics display the current inequality found between the areas considered rural and urban in 2023 — wherein rural counties fare poorer on every outcome — and provide us with a clear image of the state of rural disadvantage before moving on to the conceptual arguments that follow.

Importantly, these indicators of well-being are often the worst in communities where many people face intersectional marginalization; that is, they experience the multiplicative impacts of being both rural and otherwise marginalized in the United States.[106] In this case, we should be particularly sensitive to the experiences of rural Latino, Black, and American Indian populations. Rural America has many culturally rich nonwhite communities. However, these communities have historically faced incredible hostility, racism, exclusion, and marginalization from white-dominated local, state, and federal governments — as well as a general lack of awareness of their existence from the general American public, which continues to imagine rural America as exclusively white, working class, and pastoral. Whenever we are discussing rural development, it is vital that we keep these communities and their struggles at the forefront, so we do not inappropriately lean on romantic notions of American rurality.

The history of rural America is a topic that warrants its own bookshelf. As such, the focus here has been on providing the necessary context for the chapters which lie ahead. The primary takeaway from this history should be that (1) rural America was founded on the mistreatment, colonization, and erasure of Indigenous and nonwhite residents, many of which were brought to America against their will or "made American" through conquest; (2) the well-being of rural America is worse, and in some cases worsening, as compared with urban America, even when accounting for the paradox of rural decline; and (3) rural America is not, and has never been, a monolithic portion of the country where only white working-class people live.

CHAPTER THREE

Frameworks of Rural Economic Development

Economic development, often just termed "development," has received immense attention from scholars, activists, and practitioners of all stripes. The term can be roughly defined as the process of economic growth and rising consumption within an area.[1] From the earliest days of development theory and practice, urbanization has been pegged as a "defining outcome of development."[2] As such, questions of agrarian lands and the location of rural spaces in the global project of development have regularly been asked. Views on the status of rural areas in developed nations have varied wildly, with some scholars arguing rural spaces reflect vestiges of a time removed and others viewing rural areas as modern spaces linked to urbanity and central to the larger process of urbanization. In these arguments, the scale of focus has often been on the nation-state, with an emphasis on GDP and nationwide development continuing to dominate discussions to this day. However, a strictly nation-level perspective is ultimately lacking because all countries have significant internal variation as it relates to local levels of development, and the United States is no exception.

Because of the heterogeneity of development found within countries, there are a variety of subnational perspectives on rural economic development. However, they have generally said little about the broad concept of urbanization, instead focusing on community-level development concerns and articulating what factors are needed to facilitate economic growth and development for communities. Thus, there exists a bifurcation within our understanding of development that creates what Linda Lobao and colleagues term a "missing middle."[3] As we will see in this chapter, the missing middle leads to a disconnect wherein critical theories of development are not viewed as helpful or relevant to community-level concerns, and their important insights end up sidelined in favor of less critical views. This disconnect has fostered a continued reliance on neoliberal economic growth models within the rural economic development arena in the United States. While the inherent shortcomings of this economic growth model will be fully explored in chapter 4, first it is important to outline the relevant theoretical perspectives on development, as well as their respective strengths and weaknesses for understanding rural America. Importantly, this chapter will not provide a long-scale history or comprehensive overview of global development theory. That book-length task has already been exceptionally undertaken separately by Philip McMichael and John Isbister.[4] Instead, what follows provides an overview of dominant macro and micro perspectives on development, as well as the meso-level theories that exist and how those theories relate to rural economic development in the United States.

It is important to make it clear that in this chapter, and throughout this work, the focus is on rural economic development, not rural development writ large. This is vital to note because although terms like rural development and community development are often used as synonymous with rural economic development, the term "development" has many definitions, and there is a large body of research and practice focused on sustainable rural development outside of an economic context. At the global level, this is evidenced by the United Nations Sustainable Development Goals, a set of seventeen agreed-upon goals that set the agenda for global development efforts from 2015 to 2030.[5] These goals span a wide range of topics focused on improving well-being and the environment across the globe while also promoting sustainable environments and societies. Goals include reducing inequalities, securing access to clean water and sanitation for all, affordable and clean energy, climate action, and eradicating poverty, among others. Thus, while economic growth is still one of the goals (i.e., Sustainable Development Goal 8), economic concerns are not at the forefront, and this view of sustainable global development stands outside the focus of this book.

Clarifying this focus on rural economic development is also relevant at the local level within the United States. For example, community development can be thought of as the development of community relationships, the bringing together of in and out groups, the maintenance of social capital, and the strengthening of community ties as ends in themselves, rather than as a means for catalyzing economic growth.[6] Further, some development projects remain focused on specific local problems such as food deserts or lack of essential infrastructure for well-being. When these efforts are not pursued under the guise of broader economic development, they fall outside the focus of this book and may indeed result in sustainable outcomes for the community in question. That said, as you will see in the following chapters, the vast majority of rural development efforts in the United States remain anchored in economic growth models—even when they avoid such terms. Therefore, it should be assumed that when development is invoked going forward, it refers to economic development unless noted otherwise. In what follows, conventional views on economic development, both global and local, will be outlined and then followed by critical perspectives.

Conventional Views

The dominant conventional view of development is tied to linear notions of economic development and modernization, wherein a country or community moves from a state of being undeveloped to developed.[7] This view is perhaps best exemplified by the seemingly unshakable perspective of Walt Whitman Rostow.

In his most influential work, *The Stages of Economic Growth: A Non-Communist Manifesto*, Rostow argued that national development occurred in five distinct phases.[8] First, there is the "traditional society," where there is a ceiling on productivity due to a lack of industrialization and organized agriculture. The second stage is termed the "preconditions for takeoff," where there is initial expansion into world markets, the idea of capitalism is embraced (often by means of colonization), a strong nation-state is established, and a country's competitive advantage—meaning the goods or services it can provide cheaper than anyone else—becomes understood. The third stage is the "takeoff," where new industries and profits expand rapidly, the entrepreneurial class also expands, the national economy exploits new resources and methods of production, and there are transitions in social, economic, and political structure that allow growth to be sustained. In the fourth stage, the "drive to maturity," sectors mature, and there is movement beyond initial takeoff industries and to more advanced forms of production. Finally, there is the "age of high mass-consumption," wherein the economy shifts to durable consumer goods and services, and resources are increasingly allocated to welfare and social security.

Rostow's views, which he advocated both in his 1960 book and during his time as an adviser to Presidents John F. Kennedy and Lyndon B. Johnson, served as the bedrock for much of the development efforts from the 1960s onward. Although these views have long been subject to critique on numerous grounds and rarely directly invoked, they are still very influential today. Grounded in the experience of the United States, Rostow argued that these stages were not simply a historical observation but were instead the "bone-structure" of development.[9] As such, development is reified as something that comes from within and is a natural course that all nations will take if pushed along the correct track. Although created in the context of nation-level development, we can easily see how this linear, stage-based view can be, and has often been, applied to the subnational scale. With the obvious caveat that concepts such as macroeconomic competitive advantage fall away, it is no great leap to place counties, cities, or communities in the United States within these five stages and imagine how they may move along the spectrum from undeveloped to developed or, in a simplified context, from rural to urban.

Despite this linear perspective continuing to inform public views of local, national, and global economic development, there are many issues with Rostow's framework. First, it essentializes the experience of a few colonizing imperialist countries as the standard or natural way of progression, while also conveniently ignoring just how much internal and external appropriation, exploitation, and marginalization was necessary to accomplish later stages of development.[10] In doing so, it places the position of the United States in the mid-1900s as the end goal of development while ignoring any other possible pathways. This teleological view ultimately ignores the basic fact that we have only one world to observe and that the anecdotal experience of the United States does not provide enough data for formal theorization.

A second issue is that, similar to many microeconomic theories focused too narrowly on the individual, Rostow's macroeconomic framework focuses too strongly on individual countries and omits intercountry dynamics. Countries do not develop in a vacuum, and each country's current level of economic health is tied to its power relative to other already developed nations. The focus on individual nations forgets that many countries have not developed explicitly because the actions of, and exploitation by, more developed nations have prevented them from developing. For example, the United States would not have developed the way it did without the gross exploitation of slaves kidnapped from their homes in Africa.

Third, the linear view of development suggests that all countries can reach the age of high mass-consumption. However, even if this was something all countries actually wanted to aspire to, there is no evidence to suggest this is the case under our current model of capitalism. The need for constant growth under capitalism means that capital requires cheap labor and the ability to exploit lower-income countries. If lower-income countries ceased to exist because they had attained high mass-consumption, critical views of development argue that our current system of global capitalism would fail due to the loss of the between-nation inequality and exploitation that fuel the system.[11] Now, this may be a desirable outcome for those more interested in global equality than the success of capitalism. However, the point is that we simply would never reach this outcome while letting our current global economic model run its course. Thus, the assumption of Rostow that late-stage development is a natural long-term outcome for all countries is misguided at best.

Beyond the issues foundational to capitalism limiting the value of this linear model, our pressing climate needs and the existence of finite resources further make it clear that not every country can reach this last stage within our existing system. In short, the fact that the United States exists at the level of opulence it does means that not every country can reach the economic status of the United States within our current system.

Despite its shortcomings, internal linear development thinking—even if not formally drawing on Rostow, whose specific framework has fallen out of favor—is what dominates subnational economic development theory and practice in the United States. Because of the specific needs of communities versus nations, a number of frameworks for encouraging local rural economic development have been advanced. Key among them are the five related perspectives of (1) the Community Capitals Framework; (2) economic diversification models; (3) models of innovation and entrepreneurship; (4) the Tailored, Resilient, Inclusive, and Collaborative approach; and (5) Rural Rising. To be clear, it is not that the linear nature of these frameworks makes them completely unhelpful at the subnational level. In fact, all of these perspectives can be applied to community-level economic development goals with at least some level of success. The point here is that in practice, all of these perspectives still situate growth, urbanization, and increases in economic activity as the goal and endpoint of rural economic development while placing the responsibility of ensuring well-being within the community. As we will see later, this emphasis often cannot achieve what proponents expect.

Before discussing the five contemporary models mentioned, it is worth briefly considering a dominant historical model of rural economic development that, while largely rejected by many contemporary academics and practitioners in the 2020s, still pops up regularly—smokestack chasing. Smokestack chasing is an economic development practice where external firms are encouraged to relocate and create jobs in an area through aggressive lobbying and incentives, often in the form of large tax breaks.[12] Although this may appear reasonable on its face, the reality is that the vast majority of job growth in the United States does not come from business relocations but instead from new businesses and within-market firm expansions.[13] Further, the relocation of plants can have positive impacts on the surrounding regional economy but negative labor market impacts on the resident community.[14] Thus, it is not as if the people in the community where a firm locates will get the jobs that firm provides. Finally, the research on enterprise zones—geographic areas attempting economic growth through smokestack chasing and policies such as tax breaks, exemptions from regulations, and other provisions—has consistently found no beneficial labor market impacts from these zones and their policies.[15] As such, economic development initiatives tied to smokestack chasing are unlikely to provide what proponents hope and can often result in harm.

Moving to the contemporary subnational models, the Community Capitals Framework (CCF) is popular for thinking through the various capitals needed to advance community development and catalyze growth. In this framework, a capital is "any resource capable of producing other resources."[16] Developed by Cornelia Flora and colleagues in the 1990s, the framework initially focused on four capitals: capital goods, land, financial capital, and human capital. However, by 2016, the framework had progressed to now include seven distinct forms: natural capital, cultural capital, human capital, social capital, political capital, financial capital, and built capital.[17] These seven capitals are argued as working individually and cooperatively to ensure "sustainable communities," which are communities described as working for broad economic security, healthy ecosystems, and social inclusion.[18]

Ultimately, the CCF serves as a heuristic that rural communities, planners, policymakers, and economic development groups can use to help assess what capitals may be lacking in a community or could be leveraged for future development efforts. No single capital is positioned as most vital; instead, the goal is to balance the different capitals and seek linkages between them. To be clear, the creators of this framework are well aware of the limitations of relying on economic growth as the sole priority of development efforts—hence their choice to use the term economic security instead of economic growth. This means the CCF model can be, and has been, used for community development efforts outside of economic development initiatives. In fact, it is likely the developers of this model would argue that is its intended purpose. That said, although the creators of the framework may wish otherwise, the function usage of CCF is often as a heuristic for helping rural communities pursue economic development along the conventional linear trajectory.

This functional usage of the CCF is evidenced by its popularity and adaptation within US rural economic development efforts. For example, the

WealthWorks organization, developed out of the Aspen Institute, relies upon the capitals framework in its messaging to rural communities on how to build regional wealth—although WealthWorks takes great care in not mentioning this inspiration directly on its website.[19] Adding in an eighth capital of individual capital, WealthWorks argues these eight capitals represent the overall wealth of an area and can be leveraged to facilitate new wealth, upward mobility, prosperity, and self-reliance. The WealthWorks model consists of four steps: (1) exploring regional wealth-building, (2) identifying a market opportunity, (3) constructing a WealthWorks value chain, and (4) gauging wealth-building impact. These four steps are essentially a CCF-grounded approach to identifying a community's competitive advantage in national and global markets, which can then be used to catalyze internal linear development.

Related to the CCF's emphasis on a diversity of capitals are the arguments from industrial organization theory on economic diversity and agglomeration. In this case, economic diversity refers to the makeup of sectors and firms within a market. In general, it is believed that having a more diversified market is more competitive, less volatile, and better for future growth and well-being.[20] Through the creation of diverse markets, rural areas can grow into more active economic entities. A valuable way to achieve this diversity is agglomeration—the process of regional economic growth where related sectors site near one another to achieve cost savings, network effects, and other externalities.[21] It should be noted, though, that within this viewpoint, diverse markets without these agglomerative linkages will still receive benefits from market diversity.[22] Beyond agglomeration, market diversity is also expected to facilitate lower levels of market concentration in the rural labor market. Market concentration in this case refers to the share of a labor market captured by each firm. In a completely concentrated labor market, one firm would hold all the jobs; in an unconcentrated market, many firms hold equal numbers of jobs. The case of high concentration is known as oligopsony and is associated with disproportionate power on the side of capital relative to labor.[23] This results in limited job-changing mobility, poorer working conditions, and lower pay for labor in the market. Thus, frameworks centered on economic diversity argue that the presence of multiple sectors in a rural labor market works against this form of concentration and leads to healthier and more vibrant rural economies. In doing so, they implicitly argue that the solution for rural economies is growth into markets that more closely resemble urban markets in their diversity and concentration.

The third model to consider is the perspective centering innovation and entrepreneurship in rural areas. Because rural communities desire to develop themselves from the inside out—as opposed to through the intervention of external investors—many within the rural economic development world have long been pushing for rural entrepreneurship. In this case, the emphasis is on designing policies and programs that encourage local residents to open up new businesses. Since new and young businesses are disproportionately responsible for job creation in the United States, the expectation is that these new businesses will catalyze growth throughout the rural economy.[24] The establishment of credit access for new small businesses is therefore critical, as is the support of entrepreneurs through the development of networks, education, and access to expertise.[25]

The push for entrepreneurs in rural America is not without evidence. Beyond the anecdotal success stories of places like Holmes County, Ohio—which has leveraged a community of entrepreneurs into becoming the state's top county for small business owners—economic research has shown that entrepreneurial activities are one of the few effective drivers of income and employment growth in remote rural areas.[26] The continued dominance of this model is further illustrated in the 2021 report from Endeavor Insight and Google for Startups titled *Rural Entrepreneurship in the United States: A Pillar of Economic Development for Rural Communities*.[27] In this report, entrepreneurship is presented as an important pillar for economic development that can overcome difficulties posed by traditional strategies of economic development like smokestack chasing. Emphasis is placed on the scalability of companies, with highly productive and tech-enabled sectors given preeminence. Ultimately, the report offers multiple recommendations focused on scalability, access to lenders, talent recruitment, and regional partnerships, among others.

A further essential component of the entrepreneurial model is the concept of innovation, such as when a rural resident or community applies resources in a new way to achieve positive economic outcomes. Some argue innovation is the ultimate bedrock of long-term economic growth, and that technological innovation—anchored in the amount of human capital invested in science and technology—is the key to long-run rural growth and revitalization.[28] However, more often, innovation—whether it be in technology, marketing, process, or business structure—is viewed simply as a necessary factor for generating rural economic development, and this innovation is more likely to occur when entrepreneurship is properly incentivized and supported. In line with this thinking, the report from Endeavor Insights is broadly supportive of innovation while acknowledging that innovation alone is not enough to catalyze economic development.[29]

The fourth related model is the Tailored, Resilient, Inclusive, and Collaborative (TRIC) approach, detailed by Daniel Paul Davis and Andrew Dumont in their edited volume from the Federal Reserve Bank of St. Louis titled *Investing in Rural Prosperity*. In their chapter, they argue that the "TRIC" to rural economic development is engaging in certain activities.[30] These activities should be tailored to fit the place in question and meet the goals of the community as well as the assets already present; the activities should be resilient in that they will be adaptable to both gradual and sudden changes; they should be inclusive in order to benefit and engage the entire community; and they should be collaborative in that the activities are supported and worked upon by various sectors, levels of government, and skill sets. The TRIC is ultimately forward looking and encourages strategies that are in line with future trends and the realities of our current economy. As with the other frameworks discussed, the onus of development within the TRIC is placed on the community, and the ultimate goals of economic growth and expansion are clearly aligned with the internal linear development framework discussed previously.

A final, less academically popular model of rural economic development is one developed in 2021 by McKinsey & Company and known as Rural Rising.[31] Working with Walmart, McKinsey & Company identified five archetypes of rural communities that reflect different economic growth trajectories and priorities: Americana, distressed Americana, rural service hubs, great escapes, and resource-rich regions. Rural Rising uses these archetypes to argue there is not a one-size-fits-all way to develop rural America. After identifying sectors, workforce, and community and connectivity as the essential elements of a thriving rural community, they then position growth as the ultimate goal and identify a multistep strategy for rural economic development. The steps are similar to WealthWorks: (1) assess the current state of the region, (2) identify the value proposition, (3) evaluate existing programs and initiatives, and (4) establish partnerships and rural hubs. Finally, although McKinsey & Company acknowledges that there won't be one-size-fits-all strategies, it identifies several broad initiatives deemed worthy of pursuing nationwide, including launching "big push" investments, embracing placemaking, developing tourism infrastructure, attracting small and medium-size businesses, attracting remote workers, and increasing health care access. As is hopefully clear, the Rural Rising model may be the most steadfastly tied to linear growth thinking out of the five discussed.

These five perspectives are all tied to one another and simply reflect related ways of thinking through community-level rural economic development under a linear model. Vital to Rural Rising, the TRIC, and CCF—when the CCF is used in this manner—are rural innovation and entrepreneurship, as is the importance of ensuring regional economic diversity and encouraging agglomeration. Further, they are all related in that they ultimately look to the community as the source of rural economic development while also making many of the same uncritical assumptions as Rostow. It is not hard to see why these frameworks have focused on the level of the community. These frameworks tell rural communities that they themselves can engender real and sustainable economic growth within their community, and many times that is what these communities both need and want to hear. It is simply unhelpful to tell a rural community or rural economic development group that the only way to realize broader change is through some sort of systemic structural policy shift—the kinds of policies that naturally flow from the critical perspectives to be discussed. Communities need things they can act on now to try and make the best of the difficult situations they find themselves in.

Unfortunately, as time goes on, the situation is only getting worse for those rural areas that have not urbanized or found success as a recreation or retirement county, which means that structural change is increasingly one of the few realistic options for large-scale support of what remains of rural America. To understand why this is the case and what options we should pursue, we must turn to nonlinear critical perspectives of economic development.

Critical Views

Similar to conventional views, many critical views of development also focus on the scale of the nation-state. However, unlike the conventional views, there are very few critical frameworks of development that focus on community-level change. This is largely a product of the kinds of solutions one arrives at when considering the arguments embedded in these models. Unlike conventional economic development perspectives, these frameworks all center inequality, exploitation, and the inherent contradictions of capitalism. It should be noted that many of the community-level frameworks of development discussed in the previous section have grown to consider inequality over time. However, they have largely focused on inequality within communities as opposed to the between-community view of spatial inequality often taken by critical authors. Drawing on the valuable discussion provided by Isbister in his 2006 book *Promises Not Kept*, there are two critical schools of interest to us here: (1) the dependency school and (2) purely Marxist frameworks.[32]

The dependency school uses a broad set of frameworks from various scholars during the middle of the twentieth century. These frameworks, which were developed by Latin scholars such as Raúl Prebisch and Fernando H. Cardoso as well as German sociologist Andre Gunder Frank and American sociologist Immanuel Wallerstein, are all an outgrowth of Marxism and reflect an orientation centered on critiquing the inequalities and contradictions of global capitalism. Within the dependency school, there are several specific frameworks and points of deviation between scholars, and their differences will not be fully detailed here. Instead, what follows is a broad articulation of the central tenets of the dependency school.

To begin, all dependency frameworks rely on core-periphery distinctions. Under this model, core countries or regions are the wealthy developed nations that exploit and underdevelop peripheral nations or regions of the world. Underdevelop, in this case, refers to the explicit actions that core nations take to ensure profit and limit improvements in peripheral nations. According to the dependency school, peripheral nations face worse terms of trade and are subject to a race to the bottom against other peripheral nations. In this circular model, the creation of exports in peripheral nations is cheap because of the low labor costs that stem from uneven exchange values and heightened levels of exploitation. However, capital is motivated to keep profit high amid local (e.g., labor organization) and external (e.g., competition and innovation) factors that work to reduce profit over time. To combat this, capital from core nations works to create ever more exploitive terms of trade with peripheral nations, and wages are reduced even further. Because of the persistent underdevelopment of a region and the poverty it engenders, labor has little choice but to accept lower wages and worse conditions because they are the only options available. This cycle repeats, creating what many call a "race to the bottom," the outcome of which is the underdevelopment of the peripheral nation or region.

As noted by the use of the term "regions," we can apply this core-periphery model, which was first articulated at the nation-state level, subnationally. Although not all of the mechanisms of the dependency school are directly transferable—for example, the US constitutional ban on state-to-state trade regulation means we cannot look to state-level trade policy as a mechanism for underdevelopment—the broad contours of the dependency school apply just as well to a subnational analysis. An example of this application can be found in my earlier work on natural resource development in rural America, where I argued that rural areas in the United States can be viewed as the periphery of core urban areas, and that this peripheral status is a key way that natural resource capitalists have historically underdeveloped rural communities and fostered their dependence upon the natural resource sector.[33]

Within the core-periphery model, there are two additional considerations to note. First, some argue that there exists a middle category called the semi-periphery—namely, regions or countries that are still exploited by the core but occupy a middle zone and are able to exploit peripheries of their own. This semi-periphery is somewhat akin to the petty bourgeoisie—the management class that exists between the true working class and the capitalist— and exists to prevent a total bifurcation of the world system while also providing a sense of hope to regions and countries.[34] Although it uses terminology different from that of the dependency school, an interesting analog at a subnational scale is the economic work on spread and backwash effects. Under this model, rural regions closer to urban growth centers are expected to experience benefits from growth (e.g., semi-periphery), but remote rural regions are more likely to experience negative impacts because of their population being drawn away (e.g., periphery).[35] The second important consideration is that the dependency school can be viewed as neocolonial, meaning that although we have largely exited the era of formal colonization, colonial linkages remain and are even established in the present day, and these linkages continue to shape the exploitation of the periphery.[36]

Key to the dependency school is this notion of underdevelopment, and the central premise is that the less developed state of peripheral regions and nations is not some sort of remnant of the past but is instead a direct result of the actions of core nations or regions. Thus, the term "underdevelopment" highlights that the development process affects all areas in different ways and that a country does not develop in a vacuum. For a country like the United States to develop as it has, it had to underdevelop other nations to ensure a steady and high rate of profit for capital. This underdevelopment exists as a function of what Frank calls unequal exchange.[37]

Unequal exchange refers to a situation where a core area is able to leverage its power and wealth to obtain the upper hand on terms of trade with its peripheries. As such, the peripheral nations and regions end up giving up more than they get. This means that power and wealth continue to transfer from the periphery to the core as the cycle progresses. Although the dependency school broadly agrees that some degree of underdevelopment is an essential component to the process of capitalist development, there has been disagreement about whether and how underdevelopment is the dominant outcome for the periphery. For example, in the 1970s, Cardoso argued (1) that to assume all of the global periphery is in a dependent relationship with core countries would be shortsighted, and (2) that many of those using core-periphery models were falling prey to ahistorical oversimplifications.[38] In recent decades, scholars have expanded on the economic formulation of unequal exchange by arguing that there is also a process of ecologically unequal exchange within global capitalism—wherein environmental harms and resource depletion are relocated onto the periphery by the core, allowing core countries and regions to preserve their environmental health at the expense of the rest of the world.[39]

A final important premise of the dependency school is the focus on using the correct spatial scale for the problem at hand. At its core, the dependency school is focused on inequality and linkages between regions and nations. Thus, it is inappropriate to ever look at a region or country in isolation. While some scholars such as Wallerstein would argue that we must always use the entire world system as the unit of analysis, others would argue the more important point is to consider all contexts relevant to the issue at hand. For example, if we were interested in the economic development of a rural county in Iowa, we should not just look at the history and future opportunities of that county. Instead, we must consider that county's relationship to the rest of Iowa, as well as Iowa's relationship to the rest of the nation. If commodities traded on global markets are in question, we must also consider Iowa's placement within the world economic system.

Although very popular in the 1960s and 1970s among critical scholars, policymakers, and activists, the popularity of the dependency school declined during and after the 1980s—but it has arguably experienced a bit of a rebirth in recent years.[40] The fall of the dependency school resulted from a mixture of shortcomings within its framework and the influence of neoliberal politics in the 1980s, 1990s, and 2000s. Regarding shortcomings, there are two main critiques often levied against the dependency school. First, the framework can easily lose sight of the agency of the people, firms, and governments of the periphery. In doing so, it can oversimplify and lead to the assumption that no peripheral areas develop, or that any development that does occur in a peripheral area is simply because those in the core deemed it appropriate. As noted by Cardoso, this is obviously incorrect, and the reality is far more complicated.

Second, the policies suggested by the dependency school have not been viewed as very effective by mainstream development economists. As noted above, the critical nature of the dependency school suggests that very little can be done within a periphery to support a more positive future in the long term. Thus, those making recommendations informed by this school have tended to rely on large-scale structural solutions that remain unlikely in our current global power structure. Those policies stemming from the dependency school that do occur at the level of the peripheral nation or region have often been written off as misguided. Key among these policies is the push for import-substitution industrialization—a form of national economic development characterized by the creation of an internal manufacturing sector that produces goods previously only available through import, with the idea that this new sector can be used to launch broader industrialization and break ties of dependency.[41] Although there were some very real failures of import-substitution industrialization, one could easily argue it was unfairly written off as a method of national economic development because the hallmark examples were either (a) still dominated by external investments and thus not a fair example for evaluation, or (b) policies standing in the way of the economic goals of core nations, thus facing both political interference and unfair evaluation by economists in core countries.[42] Thus, the "failure" of import-substitution industrialization only further emboldens those who view interference and exploitation of peripheries by the core as a negative situation in need of major structural change.

Regardless of critiques, the dependency school remains a valuable framework for understanding change, linkages, exploitation, and development at varying spatial scales ranging from the local to the global. Because of its emergence from Marxist theory, the fundamental focus on inequality, power, and contradictions of capitalism gives it immense strength. While the dependency school is grounded in a broadly Marxist view of capitalism, it is worth noting that Marx himself generally viewed the destruction of agrarian livelihoods as essential for progress toward socialism.[43] Thus, one could argue Marx himself had a linear view of global development. Even though Marx was keenly aware of global issues of inequality, his class-based approach was far less attentive to geographic concerns. As such, the second critical view of development to briefly discuss is the purely Marxist view— which Isbister argues developed into a school of developmental theory unto itself in the latter part of the twentieth century.[44]

For those unfamiliar, Marx argued the basis for social change, inequality, and many other social ills was class conflict. In the basic formulation, there are two classes: the proletariat (the working class) and the bourgeoisie (the ruling class/capitalist class). The working class produces goods by selling their labor, and the capitalists sell the goods for profit because they own the means of production (i.e., the factory, inputs, and so on). Because of this inherently unequal relationship, the working class is always struggling against the capitalist class for a better life. As such, capital routinely works to subvert the working class to ensure a constant and high rate of profit. Those who apply a purely Marxist perspective to development would argue that the emphasis dependency theorists place upon nations or regions overlooks the true mechanism steering development, or a lack thereof, which they believe is class conflict.

Thus, a purely Marxist view is akin to the conventional linear model of economic development in that it generally looks within nations, regions, or communities to understand development, inequality, and how to address social problems. Perhaps surprising to those unfamiliar with Marxism, Marx himself did not think capitalism was all bad. He recognized that capitalism was a system with a remarkable capacity for growth and broad economic improvements. However, he also recognized the inherent contradictions, shortcomings, and inequalities built into the system. As such, Marx generally viewed the development of capitalism—defined by wage labor—as a necessary step countries needed to take on the path toward the ultimate goal of a socialist system.[45] Drawing on this, those focusing on development from a Marxist orientation would argue that capitalism and the development of a new or expanded capitalist class are viable means by which regions and nations may develop and improve quality of life.

That said, when we consider a situation like rural America, where capitalism is and has been dominant for more than a century, a purely Marxist model is also unlikely to suggest community-level action is going to change very much in the long term. Although increases in local labor organization would be an obvious action Marxism would inspire, Marxist views of capitalism are generally quite pessimistic regarding the outcomes for workers, absent massive structural change or large-scale nationwide labor organization. This is because capitalism leads to greater wealth accumulation by capitalists over time, resulting in less power for the working class and ever-greater levels of inequality. This accumulation can ultimately lead to crisis and a subsequent economic recession, but capital has found ways to avoid this crisis, which are discussed below. Even support for federal intervention under a purely Marxist framework is likely to be deemed shortsighted due to the assumption that the state under capitalism largely exists as an extension of capital interests.[46] Therefore, purely Marxist models still ultimately end up at a similar place as much of the dependency school thinking—large-scale structural change is all that will truly support rural and underdeveloped areas in the long term.

The assumption held by many Marxists that capital has captured the government and its interests, as well as the lack of support for community-level development efforts that emerges from a Marxist orientation, is further complicated by what Leslie Sklair calls the transnational capitalist class (TCC).[47] This term is used to describe the group of global power elite who direct the flow of capital with little regard for domestic or international borders. This class of wealthy elites is made up of four groups, according to Sklair: "(1) those who own and control major transnational corporations and their local affiliates (the corporate fraction), (2) the globalizing bureaucrats and politicians (the state fraction), (3) globalizing professionals (the technical fraction), and (4) merchants and media (the consumerist fraction)."[48] Together, these groups complicate both the Marxist and dependency school perspectives because of the way the TCC can leverage wealth and power to direct economic development in remote regions. As such, it must be recognized that the very concept of local capital versus external capital has been problematized in the contemporary era. Capital is in motion on a global scale, local capital is increasingly limited, and local interests struggle to compete with the increasingly concentrated and powerful TCC.[49] Thus, rural communities in the United States struggle to truly determine their economic future because they are constantly subject to external involvement and pressure.

Before concluding this discussion of critical viewpoints on development, it is important to detail two other related issues of capitalism relevant to linear frameworks, the dependency school, and purely Marxist approaches: (1) the spatial fix and (2) the seesaw theory of uneven development.[50] We previously saw that there is a tendency toward crises of overaccumulation within capitalism that capitalists are constantly trying to avoid. Since the nature of capitalism is such that capital continuously accrues greater and greater surplus value from labor, Marxian scholarship argues that accumulation reaches a point of imbalance such that workers can no longer afford to buy the goods they are paid to produce. This leads to a crisis where there is a massive devaluation of capital (e.g., the Great Depression). In the contemporary era, these crises are often tied to a loss of liquidity, financial mechanisms, and the risks businesses take through overinvestment during times of capital accumulation.[51] These financial crises of capitalism and how they occur through short- and long-term business cycles have been increasingly embraced by mainstream economics, thanks to the work of Hyman Minsky.[52] As such, within economics, these moments of crisis are now often called "Minksy moments." Historically, scholars of Marx discussed these crises without regard for geographic considerations; however, since the 1970s, geographic understandings of crises in capitalism—and their implications for development—have expanded.

Foundational to the geography of capitalism is the work of David Harvey in his pathbreaking 1982 work *The Limits to Capital* on the "spatial fix."[53] The spatial fix is the term used by Harvey to describe the way capital dodges crises of local overaccumulation through the reconstruction of the spatial order of production—meaning capitalists leverage spatial dynamics to keep profits high.[54] As the concept of the spatial fix is quite general, how it looks in practice can vary. For example, if there is not enough demand for goods being produced in one region, capital can export those goods to another region and continue to accrue profit while still avoiding devaluation. Similarly, if capital is unable to justify expanding production because of a lack of demand, it can invest in other markets, in other forms of production, or even encourage the in-migration of new labor. Finally, the spatial fix can also occur through investment in spatially concentrated fixed capital (e.g., improved local infrastructure and technology) that increases labor productivity and output in the long term in one location but is more difficult to move should the need arise.

At the same time that capitalism trends toward overaccumulation, the rate of profit trends lower due to processes of equalization—wherein any excess profit found within a region will decline over time owing to catch-up effects and local economic development.[55] The longer that capital and a corresponding site of production stay in place, the more profit declines because of an increasing imbalance between invested capital and labor costs. This imbalance is the result of broad effects of economic development that create lower unemployment, higher wages, stronger labor power (i.e., more unions), and agglomeration effects. Thus, as capital stays in place and becomes increasingly concentrated and overaccumulated, the rate of profit declines. These crises are even further accelerated due to larger capitalists ultimately expropriating minor capitalists to raise their own rate of profit as much as possible.[56]

This notion of the declining rate of profit serves as the bedrock for the seesaw theory of uneven development presented by Neil Smith in 1985. In short, the seesaw theory argues that capitalism creates uneven development because capital avoids the falling rate of profit by relocating to places where a higher rate of profit is available. In the simple model, capital leaves hypothetical region A, where the rate of profit is low, and moves to hypothetical region B, where the rate of profit is high. The sudden absence of capital from region A creates a vacuum of underdevelopment and reverts the area back into a high-profit context. When profit inevitably falls in region B, the capitalist then relocates production back to the now high-profit region A, and the process begins again. Thus, capital ultimately moves back and forth, creating the seesaw. Although Smith notes that this seesaw is most readily observed at the labor market or urban scale, the model can easily be scaled up to discuss regional and even international development patterns. However, it is important to note that the seesaw becomes significantly less likely to return as the scale increases.[57]

This seesaw, an admittedly simplified heuristic for understanding uneven development, helps to illustrate the considerable problems within arguments suggesting sustainable rural economic development under our current form of capitalism is possible. If development is fundamentally driven by capital, and capital is driven by the dynamics previously discussed—then it is inherently farcical to presume any capitalist would not operate within the system as it exists. For example, it may seem valuable to have new manufacturing plants set up in rural areas, but it is foundational to capitalism that the firm will ultimately exit the area once broad-scale economic development occurs and the rate of profit declines. Although historically this seesaw may have suggested relocation within cities, regions, or the nation, globalization has increasingly meant that this migration is out of the United States entirely— evidenced by the overseas migration of much of US manufacturing over the past twenty-five years.[58]

This overseas migration of manufacturing speaks to the issues of scale noted by Smith in 1985, when he wrote that "while indeed capital strives to realize the seesaw movement, as a means to counteract the falling rate of profit, the more the absolute geographic spaces that capital must create to push accumulation and localize devaluation, the greater are the barriers to the mobility necessary to realize the seesawing of capital."[59] There is no guarantee that the seesaw will actually swing back to rural America, considering the increasing friction once abroad, high-level trade policies, geographic distance, and persistent wage differentials between developed and developing countries. In fact, in 2024, much of rural America has instead simply experienced the first piece of this process, and it seems unlikely that investment— absent incentives or resource booms—will return. The specific reasons why a swing back is unlikely are detailed in chapter 4 and stem from the decreasing relevance of rural labor in the United States for contemporary industry, resource extraction, and manufacturing.

Conclusion

All told, the various frameworks presented all have some degree of viability and palatability for understanding subnational rural economic development in the United States. Unsurprisingly, linear models are still dominant in most applied and academic conversations regarding economic development in rural America. And as discussed, this is due to the positive picture those models present. Rural communities do not want to be told they are out of luck or destined to disappear; people need ideas that can help them where they are at. However, it would be negligent for those discussing rural America as a whole to argue that any community-level economic development effort will result in a broadly sustainable rural America in the long term. By projecting critical development frameworks often discussed at the level of nation-states down to a subnational level, we can fill in the missing middle in our understanding of rural development. Rural communities in the United States do not exist in isolation of broader economic context and forces. As such, we must acknowledge the very real power of the TCC, as well as the inherent need within capitalism for production and industry to constantly be in motion, leaving underdevelopment and associated hardships in its wake.

Although we can begin to see the theoretical issues baked into rural economic development through the application of critical theory to the subnational context, the theories presented still have not grappled with the fundamental fallacy built into the idea of sustainable rural economic development. That is, economic development, by definition, reduces the level of rurality—in other words, none of these models really tell us how to sustain long-term rurality. Further, none of the presented frameworks have discussed why we should or should not value rural places to begin with. To understand how we may, or may not, prevent the further loss of rural America, we have to unpack these issues. As noted, rural America finds itself at a junction. Before we can begin to discuss which road we want to take, we have to understand the fundamental mechanisms driving the loss of rural places as well as the value of those places being lost.

CHAPTER FOUR

The Limits to Rural Economic Development

It would not be an overstatement to say that rural economic development in the United States is handcuffed to notions of linear progress. In 2022, the Federal Reserve Bank of St. Louis released a volume titled *Investing in Rural Prosperity* that made this point obvious.[1] The book presents numerous chapters focused on successful rural economic development efforts written by a who's who of rural development CEOs, practitioners, and academics. In their view, communities that move from low levels of manufacturing to high, transition into multisector competitive economies, or experience long-term population growth are celebrated as successes, while communities that remain stagnant or do not effectively create their own economic development are regarded as cautionary tales. Authors in the collected volume place the emphasis for rural economic development on the agency and actions of communities, and little attention is paid to the broader political and economic context of the United States—which is largely taken as a given. Thus, to an outside observer the consensus view among rural economic development practitioners would seem to be that support for rural America in the long term means linear transitions from rural to urban, or at least from rural to somewhere in the middle. And in this impression, they would largely be correct.

The uncritical attachment to linear development thinking from all sides of the political spectrum is laid bare in other arenas as well. Perhaps one of the most obvious is the Rural Rising plan from McKinsey & Company, outlined in chapter 3, where growth indicators are detailed as the ultimate goal for development efforts. However, the focus on linear models of development goes beyond consultant groups and reserve banks and is even baked into federal funding priorities for rural America. For example, if one wishes to receive funding to study social issues in rural America from the Agriculture and Food Research Institute—the competitive research grant program of the US Department of Agriculture (USDA) National Institute for Food and Agriculture—they must couch proposals within the linear framework. Although recent calls for proposals have rebranded this funding mechanism as rural economic development, until 2019, this mechanism was called "Innovation for Rural Entrepreneurs and Communities," which makes clear the conceptual orientation of the agency toward entrepreneurship and economic growth. Consequently, those interested in improving the lives of rural Americans through USDA-sponsored research—arguably the federal agency most connected to rural populations in the United States—are forced to engage and use the logic of linear economic development, even when it may not be appropriate to do so. For example, it is not enough to propose to understand why rural poverty is so persistent. You must also propose testing solutions to poverty grounded in conventional economic development methods and outcomes. As evidenced by the critical theory described in chapter 3, the long-run outcome of this shortsighted focus is potentially disastrous for the future of rural America.

There are several reasons why the emphasis on linear economic development writ large may prove disastrous—in fact, we could argue it already is. For example, the seesaw of uneven development suggests that positive economic outcomes in any rural community likely come at the expense of other rural areas and will only be temporary because of the need to keep capital in motion.[2] However, the primary reasons this line of thinking could prove disastrous are (a) the fallacy I have briefly introduced in the previous chapters and (b) the forces within capitalism that reinforce this fallacy and its adherence. Regardless of whether we are anchoring our view of economic development in linear or critical perspectives, when we develop rural areas, we are fundamentally moving them away from a rural status. Any increase in economic development is going to result in either the direct urbanization of a rural area—meaning that rural area emerging as its own new urban core—or the integration of that rural place with a nearby metropolitan area. To be sure, there are cases where the original rural character of a place may be preserved—this has often happened in the case of rural tourism destinations.[3] However, this is a rare outcome, and many of these cases still hurt those local to the area because the cost of living increases, affordable housing becomes scarcer, and many of the jobs associated with rural tourism are low-paying, often seasonal, and service-sector positions.[4]

Thus, rural economic development inevitably transforms the thing it is purporting to help. Now, if the goal is to simply develop a rural area, this is not necessarily a fallacy. Simple ideas of rural economic development do not immediately suggest a desire to preserve any kind of rural status. In fact, many would likely argue that transitioning an area from rural to urban is the whole point of development. For example, the US Economic Development Administration, established in 1965 to provide grants for economic development, states that its mission is to "lead the federal economic development agenda by promoting innovation and competitiveness, preparing American regions for growth and success in the worldwide economy."[5] It goes on to state an interest in "sustainable job growth and the building of durable regional economies." Thus, the focus on growth within messaging from the Economic Development Administration suggests the urbanization of rural areas would likely be viewed as a positive outcome and not a tragedy at all. This perspective is similarly apparent from USDA Rural Development, which states an objective, among others, to "offer loans, grants, and loan guarantees to help create jobs and support economic development."[6] The lack of discussion of preserving rurality or supporting other noneconomic forms of sustainable rural development suggests that USDA Rural Development similarly shares an uncritical view of pushing rural America toward urbanity.[7]

However, not everyone working in US rural economic development supports these transitions. A growing number of individuals and organizations recognize that many residents of rural places do not *want* to see their communities become urban. Consequently, we are increasingly hearing about not just rural economic development but *sustainable* rural economic development. For example, the 2011 report titled *Supporting Sustainable Rural Communities* presented a unique collaboration between the USDA, the Environmental Protection Agency (EPA), Housing and Urban Development (HUD), and the Department of Transportation (DOT) focusing on not just developing rural communities but doing so in a sustainable way. Although the language in the report does a decent job of avoiding clear calls for pure conventional rural economic development, the document nonetheless highlights a clear focus on engendering regional economic growth. Further, the livability principles promoted in the report, particularly their detailed descriptions, show the emphasis on linear economic development is still baked into the vision of rural sustainability. These principles include providing more transportation choices; promoting equitable, affordable housing; enhancing economic competitiveness; supporting existing communities; coordinating and leveraging federal policies and investment; and valuing communities and neighborhoods.[8] Although these principles may sound good on their face and could lead to improvement in local well-being, when considered alongside the detailed descriptions in the report, they essentially promote the urbanization of rural places.

More recently, the Community Capitals Framework (CCF), discussed in chapter 3, focuses on "sustainable communities," which Cornelia Flora and colleagues describe in the fifth edition of their book as communities that "strive to bring economic security to all, foster a healthy ecosystem, and offer social inclusion to all residents."[9] Thus, those detailing the CCF appear to be well aware of the issues of linear thinking and instead want to see a turn to a more nuanced approach. However, as discussed previously, in practice, the CCF approach is often used by planners and other practitioners to promote linear models of rural economic development. So, even with these well-intentioned ideals, linear views still reign supreme.

Once we realize we do not want to simply make all rural spaces urban and start to talk about sustainable rural economic development, the fallacy emerges. There exists a contradiction wherein those focused on sustainable rural economic development seemingly wish to sustain rural areas in their rural status for the long term without fundamentally changing how we engage in the practice and theory of economic development. Despite how much we might wish it were so, we simply cannot sustain something by changing its very character. Thus, the practice of sustainable rural economic development is often working against its own goals. But, if we cannot sustain rural America through economic development, why does adherence to this fallacy persist? And what *can* we do to promote sustainable rural futures? The answers to these questions are complicated and require a deeper dive into the form and function of contemporary capitalism.

Rural Decline as a Feature of Capitalism

Although the application of conventional economic development techniques to rural areas is a primary way we are transforming rural America, our difficulties for supporting sustainable rural futures go beyond these practices. This is because even those who are not applying economic development strategies to sustain rural communities are still likely to foster the loss of rural places due to our broader capitalist system. As long as activities are conducted within the normal bounds of contemporary capitalism in the United States, all efforts aimed at rural prosperity and improved well-being will only accelerate the push of rural spaces toward urbanity or depopulation. This is because the path of rural development, urbanization, and integration that we see in the United States is not an aberration or happenstance. Rather, it is a natural by-product of capitalism and thus is a feature, not a bug, of our economic system. To understand why this is so, it is helpful to turn to Karl Marx and David Harvey once again.

Drawing on Harvey, one of the primary reasons that rural depopulation or urbanization can be expected under capitalism is the mobility of labor within the system.[10] Note that urbanization, in this instance, refers to both direct urbanization and the integration of rural areas into existing metropolitan regions. In general, a Marxist view of capitalism posits that two main forms of capital exist: constant and variable. Constant capital includes equipment and materials, while variable capital generally encompasses capital expended on wage labor. Labor is considered variable capital because it can be dynamically hired and laid off to meet demand. As such, labor is one of the main ways profit is achieved and that capitalists can alter their production cycles to support ever-higher profit. However, baked into this formulation is a difficult reality for the capitalist. Variable capital, or labor, is people. Except for cases of domination and slavery, people have autonomy and the ability to work where and for whom they please. Beyond just their ability to work for whichever firm they want, as long as they are hired, laborers are able to move to new markets if they desire. There is nothing legally requiring a laborer to remain in a city or rural area.

The freedom of movement experienced by labor, however, is not as free as many may initially imagine. Marx states that under capitalism, the worker "must be free in the double sense that as a free individual they can dispose of their labor-power as their own commodity, and that, on the other hand, they have no other commodity for sale."[11] Thus, it is true that workers can choose who they work for and can choose to move — insofar as they can afford the cost of doing so. However, because of the structure of our capitalist system, the only real option for survival is to find a job that pays acceptable wages. This need for employment to ensure survival has significant ramifications for the rural depopulation and urbanization we see today. Harvey perhaps put it best: "Given the general conditions of wage labor, the freedom of the laborer to move is converted to its exact opposite. In search of employment and a living wage, the laborer is forced to follow capital wherever it flows."[12] Contributing further to the (im)mobility of labor is the desire for a better life instilled in the working class. To improve one's lot in life, laborers must pursue higher wages, greater well-being, and better working conditions, and often they must try and escape exploitive situations. To achieve this, laborers must be ever more willing to move locations or jobs. Thus, by being free to move where they like, laborers are ultimately forced to move if they wish to improve their lot in life or be able to save for their future.

This false freedom of labor mobility, which others call the double freedom or dual freedom, ultimately produces a contradiction for capital. Labor must be free to move for capitalists to be successful; mobile labor allows for the efficient reshuffling of labor across space as well as the ability for variable capital to be, in fact, variable. To balance shifts in production, the capitalist needs to be able to lay off and rehire labor as opportunity warrants. However, capital also must retain a reserve labor army to keep both wages low and ensure that labor remains available for when it is eventually needed. (The term "reserve labor army" is used within Marxist theory to describe the group of people who are in the labor force but currently unemployed and who place wage-pressure on those who are currently employed.) Thus, Harvey notes that the "escape routes must be blocked off by legal requirements or other social mechanisms," and the absolute mobility of labor must be constrained.[13] Functionally, this happens in several ways, including tying labor to land through homeownership, rent leases, employer-sponsored health care, and other forms of debt that raise the income needs of households; the reduction of necessary amenities in other locales (e.g., closing rural hospitals); and the provision of safety nets that lessen the need to move, such as unemployment insurance and welfare. Ultimately, we find ourselves in a delicate balance where labor must be free and mobile, but only insofar as capital is still able to profit and pursue its preferred course.

To be clear, it is not as if rural and urban Americans are unable to move or relocate—it is about where they relocate and why. America is a highly mobile country, and there is a consistent churn of population across the country.[14] Further, it is not as if population growth always occurs because people are following jobs. In many cases, firms follow the migration of people to desirable locations. In fact, much of the US population redistribution of the twentieth century was catalyzed by the movement of people to smaller, high amenity cities in the West and the Sunbelt—with the advent of air-conditioning playing a major role in making the Sunbelt more desirable.[15] Economists explain this relationship between people, firms, and migration under a framework called the "spatial equilibrium."

Under this model, labor markets—of all sizes—exist in a self-regulating equilibrium where the desirability of locations will, in theory, balance as wages and housing costs rise and fall due to changes in the population and economy.[16] For example, if a location rich in natural amenities is highly desirable for households but less desirable for firms, then we would expect households to forgo the higher income found in more firm-centric locations with fewer natural amenities. They would do so because the lower-income location still provides them with enough benefits from the natural amenities to make it worthwhile. Key to this calculation is the fact that even if there are rich natural amenities and the ability to forgo some income, there will still be an income floor below which the natural amenities are insufficient to justify relocating. Further, implicit in this model is the notion that lower-income groups will be less able to make these trade-offs. For example, from 1980 to 2000, "higher-skilled" workers moved to pricier cities while "lower-skilled" workers moved to inexpensive ones, widening spatial inequality.[17] Over time, we would also expect firms to respond to the settlement of people through relocation and the establishment of new firms in the area. This would in turn affect wages and housing costs, and the equilibrium would continue to adjust—although this readjustment may take a long time, even generations.[18] Thus, a spatial equilibrium perspective allows us to understand the uneven (re)distribution of the US population as a product of both job availability and amenities available in an area.

In the view of many, the Marxist concept of the false freedom of labor would not be compatible with the spatial equilibrium model, a framework from mainstream regional economics. Nonetheless, we can use these concepts in tandem to help understand the plight of rural America in the 2020s. The issue faced by rural America today is that most of what remains of rural America falls short on both jobs and amenities. With the exception of the already established rural retirement and recreation destinations, most remaining rural areas have seen a marked decrease in job prospects over time (see chapter 2) while also providing few natural amenities and degrading built amenities. As such, even though Americans are highly mobile, these areas do not have the amenities or the jobs to draw in or hold population. They are either too remote, lack essential infrastructure, do not have access to necessary resources, or can only support industries that are either highly mechanized or do not pay well enough to justify moving to the area. Thus, we continue to see the out-migration of young and working-age people from rural areas for work and education. Once they depart, there are (1) insufficient economic opportunities and amenities to draw them back and (2) a multitude of mechanisms that close off their escape routes and tie them to places where their income needs can be met.

This is not to say people do not still have an interest in living in many of these rural areas. Although a rural area may not have the amenities to draw in completely new residents, local and familial connections make rural areas desirable for many former residents. The issue is that the income requirements of the modern era—including the pressures of student loan debt, the need for medical insurance, the difficulty and expense of modern childcare, the need to save for children's college, and the increasing lack of a social safety net—make it such that the wages and amenities found in many rural areas simply do not offset the need for higher absolute wages. If income was not tied to residence, or if income needs were lower, then this calculus for labor would change, and it is likely more households would move to the rural areas where they have personal connections. Unfortunately for rural areas, income remains fundamentally tied to residence in the United States. Thus, the false freedom of labor serves as a core mechanism driving the current spatial equilibrium of the US population and serves as a major barrier when it comes to people being able to justify and afford living in rural America.

Two important points about the tethering of income and place need to be raised. First, the false freedom of labor is not felt the same across industries or time periods. During the early 2020s, we saw this tether weaken through the dramatic expansion of remote work because of the COVID-19 pandemic.[19] This meant that the tether became less salient and necessary in many sectors, at least temporarily. As of 2024, the long-run impact of the COVID-19 remote work shift is unclear. Many companies have transitioned back to either hybrid schedules or fully in-person work. While some types of jobs — particularly in the tech sector — appear positioned for long-term fully remote work, a nationwide transition to remote work no longer seems likely in the long term. Even if an increase in remote work persists, it is important to acknowledge that the expansion is not felt equally. Remote work is far more likely in high-paying jobs in the service or tech sectors, such as programming, accounting, insurance, and management. Thus, many jobs still simply cannot be performed remotely, and those jobs tend to be the jobs held by the least well-off in society.

The second important issue relates to the likelihood (or not) of capital investment and subsequent labor in-migration to rural areas. To be clear, even though capital no longer appears to have a broad interest in employing individuals in much of rural America, booms in development can still happen in rural areas when it is profitable for capitalists. And during these phases of development, there is often a need for labor. Unfortunately for the rural community, labor can often be brought in temporarily. It is easier to bring in new labor than it is to try and support a steady rural population across booms and busts of development. Further, the jobs that do pop up in rural areas are often undesirable for many people because they are dangerous, low-paying, and low status. The lack of interest in these jobs found among current residents leads to alternative patterns of labor migration, wherein capitalists instead recruit workers from outside the rural area and often outside the borders of the United States. A hallmark example is the well-documented international migration networks established by rural meatpacking, wherein firms directly recruited labor in Latin American countries to work their plants in the United States.[20]

Another factor affecting rural labor market booms is that many industries still practicing in rural America have invested heavily in labor-saving technology over the past fifty years. This means that large industrial booms can have surprisingly small impacts on local employment. In many cases, one employee can now travel regionally and accomplish tasks that used to require many employees. Extractive activities like agriculture, fishing, forestry, and mining have long invested in mechanization, vastly reducing both labor demand and the need to maintain a reserve labor army in rural America. An example of this in practice can be found in the boom in hydraulic fracturing in Pennsylvania, Ohio, and West Virginia during the 2010s. Although Appalachian shale gas production exploded during this period, the counties responsible for 90 percent of gas production saw negligible returns to household income and a net decrease in both jobs and population between 2008 and 2021.[21]

The mobility of labor can help us understand why we see a general trend of out-migration and uneven growth across rural America, but it cannot provide answers to all of our questions. For example, why is it that we aren't seeing more dynamic patterns of rural seesaws, as discussed by Neil Smith? And if, in fact, there are internal core-periphery dynamics in the United States, doesn't the destruction of our internal peripheries broadly hurt capitalist development both in the United States and worldwide? To answer these questions, we need to turn back to the core-periphery dynamics of the dependency school.

Dependency and Rural America

As discussed in chapter 3, we can view the structure of the global economy as one linked by core-periphery relationships. Historically, development scholars have extended this framework and described the United States as having internal networks of core and periphery that represent a microcosm of the broader global structure. In fact, many go as far as to describe these peripheral areas as internal colonies.[22] Up to now, this formulation has broadly made sense. One can easily identify areas such as Appalachia, tribal reservations, or heartland farm regions as peripheral areas exploited for the needs of core urban areas. In general, the most peripheral regions have been those dominated by the primary production of energy, food, and fiber. However, as with any framework grounded in a Marxist tradition, we need to be able to adapt our framework to our present moment while considering historical factors.

The America of today is simply not the same as it was when the dependency school was at its peak in the 1970s. Globalization has exploded, neoliberalism led to large-scale national and global deregulation of trade, federal environmental regulations have increased and made domestic environmentally destructive activities more difficult, and the industrial structure of the United States has shifted even further away from primary production and manufacturing and into an economy dominated by private and producer services.[23] Thus, within the United States, we now have a decreased need to maintain internal peripheries and their reserve labor armies.[24] Even with the many social and economic shifts in the United States at the end of the twentieth century, the need for peripheries persisted through the 1980s and 1990s because of the boom in rural manufacturing and continuing levels of resource extraction and agriculture. But as globalization and mechanization have continued, even those needs have largely gone away. With this lack of rural labor demand, we have witnessed the continued bifurcation of former internal peripheries in the United States. Rural peripheries have been and are being incorporated into the core through processes of direct urbanization and integration into existing metropolitan areas, or else they are being left to age in place and depopulate indefinitely—where they may or may not continue on as zones of extraction for capital.

It needs to be stressed that just because an area is sparsely populated or rural does not mean it is necessarily a periphery in the sense considered here. Instead, the term "periphery," as employed here, goes further to say that not only does a place exist that is relatively undeveloped but also that the core exploits the people in that area for labor and profit. Thus, the periphery is defined by active underdevelopment by the core. Key to the point on this matter is the exploitation of labor. To illustrate, consider natural resource extraction. It is certainly true that many areas of rural America that are rich in natural resources and that have historically been considered internal peripheries continue to be heavily exploited at an environmental level by capital. The point here is that these areas should no longer be understood as traditional internal peripheries because capital, owing to advances in technology and mechanization, no longer requires a significant body of labor in these areas. Thus, it is this form of internal periphery, as defined by the exploitation of local rural labor and the maintenance of a reserve labor army, which we see disappearing across the United States. It must be stressed that just because internal peripheries go away does not mean that there is a loss of control of these areas by capital or external interests. All that is meant is that the economic conditions that previously propped up labor demand in rural peripheries have changed such that reserve labor armies are no longer necessary.

This transition away from peripheral labor can be seen in the trends in timber and mining in the United States. Once known for supporting a large number of loggers and foresters, total forest industry employment in Oregon fell 34 percent from 1998 to 2017. However, this did not correspond to a drop in total timber harvest and wood production, which remained relatively flat during this twenty-year period—highlighting decreasing labor needs in the timber industry.[25] Oregon was not alone. All regions across the United States experienced decreases in logging employment but not corresponding declines in profit or production from 1997 to 2017.[26] In the realm of mining, Appalachian coal mining has dropped precipitously in recent years—with total coal employment dropping 62 percent from 2011 to 2021.[27] The coal sector has a long history of leveraging more productive deposits (e.g., surface mining versus underground mining) and mechanization to increase output per miner, dating back to the turn of the twentieth century, so it is unsurprising this recent reduction occurred alongside an actual decrease in overall coal production and price.[28] Finally, shale gas, as discussed earlier in this chapter, has also experienced high levels of production amid declines in employment.[29] Beyond that, of the jobs that were created in shale gas areas, half were filled by residents from outside the county where the work occurred.[30] This external approach to filling positions further highlights capital's decreasing need to support or sustain rural reserve labor armies in the United States.

An additional helpful example to spotlight the loss of labor needs in rural peripheries is renewable energy. The United States is increasingly relying upon renewable energy to meet energy needs of the country. In particular, wind energy has experienced dramatic growth over the past twenty-five years, growing from only meeting 0.1 percent of total US electricity demand in 1990 to 9.2 percent in 2021.[31] This growth is only expected to continue. However, the labor needs of wind energy are dramatically different from historic forms of energy production in rural America. Gone are the needs of anchoring mining communities in place to ensure reliable labor. Instead, the best-case scenario for wind energy is large parcels of land held by willing, often absentee, landowners. Maintenance on wind turbines does not require a consistent large body of nearby labor, and after installation, local labor effects are negligible.[32] Instead, workers can travel regionally to repair turbines as needed, and the majority of jobs in wind energy are off-site.[33] Thus, the need the United States once had for an internal peripheral labor force to produce energy by mining and drilling is rapidly being replaced by a form of energy with comparatively little need for any local labor, and these labor impacts are similar for other forms of renewable energy such as solar.[34] Even if these rural areas only disappear slowly, they can no longer be viewed as the internal peripheries they once were.

In some rural areas, the transition away from natural resource extraction has been met with a shift toward nonextractive uses of the local environment, such as tourism, outdoor recreation, and real estate. Areas specialized in this form of natural resource development may, in fact, still be considered peripheries because there are still low-quality service-sector jobs in support of these sectors that need to be filled. However, even in this case, the maintenance of a reserve labor army is fundamentally altered from the historic model due to the high reliance on seasonal itinerant labor during peak seasons. Thus, although this specific form of rural economy—which, to be clear, is relatively rare across the United States—may still reflect a more classic internal periphery, the broader global dynamics mean that capital does not benefit from supporting rural labor year-round. Ultimately, this transition from extractive activities with large labor needs to renewable or nonextractive activities with few or less-rewarding labor needs is what has prompted activists and scholars to call for a "just transition," wherein policy explicitly supports or provides new jobs and opportunities for those being left behind.

Although the transition to renewable energy, the growth of nonextractive activities, and the corresponding decline of extractive labor provide clear examples for how we are seeing our peripheral labor force become increasingly irrelevant to capital, it is helpful to also discuss a more complex case. For that, we can consider crop and livestock production. We still produce a great deal of crops and livestock in the United States, and for that we need land. However, because of the consolidation of agriculture and the mechanization of much of our food production, we simply don't need as much farm labor as we used to. This is reflected in national labor statistics, which show that hired farm labor fell from 2.33 million in 1950 to 1.15 million in 1990 and then stabilized through the 2000s, 2010s, and into 2020, when the number was 1.16 million.[35] When compared to the total employment in rural America, which in 2022 was 24.2 million, farm labor accounted for just 5.4 percent—a significant but not dominant amount.[36]

Beyond the decline in overall demand for farm labor, we have also seen a transition from transient farm labor to relatively settled farm labor—wherein workers are far less likely to follow crops—suggesting the establishment of more conventional working relationships between farm supervisors and labor, the specialization of those working in the sector, and declining needs for agricultural labor because of mechanization.[37] This trend, combined with the hardening of the US border—many farm laborers are immigrants from Latin America—has resulted in the growth of immigrant destination communities across rural America. From this, we generally see two paths: (1) the settling of immigrant populations leads to new growth or integration with nearby metropolitan cores, or (2) the settling of populations is not enough to offset the broader processes of out-migration previously discussed. This is because rural immigrant destinations are still subject to the same struggles as all other rural places. That is, young people have little interest in becoming farm workers themselves, and capital is consistently drawing them to urban parts of the country. Consider the rising ages of farm labor over the past fifteen years, where the average age of immigrant farm labor rose from 36 to 41.6 between 2006 and 2019, as well as the continuing rise in natural decrease and persistent levels of out-migration.[38] Thus, absent major migration booms, the story of farm communities in contemporary rural America is still one of either movement into urbanity or depopulation and lag.

It is important to address the inequality inherent in this bifurcation. The process of development is never random. It is influenced by the needs of capital, the preferences of capitalists, and the profit available in the location. As such, it should not be surprising that many of the most languishing rural places have historically been the most peripheral and inhabited by population groups that experience the most marginalization. In the United States, our white supremacist and classist underpinnings mean that tribal reservations, rural Black communities, border colonias, and the most remote parts of Appalachia continue to face some of the highest levels of hardship in the country.[39] If this rural bifurcation continues, conditions will likely deteriorate even further. It is possible that some areas will experience development into urbanity. For example, some Mississippi Delta communities experienced significant growth following the siting of new casinos—although even that boom seems to have likely been short-lived.[40] Although some communities may grow, the prospects for many of these persistently impoverished communities are bleak. This situation has many ramifications for the well-being of residents, many of whom cannot afford to move to where capital demands. Further, existing theory and research on rural inequality and local power dynamics suggest that even if things improve, many of the benefits that do occur will be captured by the elite and held unequally.[41]

What this means when we consider the whole country is that the United States is in the process of moving from a core nation with internal peripheries to an entirely core nation where capital has no need to maintain internal peripheral zones. Importantly, this does not mean that the seesaw of development does not still occur. At the local level, the seesaw will continue to dynamically create zones of underdevelopment across space, only these will be urban zones of underdevelopment and not rural. Within our once-rural spaces, international competition, US wage expectations, and persistent rural disinvestment make it so that the seesaw has already fallen and is unlikely to rise in the foreseeable future. It does not mean that areas that we may look at and visually describe as rural will go away. Pastoral land remains in many metropolitan areas, and remote undeveloped areas are not going to suddenly support a city. What it means is that rural areas—as defined by both low population density and a lack of connectivity to urban cores—that have historically served as internal peripheries of the United States are of little and decreasing use to capital in contemporary America, particularly when it comes to labor. As such, the false freedom of labor mobility built into capitalism fosters the continued depopulation of many rural hinterlands and small towns.

Conclusion

The fallacy we face in sustainable rural economic development is produced and reinforced by factors deeply embedded within capitalism. Thus, it is not enough to simply point out the inherent contradiction found within the idea of sustainable rural economic development. We cannot realistically support sustainable rural livelihoods unless we identify the issue at its source, as done here. The dual patterns of out-migration and urbanization that we see in rural America are the end result of the false freedom of labor under capitalism. Labor is free to move, but only to where capital will support that labor with an income. Further, the restructuring of US industry, the mechanization of many sectors, and the full expansion of global capitalism place the United States in a position where the maintenance of internal peripheries is no longer necessary or desirable. Thus, the need for internal peripheries and their labor force, which once pushed against this trend of urbanization, is no longer there—allowing the bifurcation of rural America to proceed unfettered.

Ultimately, we arrive at the conclusion that the main reason we are currently unable to support sustainable rural futures is that the false freedom that labor currently experiences under capitalism isn't really freedom at all. Thus, any model going forward that continues to tether income to place of residence will further facilitate the decline of rural America and leave what remains as a combination of empty towns, mechanized agriculture, rural tourism destinations dominated by the elite, renewable energy installments, or depopulated wildlands.

To be clear, the depopulation side of the bifurcation of rural America has been well documented, and more proximate reasons for these trends are well known. For example, *Hollowing Out the Middle* by Patrick Carr and Maria Kefalas (2009) richly documents the inequality and pressures found within rural education, where those viewed as the best and brightest young people—a fraught concept to be sure—are given a disproportionate share of resources and pushed to urban areas for education and the service of capital.[42] Similarly, there is demographic work that speaks to population aging, retiree migration, and decreased fertility rates in rural areas.[43] While these are important processes to consider—and they will come up again—here we have seen that rural out-migration and depopulation are not the result of some unfortunate set of incentives in our economy or "failures" of specific communities. Instead, they stem from the bedrock processes of an increasingly global capitalism. Thus, solutions to this problem lie within our economic system generally and will not be solved by more proximate solutions such as community-level rural development initiatives. Instead, what this tells us is that supporting sustainable rural futures requires dealing with the root process at hand—the false freedom of labor. From this, it appears the only way we will support the persistence of rural communities is to sever the link between the places where we live and how we obtain the resources we need to survive.

This conclusion—that if we want a sustainable rural America we need to decouple where we make our money from where we live—could be implemented in multiple ways. However, before we discuss how to move forward, we first have to decide whether that goal is worth pursuing. Just as with the tacit acceptance of linear models of rural economic development, many people uncritically push for the preservation of the rural way of life in the United States. Unfortunately, this lack of critical analysis weakens the stance of those pushing for a sustainable rural future while often leading to the romanticization of rurality and an inattention to inequalities in development and well-being. Thus, if we are to consider any proposal to "save" rural America, we first need to decide whether that is even an appropriate cause to begin with.

CHAPTER FIVE

Should We Care If Rural America Goes Away?

So far, we have examined the case for why we are seeing the bifurcation of rural America into either urbanity or depopulated territory. As such, one may be compelled to ask, "How do we save rural America?" This is a good question that will be taken up shortly. However, before we discuss possible solutions to the decline of rural America, it is vital to ask whether this is a bad thing in the first place. We cannot approach stopping the further decline of rural America as we know it—which is a result of the false freedom of labor combined with the decreasing need for internal peripheries in the United States—without first deciding whether that is the correct goal in the first place. As it happens, why the decline and disappearance of rural America matters is a popular question. Scholars of rural people and places are often asked this question, and at times, we find ourselves at a loss. To many of us, the downsides seem self-evident. However, if we are to truly argue that rural America is worth saving, we need to understand just what is being lost.

To begin, what exactly do we stand to lose when we say we are losing rural America? Recall that the broad place-based definition of rurality has two dimensions: (1) low population density and (2) remoteness. Thus, a rural place is one that has low population density and does not have access to metropolitan amenities or labor markets. These isolated zones have historically functioned as peripheries serving the needs of a variety of industries. However, in the 2020s, they largely find themselves with either limited opportunity and depopulation or urbanization through internal growth or annexation. What this means is that *we are not* losing all of our pastoral lands or lands that visually may appear rural. There remain many places within metropolitan areas that still possess a character many would argue feels rural. The distinction is that these places are now able to access labor markets and amenities associated with urbanity. Further, in these contexts of urban expansion, this pastoral land is being used less for commercial agriculture and instead becomes either an idyllic retreat for wealthy urbanites, a smaller-scale hobby farm, or the land is earmarked for future urban development.

The loss of rural America also does not mean that we are paving over all of our natural or wild spaces. In areas where we are seeing depopulation, it is quite likely the opposite. When rural parts of the country, particularly the more remote areas, become less populated, the land still remains and is likely to either be left fallow, farmed, or used for recreation. Thus, the long run of these processes does not ultimately look like some futuristic scenario where the entire country is a version of New York City.[1] Instead, what it means is that the economic opportunity is gone from these areas, and given the tethered nature of income and residence, people can neither afford nor justify living there. Since there is limited economic opportunity in these areas, it remains unlikely they will be integrated into existing metropolitan areas any time soon—although it could certainly happen in the more distant future.

Finally, this also does not mean that we are losing all of our small towns. Indeed, many metropolitan areas have thriving small towns that serve as bedroom communities to metropolitan cores, thus providing an ideal residential location for high-income urban workers who prefer a rural pace of living.[2] Recall, for example, Butler County, Pennsylvania, which was discussed in the introduction. Butler County is within the greater Pittsburgh metropolitan area and has a population of 197,763. While Butler County was classified as rural in 1980, since 1990 this has not been the case. However, it is not as if Butler County has become akin to downtown Pittsburgh. For example, Marion Township in northern Butler County has a population of just 1,167, and the Google Maps view shows that driving through the area would still provide a very pastoral and small-town feel. Thus, small towns in general are not necessarily all disappearing. Instead, it is *remote* small towns and their surrounding region that we are seeing persistently depopulate, some at an unprecedented pace.

So, if we are not losing all our pastoral lands or paving over all of nature, and if we aren't necessarily losing our small towns, what are we losing, and is it worth saving? As we will see, the loss would be severe, and rural America *is* worth saving for a mix of cultural, political, and social reasons—which will be presented shortly. First, however, it is important to revisit the concept of the rural idyll.

The rural idyll is the term used to describe the view of rurality as a social construction, often applied in European academic settings.[3] This framework argues that how we determine "what is rural" stems from the signs and symbols associated with rurality. As these signs and symbols evolve over time, we as a society reconstruct rural areas to match this idyll.[4] For example, when rural areas were synonymous with mining and extraction, our expectations and planning reflected and supported this kind of development through how we structured and placed our settlements as well as the kind of culture we expected to see. However, as rural areas are transitioning to bastions of re-newable energy, we are growing accustomed to views of wind turbines and solar farms. Thus, we might be surprised to see a new coal mine and find that it no longer fits in with our conception of a rural place in contemporary America. Importantly, the specific idyll and culture of a rural area is a product of a back-and-forth relationship between the material reality of living in a place with its specific rural qualities and our ever-changing sociocultural system. As such, there are competing rural idylls across different populations and subcultures. Remember that "idyll" does not mean it is always a positive view. Rather, it is simply the social construction of what it means to be rural at that time. We cannot talk about why we should or shouldn't care if rural America goes away without invoking the rural idyll.

Consider two different rural idylls found in the United States.[5] In the first, we have the version arguably most prevalent among those who live in, want to live in, and defend rural spaces. This idyll includes visions of small towns where everyone knows everyone, people largely get along, agriculture is the dominant industry, there are many family farms, and there are red barns, wide open spaces, and clean air and water. This rural idyll valorizes the rural working class, asserts that rural people have a deep connection to the land, and paints rural America as an area with a slower pace and kind people.[6] This version of the rural idyll generally ignores the ethnic and racial diversity found in rural areas and portrays rural America as a historically and continuously white-dominated portion of the country. Further, although hardship is likely known to exist, the extremes of rural poverty are generally excluded from this imaginary.

In the second rural idyll, we can consider a far more negative view—which we may associate with urban residents of the United States or possibly those who grew up in rural America and were desperate to leave. In this version, rural America is viewed as backward, racist, classist, and eager to exploit and destroy the environment. Rural areas are still viewed as white, but this is seen as a negative and evidence of the displacement of Indigenous people and racism. In this model, the rural working class is not valorized; instead, it is viewed as uneducated and often voting against its own interests to support right-wing conservative causes. Depending on who holds this idyll, the extremes of rural poverty may factor into the idyll, or they may not.

As is hopefully clear by this point in the book, neither of these idylls are accurate. Rural America is both of these and neither of these. Each rural idyll is ultimately harmful in that it flattens the diverse reality of the rural American experience. Beyond that, it others rural people in a way that is detached from reality. Although rural America is comprised of places distinctly different from urban America, rural Americans are far more similar to urban Americans than many of us appreciate. For example, the assumption many people have that rural families tend to be larger than urban families is incorrect—rural family structure is basically identical to urban family structure and has been for a long time.[7] As a result of persistent rural outmigration, many current urban residents once lived in rural areas, and research has historically suggested a significant share of these rural-to-urban migrants would like to return to rural living.[8] For example, a 2021 Gallup poll found that 48 percent of Americans would prefer to live in a town or rural area, and a 2021 Pew Research report found that 35 percent of Americans have a preference for rural living.[9] Given that only 14 percent of Americans live in rural areas (i.e., nonmetropolitan counties) currently, this reflects a significant imbalance.[10]

The point of invoking these two idylls is to illustrate that whether or not we should "save rural America" is fundamentally attached to what we envision when we imagine rural spaces. Certainly, we would not wish to save *all* of rural America as it currently exists. It is hard to imagine that those who are unable to drink safe water, find employment, or go to a nearby hospital would like to see those conditions preserved for time immemorial. When we discuss saving rural America without acknowledging the diversity and heterogeneity of the areas we are discussing, we are likely to fall on deaf ears or worse, depending on the idyll people internally hold. As such, we must resist the urge to lean on idyllic tropes when we discuss whether or not to fight for a sustainable rural future in the United States.

What Is Lost?

Stepping outside rural idylls and addressing rural America as it is and not as we imagine it to be, there are some very good reasons why we may want to support a sustainable future for rural America. To begin, there are strong cultural grounds for supporting these communities. Outside of romantic notions, there are rich and distinct cultures found across the rural reaches of the United States. Thus, from the standpoint of cultural preservation and the preservation of diverse ways of being and knowing, these distinct cultures represent something very real that we stand to lose.

Importantly, there is not a single "rural American culture" worth saving, but instead there are many. For example, Indigenous cultures, both on and off official reservations, contain deep histories, languages, knowledge, and traditions that risk being lost forever if tribes cannot continue living in rural spaces and are forced to move into settler-colonial cities, where the preservation of culture is even more difficult.[11] Given that there are 574 federally recognized and around 400 unrecognized tribes in the United States—within which there exist many subcultures—this represents a staggering number of unique cultures put at risk by the current trajectory of rural America.[12] While reservations certainly have unique needs and concerns relative to other rural areas, they face similar population pressures. Consider that 75 percent of the US American Indian or Alaska Native population lived outside of reservations in 2000, and by 2020, that number had increased to 87 percent.[13]

We can also consider rural Black culture, particularly in the South, which reflects the long-term resistance and struggle against slavery, Jim Crow, and gross inequality while being rich in food, music, agriculture, and fishing, among other cultural elements. Although many strong rural Black communities remain in the 2020s, they continue to vanish quickly, and residents are struggling to retain their land and culture. For example, rural Daufuskie Island, South Carolina, used to support a strong community of Gullah/Geechee people—an African American ethnic group found in pockets across the low country region of the US South.[14] Today, there are only a handful of Gullah/Geechee residents remaining on Daufuskie Island.[15] This is not a unique experience among the Gullah/Geechee or other rural Black communities, as more and more historic Black towns continue to disappear.[16]

The risk of cultural loss felt by American Indian and Black communities in rural America is severe, but these communities are not alone. Across the United States, there are many distinct rural cultures that we stand to lose—for example, Cajun communities in Louisiana; Danish settlements in places like Dagmar, Montana; the historically Bohemian town of Spillville, Iowa; and the Hispano peoples of New Mexico who have lived in the American Southwest since before the Mexican-American War. Finally, there are also many cultural elements of rural America that simply fit, in part, into the positive rural idyll previously described. Many small towns in rural America are dominated by descendants of white settlers and have unique cultures tied to mining, agriculture, fishing, and other activities that we risk losing if we let rural America disappear.

The risk posed by this loss of culture goes beyond basic concerns over preserving history and ways of being and knowing. The loss of culture and cultural practices is associated with poorer mental health, more stress, a loss of identity, and a diminished sense of belonging.[17] Further, rapid changes in culture, such as the experience of a town rapidly disappearing, have been associated with increased anxiety and concern for the future.[18] Appropriately, the majority of work on the consequences of cultural loss has been on Indigenous populations across the globe. However, there is no reason we should not expect this loss of culture to impact non-Indigenous populations as well.

Beyond the value of preserving local rural cultures, there are also national cultural considerations for why we may wish to support rural America. First, if we lose rural America, then the history of how America came to be risks erasure and being forgotten. Rural America, as described in chapter 2, was built upon genocide, slavery, white supremacy, and environmental exploitation.[19] As such, the bifurcation of our former internal peripheries risks smoothing over that history by erasing its evidence on our landscape. Given that there are many in the United States who wish to avoid discussing our real history—evidenced by the recent spate of states banning discussions of race, privilege, and critical race theory—this potential for ignoring history and the need for reparations is a real concern for our present course.[20] Second, the United States has a culture of Jeffersonian democracy and an aligned support of rural farming that we stand to lose if rural America goes away. Although it is fair to say that yeoman farmers have not really been a significant part of rural America for a very long time—and when they were, it reflected a deeply problematic colonizing model—the ongoing interest in propping up the views of the founding fathers suggests that this element of US culture is still quite relevant and important to many.[21]

While the many distinct regional rural cultures of the United States are rich and full of history and tradition, the hard truth is that many of these cultures have long been marginalized and have had to endure mistreatment and gross inequality. This brings up the social reasons for why supporting sustainable rural futures is necessary. Even before the contemporary era of true rural depopulation and urbanization, many rural areas—particularly those inhabited by Indigenous, Black, and Latino populations—have faced higher poverty, worse health outcomes, environmental injustice, and multiple forms of violence.[22] Thus, there is an ethical imperative for supporting these communities through reparations and continued support so that people in these areas can live the lives they choose.[23] Beyond historical reasons for support, there is also a very real social justice consideration for the current trajectory of rural America—people still live there. If we as a society decide to let capitalism determine the fate of rural America, the path will be incredibly painful for those who currently live in our remote reaches. Just as we have seen calls to support those who are bearing the brunt of the initial impacts from climate change, we must support those who are bearing the brunt of capital's diminishing need for labor in rural America.

Not saving rural America, or at least not supporting current residents through its decline, will amount to a grave social injustice. The parts of America that can be considered rural in the 2020s are those that have historically had the highest mortality rates, slowest growth, and most persistent poverty.[24] As former internal peripheries continue to decline, the ability to earn enough income to support relocation will also disappear, leaving residents with a very hard road ahead. This will affect marginalized populations far more than others due to the persistent gap in intergenerational wealth, which makes resources for moving even harder to come by. Further, with a nationwide affordable housing crisis, it seems increasingly unlikely that many rural residents will be able to pick up and move to find an affordable place to live. These increased struggles for those already experiencing marginalization will interact with the impacts stemming from cultural loss and are likely to be associated with numerous deleterious consequences for depression, anxiety, and overall well-being among rural Americans.

While the social injustice of rural decline will affect children, families, and working-age adults, there is elevated concern for older adults who face difficulties in relocating, have lived in areas for long periods of time, and are likely living on fixed or limited income.[25] The concentration of older adults is high in rural America and only rising. Although some of this concentration is found in relatively well-off rural retirement destinations, a similarly high concentration of older adults is found in counties that are dependent on farming and losing population. Thus, a large portion of older adults in rural America are highly vulnerable to the effects of rural bifurcation.[26] This vulnerability is unfortunately paired with the stagnation and decline of rural health care services, so we will inevitably find ourselves in a situation where struggling rural areas have a high concentration of older adults with limited opportunities for receiving necessary health care.[27] This outcome will ultimately present an economic issue, as providing care for these populations will become increasingly expensive for local, state, and federal governments.

The final social consideration to discuss is the notion of simply allowing people to have the freedom America often argues it supports. Many people do not want to live in an urban area for a wide variety of reasons. The "American dream" is still widely espoused and usually means you can live the life you want and achieve success if you work hard enough. Even if we set aside the fact that inequality continues to rise and that meritocracy in America has always been a myth, in practice, this dream is currently more about living the life capital wants you to live than it is about charting your own course. If the United States is truly to be a nation standing as a hallmark of freedom, then we must find a way to support people living the life they wish, without being forced to live only in locations where capital will employ them.

There are also strong political incentives for saving rural America, for Democrats and Republicans, as well as the overall health of our political system. Rural America matters for the future of our political system because of the geographic nature of both state and federal legislatures. Although land doesn't vote and it is the votes of people who determine elections, some land conveys more power to its residents than others. It is well understood that we have seen the geographic sorting of political interests in the United States.[28] Although rural and urban counties voted fairly similarly in presidential elections from the 1970s until 1992, since then there has been a sharp divergence.[29] In 2020, 64 percent of votes in rural counties went to the Republican candidate, relative to just 43 percent in urban counties.[30] As such, Democrats tend to dominate cities while Republicans dominate suburbs and rural areas. That said, in recent years suburbs have become more complicated, with the outcomes of the 2016 and 2020 presidential elections hinging more upon suburban battlegrounds than urban or rural areas.[31]

Given the way political districts are designed for representation, how the US Senate provides two seats to all states, and the way the electoral college assigns votes, if rural America continues to depopulate, smaller and smaller absolute numbers of people will be able to sway politics in the United States at the state and federal level. In fact, with the stagnant nature of rural populations over the past twenty-five years, we already see this reflected in the divergence in voting patterns between rural and urban areas, the increasingly wide berth between congressional politics and public opinion on key issues, the frequency with which states have Democratic governors but Republican legislatures, and the increase in electoral college/popular vote disagreement in presidential elections.

Beyond sorting and representation, we have also seen a dramatic rise in what political scientists call affective polarization—wherein members of the two main political parties associate the other party with negative feelings and distrust.[32] The many implications of this polarization are a major factor in the increasing dysfunction and hostility we see playing out at state and federal levels. Unfortunately, the continued bifurcation of rural America is likely to only increase these negative sentiments. A protracted rural decline will likely continue to fuel feelings of resentment among rural residents as well as among suburban and urban residents sympathetic to rural concerns. These negative political impacts are not independent, either. Growing concerns about minority rule and the disagreement between popular vote and electoral vote outcomes will likely deepen affective polarization among the American electorate.

Clearly, these political considerations are most likely to be immediately negative for Democrats or other liberal groups because rural America is still largely dominated by conservative politics. Somewhat perversely, Republicans are currently benefiting from these processes of rural decline and stand to do so in the future. However, not supporting rural futures because it facilitates minority rule and political victories is a dangerous game for Republicans to play. These processes will lead to an increasingly precarious democracy, wherein urban voters become ever more frustrated and political vitriol rises to even higher levels—vitriol that is only heightened by both Democrats and Republicans continuing to pursue gerrymandering nationwide. Depending on the level of vitriol and the extent of minority rule, the whole political system in the United States could be made vulnerable to restructuring. Further, should Republicans ever lose the vote of rural Americans—a very real prospect given changing patterns in voting, diversity, support for labor causes, and the rise of an increasingly leftist polity in America—the system that once supported them could ultimately render them obsolete.

Are There Any Benefits to Losing Rural America?

It would not be doing the argument for saving rural America justice if we did not consider some of the plausible reasons why we may not want to save rural America. First, as outlined at the start of this chapter, we are not necessarily losing what many people think we are losing when we say rural America is disappearing. Open landscapes will remain, pastoral lands will carry on, and small towns—if they are near metropolitan areas—are still likely to exist. It is true that the remote rural towns will likely disappear and that the transition will be painful. But, if all we really care about is having an ability to appreciate bucolic landscapes and still believe that a growing economy is a good economy, then we may wish to let American capitalism proceed along its current course.

Second, there are climate-associated reasons some might advance against rural America. Some people argue that dense city living, especially when we can rely on low-emission public transportation instead of cars, results in fewer carbon emissions than living in rural areas.[33] However, research suggests that this rural-urban difference is not very large to begin with and that the imbalance in vehicular emissions is largely offset by the consumption patterns and higher incomes of those living in cities.[34] Research also shows that the areas of greatest concern from a carbon emission standpoint are suburbs, not rural areas.[35] Given that most US cities expand by suburbanization, there may actually be an argument to be made that saving rural places is likely to lead to lower per capita emissions, not higher. Thus, this argument seems shaky at best and should not be a basis for allowing all the negative outcomes discussed earlier to come to bear.

Third, there are clear economic reasons to not support sustainable rural livelihoods. For one, rural infrastructure is, in many cases, nearing the end of its life and will be incredibly expensive to repair or replace.[36] Many rural areas lack the tax base to internally raise funds for infrastructure overhauls. This means that these overhauls, if they are to happen, must be financed by either state or federal governments. Even if these overhauls are financed by some kind of debt, it appears increasingly unlikely rural areas will ever be able to pay it back. Thus, there are obvious cost savings on the part of state and federal governments if they choose not to invest in rural communities. Beyond a cost-benefit analysis for rural America, if you are of the view that the best way to support the future of the United States and our planet is to simply support the unfettered march of capitalism, then obviously you would want things to continue following their course. As we saw in chapter 4, the reason we are seeing the loss of our rural areas is because of the changing demand for rural labor in our globalized system. This means that the current global economic incentives are squarely aligned with the continuation, or even acceleration, of rural decline.

Fourth, we could argue that rural America is in such a state that its removal will ultimately lead to better conditions for those who currently live there, as well as future generations. As discussed, popular rural idylls in the United States are largely incorrect. Rural America is neither universally good nor universally bad. As diverse as it is, rural America has many positive aspects, but there are many massive challenges, too, and a sizable portion of rural areas in the United States have persistently low levels of well-being. Drawing on these negative outcomes, one could argue that we are better off completely rejecting rural idylls and the preservation of rural ways of life and instead should focus on moving rural people into cities as a means of improving societal well-being. This argument is fundamentally grounded in a mindset where we would actively accelerate the destruction of rural America as a way to reduce national poverty, alleviate health disparities, and improve the lives of children. This argument is not without precedent. For example, in Fuping County, Hebei Province, China, the county government provided resettlement assistance to poor populations in depopulated rural towns as a means of poverty alleviation.[37] Although the argument that rural America is a lost cause and we should simply accelerate its demise is possibly one of the strongest entertained here, it still ultimately supports the interests of capital and gives up everything that is valuable about rural America. As such, whether or not to support this argument ultimately boils down to individual and societal worldviews regarding the balance of supporting capital versus supporting people and communities—an issue that will be taken up more fully in the following chapters.

Finally, there is an ethical argument we must consider when discussing whether or not to invest resources in rural communities. This argument is grounded in an ethic similar to what Gifford Pinchot, the first head of the US Forest Service, espoused—that is, we should pursue "the greatest good of the greatest number in the long run."[38] In this vein, one could argue that preserving rural spaces will direct resources from state or federal governments to areas that are relatively less populated. As such, those dollars could instead be spent where those resources would support a greater number of people's well-being. This argument stems from a normative utilitarian ethic where a decision is considered right or moral if it maximizes the well-being of society.[39] This utilitarian view can be contrasted by other families of normative ethics such as deontology, which argues that whether something is right or wrong is determined through moral duties and principles, or virtue ethics, which argues that ethics are determined more by inherent virtue than actions or duty. On its face, the broad utilitarian argument makes sense. Resources are constrained by a variety of factors in our political economic system; directing scarce resources to small populations instead of large populations would go against a utilitarian ethic.

Even if we accept a strict utilitarian view of the world—which we have no clear reason to do—this argument carries with it some questionable assumptions. First, if we were to develop a way to sever the link between where people live and how they make their money that was universally beneficial and not just beneficial to rural people, then the unequal distribution of scarce resources argument does not apply. Thus, the utilitarian critique assumes universal benefit is not possible—an assumption we will see is incorrect in following chapters. Second, many remaining rural communities are those that have long been the most marginalized. Thus, even if resources were directed unevenly, they would arguably be correcting past wrongs and thus would be reflective of the enactment of social justice. This element of justice highlights a further issue with a strict utilitarian view—if we are only evaluating our current actions based on future utility or benefit, then the historical nature of justice simply cannot exist within the framework.[40] Given the broad interest in justice we see throughout American society, a strict utilitarian ethic appears a questionable position from which to make national decisions. That said, even if a belief in justice and strict utilitarianism appear somewhat at odds, many Americans still espouse an ethic of fairness and utilitarianism. For example, much of the discourse surrounding student loan forgiveness has centered on who benefits and overall fairness. As such, it is important that any approach to saving rural America at least addresses these concerns. Thankfully, as we will see in the following chapters, a universal approach is possible. Thus, the utilitarian argument can largely be sidestepped.

Conclusion

When deciding whether or not to save rural America, we have to grapple with the arguments both for and against taking action. This is because it is not obvious from the outset that saving rural America is the most prudent course. While navigating the various arguments, we must also be attentive to the distracting nature of competing rural idylls in the United States. If we romanticize rural America when deciding whether or not to save it, our decision and subsequent actions will likely only exacerbate existing injustices because our romantic views of rural America are shaped by continuing forces of racism and inequality. If we do the opposite and view rural America as a pariah, we will again wash over the richness and value of rural people and places. Thus, we must make our decisions with as clear a view as possible of the reality of the diverse nature of rural America and its many needs, opportunities, and problems.

When we consider what is lost versus what is gained by the disappearance of rural America, the benefit of supporting sustainable rural futures appears to outweigh the costs, although it is important to admit this is fundamentally anchored in values in addition to facts. When weighing what we stand to lose versus what we stand to gain, in light of the possible solutions available, supporting a sustainable rural future for America seems immensely valuable. The cultural, social, and political ramifications of inaction, or an acceleration of rural out-migration, are simply too much to bear. When we turn a clear eye to the situation in rural America, the diversity of its cultures, and the legacy of neglect many communities face, we have an imperative to set aside notions of rural idylls and act.

However, utilitarian concerns and a recognition of the abject squalor endured by many nonrural areas should not go unheard. Just as there are those marginalized in rural America, there are even more people experiencing intergenerational hardship in urban America. Many populations that once lived in rural hardship have been absorbed by urban areas and may not have received any clear benefits from this annexation. It would be unfair to ignore their plight simply because they no longer fit our current definition of rurality. Further, saving rural America cannot mean just preserving things as they currently are. Many rural areas have incredibly persistent poverty and very little wealth. For these areas, saving must mean improving. To accomplish this delicate act of sustaining rural communities into the future, we have to identify a solution and path forward that addresses the fundamental issue at hand—the false freedom of labor under capitalism—while also finding a way to raise all ships and reduce existing rural hardship. Thankfully, there are paths we can take, and it is these paths we will now consider.

CHAPTER SIX

Branching Paths for Rural Futures

As we have seen throughout this book, rural America is currently at a crossroads. There are several paths in front of us, however, it remains unclear which one we should take. Taking stock of the situation, there are four main paths rural America could pursue, and these paths would all result in incredibly different outcomes for both rural and urban Americans, as well as the capitalist class. In what follows, we will consider each path while also discussing its merits and drawbacks. This chapter will cover the first three paths. The final path, which is the path most likely to lead to a sustainable rural future, will be saved for chapter 7.

It must be made clear from the outset that it is not as if rural America will "choose" any one of these paths. Large-scale policy decisions are made at the federal level through dynamic networks of power, bureaucracy, and capital-intrusion. Further, rural America is not monolithic. It is not as if we could go ask rural residents their opinion and expect any single overall view to emerge. Thus, the possible paths are simply that—possible paths. You will also find this chapter does not spend much time considering the plausibility of these paths being adopted by those currently in Washington, DC. Doing so would likely lead to an ultimate weakening of each proposal because they would be overly tailored to the current policy preferences of lawmakers at time of writing.

Instead, what is presented here are ideal types or utopian versions of possible paths forward. Ideal types—popularized by Max Weber, who is often considered one of the founders of sociology—are descriptions of phenomena that elucidate the most important characteristic of the phenomenon in question.[1] They are heuristic simplifications that are not designed to perfectly capture all details; instead, they capture the contours of how we may expect something to be. In practice, ideal types are used as a tool for comparing conceptual types to the real world so that we can better interrogate the why and how of social processes. Ideal types are utopian in that they accentuate one or more points of view and allow us to step outside reality to imagine how things may or could be.[2] Importantly, the use of the words "ideal" and "utopia" does not mean these are all positive paths to go down. The use of these terms is value neutral; we can have both positive and negative utopias. But just because these paths reflect idealized versions of the future does not mean they are not valuable. By invoking utopias, we can generate valuable insights into our possible futures and discern what steps are truly necessary to achieve a sustainable rural future.[3] Ultimately, if we do not engage in utopian thinking, it is hard to discern what steps we may need to take to create a better world than the one we live in.

The Status Quo Path

The first path we must consider is arguably the one that least represents an ideal type—namely, the status quo. As we have seen, the decline of rural America is real and rooted in the core of capitalism, and it is an undesirable situation. Yet there is a very real and unfortunate likelihood that things will continue on their present course. Under this model, trends would persist and the bifurcation of rural America into either metropolitan areas or unpopulated zones would continue at its current pace. Population aging, natural decrease, the exit of services, and the decline of infrastructure would continue to be the norm in those areas that do not become incorporated into larger urban cores. Those rural spaces that do not decline would continue to become retreats for the elite, since only those who have wealth and stability beyond what can be found in the locality will be able to afford to live there.[4] Along this path, we would continue to rely on linear development thinking and position a greater degree of urbanity as the only way rural communities can "succeed." Economic development efforts would focus on entrepreneurship, innovation, agglomeration, and rural tourism. Existing development frameworks—such as the Community Capitals Framework (CCF), Rural Rising, and the Tailored, Resilient, Inclusive, and Collaborative (TRIC) approach—would continue to be uncritically applied. As such, increases in indicators of economic growth would continue to serve as the marker of a job well done.

A path that maintains the status quo would continue to allow capital to mask the decline of rural America as some sort of unfortunate outcome to blame on regulations and politicians as opposed to correctly articulating its root within capitalism and the pursuit of profit. This laissez-faire approach is the friendliest to capital because it essentially allows the incentives of profit to continue shaping the trajectory of rural America. As such, the transnational capitalist class would be allowed to continue leveraging its global power to influence local rural economic development trajectories from afar. Although unpalatable to many, if you happen to be someone who vaults the success of capital above all social outcomes, this would likely be the preferable option.

Politically, this path would continue to push along the increases in affective polarization while also creating power vacuums for even higher levels of minority rule. We would lose the vast majority of the culture and cultural practices found in rural America and risk creating a revisionist history of rural America where the atrocities committed against Indigenous, Black, Asian, and Latino populations are ignored. Importantly, this path would dramatically exacerbate social injustices for marginalized populations in rural America. Native, Black, Latino, and poor populations would face the brunt of this unplanned and unmanaged transition. Due to the attachment to the status quo, this path would not provide any new form of aid or assistance to populations living in our declining rural areas. This would mean that aid would continue to be largely comprised of programs focused on conventional development efforts through agencies such as the US Economic Development Administration or those focused on rural infrastructure through the Infrastructure Investment and Jobs Act of 2021.

Given that our existing programs are not likely to resolve the dilemmas rural America is facing, this path would ultimately amount to a slow war of attrition against rural areas in the United States. As the prolonged decline continues, those without money or wealth would have the hardest time either moving away or making ends meet. To be clear, residents living in one of the rural areas that are ultimately integrated into growing metropolitan areas may actually find themselves with access to more resources instead of less. However, the place they call home will still be fundamentally altered. Given the dynamics of rural gentrification in amenity-rich areas, they may ultimately be forced to relocate because of unaffordable property taxes and cost-of-living increases.[5]

The Accelerated Path of Rural Destruction

While the path that preserves the status quo would largely ignore any social imperative to help those facing the brunt of the ongoing decline of rural America, we can consider another path that would continue current trends with a higher degree of social responsibility. This path, termed the Accelerated Path of Rural Destruction, would aim to continue and even accelerate current trends through political and financial support. As discussed earlier, it can easily be argued that living conditions in many parts of rural America are undesirable—or at least result in worse outcomes for public health and overall well-being. Thus, those with a utilitarian view of the world would argue that administering scarce resources to support a declining rural America, instead of aiding other causes or locations with more people, is an unfair allocation of resources. It is not hard to see how a utilitarian-minded individual could come to that conclusion. Rural areas already receive a disproportionate amount of social spending because of their poorer and older populations, their heightened infrastructure needs, and their dominant industries (e.g., agriculture) receiving significant federal subsidies.[6] Thus, one option is to simply support the end of rural America as we know it through the encouragement and facilitation of out-migration.

The idea of incentivizing rural residents to leave their homes is not without precedent. In fact, this idea was the impetus behind the creation of the oft-forgotten New Deal agency known as the Resettlement Administration in July of 1935.[7] Led by Rexford G. Tugwell—an American economist who was a strident advocate for urban planning—one of the Resettlement Administration's principal activities was to relocate impoverished farm families and communities off blighted dust bowl land and into planned communities structured around either local industry or farming cooperatives. The Resettlement Administration was short-lived, only lasting eighteen months before it was transitioned into the Farm Services Administration.[8] An immensely controversial agency, the Resettlement Administration was decried as a communistic overreach of state control, and its efforts at raising a model community were deemed unconstitutional by the courts in 1936.[9] Although well intentioned, the initiatives of the administration drew the ire of both rural and urban residents because of perceived government overreach, tax implications, concerns of cost, and anti-communist sentiment. Although a variety of resettlement activities were still completed by the Farm Services Administration, the relocation programs were unpopular and ultimately abandoned.

More recently, China has used rural-urban resettlement as a means of alleviating rural poverty.[10] Within Fuping County in Hebei Province, rural residents have been incentivized to move to urban areas through two different programs. In one, they forfeit their homes to the government in exchange for standardized government housing in urban areas. In the other, they purchase a new home in an urban area and then receive fair market value for their land from the government. Although this has been vaulted as a successful means of poverty reduction in China by some scholars, the acceptability of such an approach in the United States remains open to debate.[11] If the history of the Resettlement Administration is any indication, it seems unlikely it would be well received.

The Accelerated Path of Rural Destruction's level of aggression would be highly dependent on the specifics of the programs that were ultimately developed. For example, if the United States adopted a model of forced out-migration from rural areas, similar to how the US government historically treated American Indians, it would be a very hard path, indeed. However, an approach similar to the program in China, or even more relaxed, would likely be more palatable and humanitarian. We already have a variety of programs in the United States focusing on incentivizing migration *into* rural areas. For example, in 2012, Kansas implemented the Rural Opportunity Zones program that provides college-educated adults with economic incentives such as tax breaks and student loan relief if they move to a select set of identified rural counties.[12] It is not hard to imagine an inverse of these programs should federal or state governments decide that giving up on rural areas is the more prudent approach. Further, if policies designed along this path were sensitive to historic patterns of marginalization and discrimination, then it is possible this path could result in a higher quality of life for nonwhite and poor residents of rural America. Incentive programs that take into account current wealth, education, and historical treatment would be able to provide more resources to the most marginalized and help tip the scales for Black, Native, Latino, and poor residents of rural America.

Although the Accelerated Path of Rural Destruction may avoid some of the injustice of the status quo, there are still significant issues with this approach. The underlying fact is that this approach does not address the fundamental issue at hand—namely, the false freedom of labor mobility under capitalism. As such, this path not only continues to yield the direction of the United States to the desires of capital, but it actually accelerates the hand-off.

From this, several issues emerge. First, absent an unlikely degree of highly intentional political planning, we would still see the negative political consequences of rural out-migration. Unless we were to see a complete redrawing of our political maps or a mandated transfer of property to the government, pro-migration policies could very easily leave a power vacuum in depopulated rural areas for wealthy, politically driven investors. This approach would likely accelerate a transition of rural America from its current state to a high-status realm only inhabitable by the most independently wealthy individuals. This would only exacerbate our ongoing political dysfunction because these elites would be able to influence politics through the geographic structure of our system. Second, the loss of our many rural cultures would still occur. Obviously, we can imagine policies that attempt to preserve culture even amid migration, but losing one's home fundamentally makes it harder for people to maintain their cultural traditions.

Third, the relationship between any version of this path and American Indians is fundamentally fraught and unjust, particularly as it relates to tribal lands. Although not all tribal lands are rural, the vast majority of them are.[13] American Indians have lost almost all of their ancestral homeland since colonization, and the land tribes now occupy was often given to them because of its remote and often marginal nature.[14] Thus, even absent intergovernmental concerns, this kind of policy risks further decimating tribal cultures while continuing to push Indigenous populations where the federal government and capital would prefer they live. Beyond issues of justice, the relationship between this path and tribes is also complicated by the complex nature of the relationship between federal and tribal governments. Tribal governments, unlike county or state governments, are sovereign entities that often have treaties between themselves and the federal government. As such, tribal governments can create their own laws, are not subject to many state laws, and are afforded greater autonomy over controlling their own interests than other nonfederal governments in the United States. If this sovereignty meant that state or federal relocation efforts would not include tribal reservations, then the quagmire posed by forcibly moving Indigenous populations might be avoided. However, if this were the case, then it also means tribal populations would not be receiving any support while the government essentially gives up on the broader rural regions surrounding their territory. Thus, when considering tribes, the Accelerated Path of Rural Destruction is fraught from all angles.

Finally, this approach would require Americans to squarely face the false freedom of labor mobility and accept that they are not as free as they thought. Despite the actual degree of freedom in the United States being debatable, given the continuing internal attacks on human rights, it is undeniable that freedom to live where and how you please is a bedrock tenet in American culture. In many cases, American adherence to the idea of freedom is akin to a religion. As such, the Accelerated Path of Rural Destruction would likely face dramatic levels of resistance from the left and the right. Historically, the use of eminent domain—wherein the government annexes or takes privately held land for necessary purposes—has been incredibly unpopular and viewed as a violation of basic rights.[15] Given that this path would essentially mean state and federal governments are giving up on places entirely—places that the public often imagines have a homogeneous conservative political opinion—there is no reason to expect we wouldn't see similar levels of vitriol and claims of anti-conservative discrimination similar to what we already see from far-right political groups.

The Soft Path for Rural Sustainability

Not all paths for rural America require toeing the line for capital. There are two paths that would actually work to address the fundamental issue at hand—that being the tether we currently have between where we live and how we make our money. Remember that if we choose to save rural America, we must attempt to stall or even reverse the bifurcation of rural areas into either depopulated zones or urban areas. Neither of these paths would likely stop the annexation effect stemming from urban expansion. The growth of metropolitan areas and shrinkage of others is a function of the broader seesaw discussed by Neil Smith, as well as other migration concerns related to climate, amenities, culture, and industry. Thus, it is hard to imagine any paths that would truly address that side of rural bifurcation without resorting to forced migration. Instead, these paths work to sever the link between work and place and thus allow labor to stay in or move to rural places they find desirable. The first of these approaches is called the Soft Path for Rural Sustainability. Under the soft path, we would seek to partially sever the tether without radically altering our political or economic system. In some ways, we are already starting to see this soft decoupling occur. This is evident in both pre–COVID-19 trends as well as the dramatic changes induced by the COVID-19 pandemic. The shift to remote work represents one of the key anchors of the soft path.

Remote work is one of the primary mechanisms available for allowing people to live where they want while still earning an income sufficient to support them and their family. This form of work was already increasing pre-pandemic, leading Alan Felstead and Golo Henseke to argue in 2017 that we were seeing a "detachment of work from place."[16] However, during the COVID-19 pandemic, we saw a dramatic yet uneven increase in remote work, and it appears as if this transition is poised to at least partially continue—with Jose Barrero and colleagues arguing in 2021 that COVID-19 represented a "persistent reallocation shock."[17] Although remote work may help us decouple work from place, the ability to work remotely is not shared across sectors. Research shows that the sectors classified as skilled scalable services—such as information services, finance and insurance, professional services, and management of companies—not only have the highest potential for remote work but also accounted for more than twice the amount of remote work during the pandemic compared to the rest of the US economy.[18] These services are generally high income and require a bachelor's degree or even graduate-level education. As such, relying solely on this sector for a broad scale decoupling of work from place would undeniably exacerbate existing inequalities while also creating new ones.

Under the soft path, the increases in inequality stemming from this uneven access to remote work across sectors would be further complicated by the lower participation in remote work found in rural areas. Data from the US Current Population Survey—the data source used to generate employment statistics for the United States—shows that those in nonmetropolitan counties were far less likely to engage in remote work during the COVID-19 pandemic.[19] This rural-urban imbalance in remote work has also been shown to fall along measures of overall population density.[20] The reason is twofold. First, rural areas simply support fewer jobs with remote work potential. For example, like urban America, rural America is now a service-dominated economy, but the kinds of service jobs available in rural America are fundamentally different. Rural service jobs are often lower paying, not in the skilled scalable services sector, and tend to be rooted in face-to-face contact.[21] Thus, current rural residents were less able to transition to remote work during the pandemic and will continue to face this disadvantage unless these trends change.

Because of this imbalance between rural and urban industrial structure, if we were to support rural areas under the soft path, it would require a substantial investment in the acceleration of remote work across sectors and space. As such, an important step would be the formal encouragement of companies in all sectors to increase their acceptance and promotion of remote work. As it happens, some businesses are already accepting this transition due to labor demands and lessons learned during the COVID-19 pandemic. One example is Brian Chesky, the CEO of Airbnb, who in May 2022 unveiled plans to support remote work of Airbnb employees indefinitely.[22] Under this plan, workers are permitted to work from any state with an active Airbnb entity, which includes all but seven states. Within these states, they can live where they wish and will not receive a pay cut regardless of whether they live in an expensive place like San Francisco or a cheap place like Dillon County, South Carolina. In implementing this plan, Chesky stated that the current office is dead, and he believes this is the future of work. As of November 2024, this policy was still in effect.

Perhaps perversely, the shift to remote work not only works to decouple our link between place and work but also provides several clear benefits to capital. First, shifting to remote work dramatically reduces overhead for businesses. No longer do businesses necessarily need to pay as much for rent or utilities on office space. This allows them to displace risks associated with office spaces to remote workers who pay for their own internet and have an office in their home. Second, as Chesky notes, the shift to remote work greatly increases the talent pool available to employers—with labor supply no longer restricted to those willing to live within close proximity to company headquarters.

An additional reason for the lack of remote work uptake in rural America is related to infrastructure. Internet access in rural areas continues to be much more limited than many people in the United States appreciate. As of 2020, 22.3 percent of Americans in rural areas and 27.7 percent of Americans in tribal areas lacked broadband speeds at the Federal Communications Commission (FCC) high-speed benchmark. This is made worse when we consider that the benchmark for what counts as "high speed" is viewed by scholars as too slow and ultimately harmful to rural areas because it allows providers to get away with the implementation of outmoded technology.[23] Indeed, even in those places where the FCC reports that rural residents have access to reliable broadband, independent speed tests reveal that internet speeds are far lower than reported by the FCC.[24] As such, rural residents have far more trouble accessing infrastructure essential for effective remote work than even government reports indicate. Thus, the 22.3 percent statistic reported by the FCC represents a severe lower bound on the actual portion of rural America without access to internet service that is fast and reliable enough to support remote work. Ultimately, the lack of reliable and fast rural broadband internet is one of the key barriers to address if we were to support the soft path. Thankfully, many are well aware of this issue. For example, the Montana Department of Commerce has launched the Come Home Montana initiative to position Montana as an ideal remote work destination so people can return to where they grew up. In doing so, the initiative's website directly states that "efforts to expand broadband infrastructure are underway."[25]

While an important step for supporting the remote work transition under the soft path would be the expansion of fast and reliable broadband in rural areas, at least some attention would also have to be paid to other ongoing rural infrastructure issues. Many rural places have experienced decades of neglect and infrastructural decay. If we are to support people living in rural areas and working remotely, we will need an initial infusion of support for rural infrastructure across the country. The idea of rural sustainability baked into this path is that if enough people work remotely in rural areas, then the tax base will be enough to support at least some degree of maintenance and upgrades. However, to catalyze that initial movement, an infusion of resources would likely be necessary. People simply won't want to move to places they view as unsafe or unsupported. For this reason, improvements to the physical infrastructure for water, transportation, and health care would be necessary if this path were to be successful. Importantly, this infusion would likely need to go beyond the resources already being provided to rural America under the Infrastructure Investment and Jobs Act of 2021.

Investing in physical infrastructure, however, is unlikely to be enough. Many rural areas would benefit from renewed investment in social infrastructure such as schools, childcare, and gathering spaces. Even if adults want to move to a rural area and work remotely, if there are not nearby schools and childcare options, they may deem the move simply unrealistic. How this looks will likely be variable, and government investment and support for social infrastructure initiatives will need to be flexible. For example, childcare services could be home-based, church-affiliated, or commercial, depending on community size and need. What is clear is that traditional funding mechanisms are likely ill-equipped to support this kind of essential infrastructure, so creative policies delivering material support will be needed. At present, rural communities with functioning social infrastructure appear far more poised to support sustainable populations; however, expanding this form of infrastructure to all rural communities will be necessary if widespread rural-urban migration were to occur.

Beyond remote work and infrastructure improvements, there are other strategies we could pursue under the soft path to support our rural regions. For example, there are many individuals who would like to live in rural areas, but the wages they can earn are so much lower in rural markets that they cannot earn a wage that rewards their expertise and allows them to pay off student loans. For this, programs such as the Kansas Rural Opportunity Zones—which provide financial incentives to encourage professionals to locate to rural areas—would likely be worthwhile. Thus, instead of severing the link between work and place, this strategy would provide workers with the freedom to move where they want by subsidizing their choice. That said, programs focused on incentivizing rural labor migration have historically provided far too little, and this lack of sufficient incentives has led to these programs having limited impact. For example, a study on Health Professional

Shortage Areas (HPSAs) reported that from 1970 to 2018, the HPSA program—a federal program designed to recruit doctors to rural areas in need of physicians—had no significant impact on mortality or physician density.[26] Even if there are sufficient incentives, these programs are still premised on the existence of jobs in the first place; if a program intends to recruit doctors to rural areas, the rural area still has to have a hospital or clinic. Unfortunately, this is increasingly rare because of the consolidation of health care services and the reduction of services offered or even the closure of rural clinics and hospitals due to a lack of profit.[27]

Many of these rural relocation incentive programs offer to pay off student loans, an important form of debt relief that significantly affects labor migration decisions. However, these incentive programs tend to only exist for the most highly trained professions. As such, the final piece of the soft path would be student loan forgiveness for a wider swath of Americans. Student loans are now the second largest debt category in the United States, second only to mortgages, and are in excess of $1.74 trillion.[28] These loans represent a significant factor driving labor (im)mobility, with the need to pay off loans dominating the decisions of many workers. Although various programs to help pay off student debt exist, these programs are notoriously hard to complete and comply with, and they have rarely resulted in the actual forgiveness of student loans.[29] As such, student loan forgiveness at any level would reflect a soft path approach for catalyzing greater labor mobility.

While many have argued student loan forgiveness is regressive because it would benefit the wealthy more than the poor, this argument is misguided because it misunderstands the distributional structure of student debt. Although the majority of the total dollars of student debt are held by those earning very large incomes, such as doctors and lawyers, the majority of *loans* are held by those making very little who often belong to marginalized ethnic and racial groups.[30] Further, as a ratio of total student loan debt to income or wealth, it is those with low incomes and low wealth who face the largest proportional burden. Given that many of these loans are relatively small but large enough to hold people in place, forgiveness is a valuable approach for increasing the freedom of labor mobility in the United States. In the summer of 2022, this issue was taken up by President Joseph Biden when he issued an executive order forgiving up to $20,000 of student loan debt for individual's making less than $125,000 a year. Although Biden was able to forgive a smaller amount of debt through other channels, the sweeping debt relief program never materialized because the Supreme Court blocked the order in June 2023.[31]

All told, the anchors of the Soft Path for Rural Sustainability are remote work, improvements in infrastructure, the pursuit of individual labor incentive programs, and student debt forgiveness. Ideally, this path would support sustaining rural communities by allowing individuals to move back to areas they once called home while also allowing others to stay in an area if they wish to. The broad nature of this approach would allow for migration effects across all of rural America while hopefully avoiding many of the ethical dilemmas associated with providing scarce resources to communities with small populations. Further, this path would preserve at least some of the diverse rural cultures in the United States while avoiding the large-scale urbanization or out-migration we are currently facing. Politically, it is not clear one way or the other if this approach would address the issues of minority rule and polarization. While the soft path may work to restore some balance to our current system through the redistribution of populations, this appears heavily subject to the specific programs implemented and would also be influenced by the issues of inequality, gentrification, and culture clash described below.

Although the soft path may seem like a valuable approach, there are some important limitations to acknowledge. First, this path is largely focused on those already occupying elite professions. Jobs that can be performed as fully remote tend to be in the skilled scalable services sector. The transition to remote work in occupations that do not require a credential or college degree has been slower and may be simply impossible for many forms of labor, such as skilled trades. For example, auto mechanics, construction workers, plumbers, and machinery operators seem unlikely to ever become remote positions. Additionally, current incentive programs largely support the relocation of elite professionals such as doctors and lawyers, meaning they provide little help to those trying to sustain themselves who are already living in rural places. This emphasis on elites has two possible ramifications to note.

First, it is truly possible that an infusion of professionals to a rural community would catalyze enough activity to support other jobs in the area and thus generate enough of an economic engine to sustain a rural area without fundamentally altering its rural nature. For example, the in-migration of professionals could lead to more demand for restaurants, schools, and grocery stores, representing a large multiplier effect. However, it should be obvious to the reader that this trajectory still ultimately leads us to linear development thinking. It would also create two classes of worker—one who has been able to detach work from place and another who has been unable to do so.

These two classes of worker bring up the second ramification—an increase in both local and spatial inequality. In terms of local inequality, scholarship on rural America has often reported an in-group/out-group dynamic between new in-migrants and those who view themselves as being "born and raised" in an area. This research has shown that in scenic areas like the intermountain West, where people migrate for natural amenities, there are often strong tensions, including culture clashe, resentment, and exclusion.[32] New migrants, especially when tied to a different socioeconomic class than current residents, often have very different values and ideas on how a community should function. Although some may write this off as current residents being resistant to change or not being open to external viewpoints—and some research has indeed shown this to be the case—the turmoil it creates should not be overlooked. Notably, this dynamic has also been associated with rural gentrification processes that make it so that residents can no longer afford to live in the rural areas they call home.

The notion of a rising cost of living brings up the likely impact of elite migration on spatial inequality. Historically, the places that mobile skilled labor have chosen to move to are areas rich in natural amenities or other highly appealing qualities—a pattern observed during the COVID-19 pandemic.[33] As these are the rural areas most likely to be thriving, an imbalanced rise in remote work may ultimately exacerbate our existing patterns of spatial inequality in rural America. To be clear, if we managed to expand remote work to all Americans while also improving rural infrastructure—these distributional issues may be avoidable. But this seems incredibly unlikely. Thus, unless careful attention is paid, many of the social justice reasons for sustaining rural America would not be met under the soft path approach.

Finally, it is worth noting the resistance this path would likely face from capital. As David Harvey notes, to ensure access to a reserve labor army, the escape paths must be cut off.[34] Thus, it is likely that a push from government sources to further expand remote work would likely be met with at least some degree of resistance. Importantly, resistance would probably come from both the sectors transitioning to remote work as well as the sectors unable to do so. For the first, remote work may experience resistance if companies see it as standing in the way of profit. There are those who argue remote work is ultimately a win for both labor and capital—for example, the flexible firm hypothesis argues that remote work allows for a more flexible and cost-effective allocation of labor resources.[35] Yet it is clear this opinion is not held by all firms.

Although the CEO of Airbnb believes remote work is the future, the number of companies resisting calls for remote work makes it clear not all corporations agree. This resistance is well illustrated by the emergence of hybrid work—wherein employees spend some days in the office and some at home each week—which has quickly overtaken fully remote work as the dominant modality in the immediate years following the COVID-19 pandemic. According to Gallup, although 70 percent of workers were remote in 2020, that number had declined to 29 percent by May 2023.[36] By contrast, hybrid work jumped from 18 percent of work arrangements in 2020 to 52 percent in 2023. Hybrid work provides employees with a degree of flexibility and some relief from the daily grind of commuting, but it still requires them to be within a reasonable distance to a main office. This normalization of hybrid work might actually work against a push toward a more fully remote labor force and rural living going forward.

Beyond the companies actually providing remote work opportunities, we would also likely see resistance to the soft path approach from sectors with low remote work potential. This is because our modern working environment has a spatial arrangement built to support people going to work. As such, food, retail, and other services in cities are clustered around places of employment and stand to lose significant revenue should remote work become the standard.[37] This is further complicated by commercial real estate, which supports multiple businesses and has a wide array of ownership structures. As such, it is likely that this reshuffling would face resistance from a wide range of urban businesses and real estate interests.

Conclusion

The three paths we have seen—the Status Quo Path, the Accelerated Path of Rural Destruction, and the Soft Path for Rural Sustainability—are three possible futures for rural America. While the first two would lead to the loss of rural areas in the United States, the third would attempt to sustain rural regions for the long term. Importantly, all three of these paths remain committed to our current political economic system and are thus subservient to the whims of capital. Although the soft path does attempt to destabilize the false freedom of labor mobility, it does so while trying to not upset capital *too much*. Further, for the soft path to work, capital would have to be willing to go along with transitions to a largely remote workforce—and it seems increasingly unlikely this would happen. With their adherence to the desires of capital, none of these paths truly fix the core issue driving the loss of rural America—the tethered nature of work and place.

CHAPTER SEVEN
The Hard Path for Rural Sustainability

The final path for us to consider is called the Hard Path for Rural Sustainability. This path is premised on the notion that only a radical decoupling of where we live from how we earn our income will save rural America in a way that is attentive to the important issues of injustice while also being appropriately considerate of utilitarian concerns. While still squarely focused on saving rural America, this path is notable for the fact that it focuses on improving the lives of all Americans, not just those living in rural areas. Whereas the soft path focuses on incremental changes that would disproportionately benefit elites, the hard path is a universalist approach acknowledging the linked fate of rural and urban Americans.

So, what is the hard path? Although there are several ways one could design a radical restructuring of the mobility of labor, here the focus is on four activities that, while still utopian, seem the most realistic and plausible in the near term: (1) the establishment of a universal basic income, (2) the creation of a single-payer health care system, (3) the payment of reparations to Black Americans, and (4) the establishment of a federal program of tribal restitution.

Universal Basic Income

The establishment of a universal basic income (UBI) is the foundational anchor of the hard path. The idea of UBI has become increasingly popular in recent years and would amount to providing all residents of the United States with a regular income to support a "life free from economic insecurity."[1] Under the UBI proposed here, which is broadly within the vision described by Juliana Uhuru Bidadanure in 2019, cash payments would be distributed at the individual instead of household level, the benefit would be an unconditional entitlement, and all adult residents would universally receive income regardless of current employment or earned income.[2] It is valuable to briefly detail each of these mechanisms in turn.

First, the individual focus of UBI means that UBI would be agnostic to relationship status or the pooling of household resources between adults. To ensure economic security for families with children, the amount of UBI would be increased for each child dependent upon an adult, but the individual focus means each adult would receive their own independent benefit. From a gender equity perspective, this would have the potential to facilitate broader gender equality by providing women with the resources necessary to leave unsafe situations while also allowing both men and women to engage in active parenting and care work without a loss of economic security.[3] Further, the individual focus would also allow young adults to make their life decisions from a place of security, free from the concerns of household or parental income and resources.

Second, the benefit of UBI would be unconditional. There is no work requirement. UBI is seen as supporting true freedom and allowing individuals to lead the life they would choose. This unconditional nature stands in stark contrast to the vast majority of existing US safety net policies that often require evidence of searching for jobs to continue receiving benefits.[4]

Third, UBI would be *universal*; all people receive it regardless of wealth. This means that UBI would not just go to those who need it; instead, it would go to all people. This universality means that all permanent adults in the United States, regardless of citizenship, would receive UBI. Thus, noncitizen populations would still be afforded the ability to live the life of their choosing. This approach would prove vital in sustaining the growing rural Latino communities where many residents, although legally in the country, may not be citizens of the United States. To be clear, the extension of UBI to noncitizens would certainly not be a guarantee if UBI was adopted. Many social programs in the United States do not allow for noncitizen participation. The point is that under the ideal type of hard path presented here, all adults — and indirectly their children — would receive UBI.

Within the broader world of social policy, this universality has often been a sticking point — particularly as it relates to giving UBI to those who are already financially well-off. After all, why should we give resources to those who do not need them? The commonly cited rationale is twofold. First, in the United States, universal policies have a long history of being more enduring, popular, and successful. For example, Social Security and Medicare continue to be the most broadly supported safety net programs across the country. These are two policies that everyone can access past a certain age. This is sharply contrasted by the assault on means-tested programs we have seen, wherein persistent and unfounded fears of systemic abuse continue to foster low overall support for means-tested programs like food stamps, Medicaid, and unemployment. This reproach of means-tested programs feeds directly into the immense stigma associated with receipt of welfare and reduces overall uptake.[5] For these reasons, universal policies must be a priority. The second response to those unsupportive of UBI's truly universal nature is that even if people are making decent money, they may not be living the life they desire. If we believe living one's conception of a "good life" is equivalent to a high level of well-being and the expression of true freedom, then UBI is valuable for raising the well-being of individuals regardless of their current income.[6]

Although responding to critiques of universality is valuable, the entire premise of the critique of universality is less relevant to our application of UBI. This is because the whole point of UBI in the context of saving rural America is to universally decouple income from place. We do not only care about improving the lives of those at the bottom of the income distribution or those living in rural places. In fact, the goal of the hard path is to radically decouple all of labor from residence. This means that we need to support true freedom of mobility at all income levels.

It is worth noting that the emphasis on freedom within UBI has an inherent libertarian bent that has been viewed suspiciously by those on the left.[7] And to be clear, while it is true that UBI may make some social programs redundant and thus justify their termination, if UBI were to be implemented as a backdoor for removing minimum wages, collective bargaining, or other essential safety net programs, then it would be a libertarian policy out of step with hard path goals and not worth supporting. However, the focus on implementing UBI at a level that would universally remove economic insecurity means that the hard-line libertarian values are substantially downplayed under this proposal.[8] Further, because the hard path combines UBI with the other mechanisms discussed below, it ultimately stands as a far more social democratic than libertarian strategy. Finally, it should be acknowledged that the framing around freedom would likely be quite effective in the United States given the cultural attachment to the concept.

It is at this point that one might be tempted to argue for the value of UBI on the grounds of spurring economic growth or inspiring innovation. However, that won't be pursued here. Instead, we need to remember that these considerations are irrelevant to our goals. To embrace UBI and the Hard Path for Rural Sustainability, we have to make the radical decision to cast aside all notions of catalyzing economic growth when evaluating UBI as a path forward for a sustainable rural future in the United States. Focusing on growth or innovation is antithetical to the purpose of UBI in this context. What we are doing with UBI is resolving the false freedom of labor mobility by allowing individuals to decide where and how to live without worrying about economic security. If this catalyzes growth in urban or rural areas, that may well be an upside for people in those areas—but it is not the goal and stands as a red herring to progress.

Although evaluating UBI on the grounds of economic growth is not relevant to the goals of the hard path, to ensure we have a fair understanding of the scope and impact of UBI, it is worth examining some of the current thinking on the overall cost and efficacy of various UBI experiments. Although the testing of UBI at a scale similar to what is proposed here has not been undertaken, there have been a number of small-scale tests of UBI and UBI-like programs across the world. Perhaps the most famous UBI experiment occurred in Finland in 2017 and 2018, where 2,000 individuals received monthly payments and an additional housing supplement if the monthly payment was their sole income. The results were generally favorable, with improvements in mental health, physical health, and modest increases in employment among those receiving the benefit.[9] The finding related to employment is particularly notable because a major critique made against UBI is that it may discourage workforce participation among recipients.

During the COVID-19 pandemic, similarly favorable results were found in rural Kenya, where the longest trial of UBI to date—which will run for twelve years—is ongoing.[10] Over the first two years of this trial, cash transfers led to improved well-being, increased resilience, and lower reported occurrence of hunger during the vulnerable periods of the pandemic. Additionally, transfers were found to have led to greater income-based risk taking among participants, particularly among those who were in the portion of the experiment that guaranteed long-term support (e.g., ten years), with individuals investing their extra income in new business ventures.[11] This increase in self-started business ventures supports the notion that long-term UBI in the United States would allow individuals greater freedom to pursue a life of their choosing. Importantly, the commonly feared adverse effects of UBI—namely, fewer people working or people earning less on their own—were roundly refuted by study results.[12]

Within the United States, experiments and programs similar to UBI have been found to result in a number of positive outcomes related to health, poverty, and education. For example, the Alaska Permanent Fund, established in 1976, continues to provide income transfers from oil proceeds to Alaskan residents annually. Although structured in a very different manner than the UBI we are considering, this payment has been found to result in improved health among young children, no decrease in labor market participation, and substantial reduction in poverty—particularly among older adults.[13]

Although many findings are favorable, it should be noted that one analysis found payments from the fund were associated with an ultimate increase in income inequality, and another found no impact on high school completion.[14] Unlike the Alaska Permanent Fund, negative income tax experiments in the 1970s in Indiana, North Carolina, and New Jersey-Pennsylvania showed a positive education effect, wherein children in families receiving payments scored notably higher on tests. More recent experiments in India and Namibia also showed positive educational impacts of UBI.[15] All told, the body of work on experiments and programs testing UBI or UBI-like programs suggests generally positive but variable and sometimes negligible impacts of UBI related to health and education and little, if any, impact on overall labor force participation among those receiving the benefit.[16]

Although the experimental work suggests UBI would result in benefits to society and have limited negative effect on overall labor force participation, it is of course vital to briefly discuss the affordability of such a proposal, as well as what level of benefit may be required. Importantly, although experiments have been performed on UBI, no full UBI program has been implemented at scale. Further, many of the experiments that have been performed have not been true tests of UBI; rather, they have been tests of scaled-down and often overly pragmatic models.[17] A major reason that UBI has not been truly tested is likely because people are uncomfortable with such a radical shift in government spending.

At present, it is not entirely clear how impactful UBI would be on the overall federal budget—largely due to the fact that the cost of such a program would be contingent on many specifics. For example, a proposal presented by the Green Party in the United Kingdom in 2015 argued that their model of UBI would ultimately be revenue neutral because it would make means-tested programs redundant and lead to their termination—a conclusion tightly tied to the specific income benefit they proposed.[18]

Fully costing out a UBI program is difficult because there are so many details to be arranged, and it is not clear what level of UBI should be implemented. One starting point we may consider would be setting the benefit at an amount sufficient to ensure no individual is in poverty. As such, if we use the conventional poverty guidelines of the United States—which to be clear are often viewed as being too low for actually living a decent life—a single adult would receive $15,060 per year (in 2024 dollars) and then additional support depending on their number of children.[19] If we only provided the $15,060 to the roughly 262 million adults in the United States and gave nothing to children, this would generate an annual bill of $3.9 trillion—equivalent to 16.9 percent of US GDP and $2 trillion larger than the 2023 Omnibus Appropriations Bill. Even if UBI did create redundancies in the US safety net and thus consume existing programs, it seems implausible any sufficient UBI proposal would not lead to a radical increase in federal spending.[20]

Beyond the simple cost, it must also be noted that the macroeconomic impacts of a full-scale UBI remain unknown. While opponents of UBI have often argued it would immediately lead to inflation and thus a negligible real benefit to recipients, economic theory remains mixed, and recent scholarship suggests a negligible or extremely modest effect of transfers on inflation.[21] In many ways, these impacts are unknowable without actual attempts at implementing the policy. That said, this uncertainty should not be a reason to avoid the implementation of such a program. We live in the society we create; we can decide to sever the link between work and place by supporting all people with a universal basic income. A key step in this will be funding targeted research to inform the specifics of such a policy.

Drawing from this, it is clear that a major hurdle for UBI in the United States will be financing the program. Although the utopian approach taken in this work means we should not try and outline specific details for UBI, there are several avenues for financing UBI worth discussing. First, although ideally a UBI would be truly universal, there is certainly an income threshold wherein UBI becomes unnecessary for an individual. For example, research on UBI in India suggests that those in the top 25 percent of earnings should not receive the benefit—a measure that would surely cut costs. Second, as UBI represents a refocusing on the importance of meeting the basic needs of working people relative to capital in the United States, raising income taxes appears a valuable, if politically contentious, way forward. At present, top earners in the United States are only taxed 37 percent on every dollar over $539,901. This pales in comparison to the equivalent upper tax bracket of 70 percent in 1980—a time where the US social safety net was appreciably stronger. Thus, an obvious approach would be to raise taxes on top earners to finance UBI. Finally, although income taxes would be a valuable way to finance the program, other forms of taxes would also likely be worth pursuing. For example, many of the wealthiest in the United States do not draw a large annual income, instead letting their wealth grow in the form of stocks, bonds, and real estate. The exploration of new tax mechanisms to actually redistribute wealth from the wealthiest to the rest of the population would need to be pursued.

Single-Payer Health Care

The second fundamental anchor is the establishment of a single-payer health care system, often labeled "Medicare for All" in the United States, wherein the federal government would replace the current health insurance system and become the "single payer" for health care. In the 2020s, the United States stands alone as the only high-income country without universal health insurance.[22] Instead, health insurance in the United States is uneven and either tied to employment, purchased through the Affordable Care Act (ACA) Health Insurance Marketplace, or provided by the government in the form of either Medicaid, which is for those experiencing hardship, or Medicare, which is for adults over age 65. Although the passage of the ACA led to a drop in the uninsured population from 46.5 million in 2010 to 25.3 million in 2023, corresponding with our lowest uninsured rate in history, progress has been relatively limited since 2016.[23]

A combination of factors explain why so many people are without health insurance: states are reluctant to expand Medicaid, undocumented immigrants are excluded from Medicaid and the ACA marketplace, the individual mandate's tax penalty for not having health insurance was eliminated, and the health insurance plans on the ACA marketplace remain expensive.[24] This large uninsured population and lack of universal health care are unfortunately aligned with our performance on health indicators, with the United States falling well below peer nations on the majority of health outcomes.[25] Tragically, the number of uninsured individuals is expected to have substantially increased by as much as 3.1 million in 2023 because of the sunsetting of COVID-19 coverage protections, thus erasing the gains of recent years.[26]

Although decreasing the size of the uninsured population is an important benefit of single-payer health care, in many ways, it is an indirect benefit of the true reason it is included within the hard path. When considering our prime directive of separating where we work from how we make our money, single-payer health care is primarily focused on transforming the way American's access and pay for their health care. In terms of access, when insurance is attached to employment, as is the most common arrangement in the United States, the tether of work and place is strengthened. Employer-sponsored health care serves as one of the ways that "the escape routes" for labor mobility are blocked.[27] In fact, employers acknowledge this to be the case, with benefits executives nationwide agreeing that employer-sponsored insurance serves them as a valuable retention tool.[28] The impact of this "job-lock" nationwide is significant, with job-lock reducing voluntary turnover by 20 percent per year.[29] This means that even if UBI met the base needs of economic security, labor would likely still be insufficiently mobile due to the link between work and health insurance.

Beyond the notion of job-lock, health insurance in the United States adds even greater friction to mobility through provider networks. Private insurance in the United States uses networks of providers with negotiated rates to contract services for their members.[30] These networks are often difficult to understand, and it is exceedingly expensive to use out-of-network options.[31] Because the vast majority of US residents cannot afford care at an out-of-network provider, these networks formally tie us to specific providers within a given region. Thus, even if one takes a remote position, absent single-payer health care, they may still encounter difficulties in choosing where to live because of the importance of these provider networks in ensuring affordable care.

Another reason adopting single-payer health care is vital to the hard path is cost. Health care in the United States is simply expensive, and affordability remains the number-one reason individuals forgo health insurance.[32] Unaffordable monthly premiums, high deductibles, coinsurance, large maximum out-of-pocket totals, and so-called balance billing—where individuals are expected to pay the difference between what insurance will cover and the hospital is charging—alter household balance sheets and elevate the income required for true economic security in the United States.[33] Thus, without a single-payer model, the economic security provided by UBI would be curtailed because many people would have to use that money to cover monthly premiums, pay out-of-pocket costs, or save that money for inevitable future health care bills. Given that health care needs are often concentrated among marginalized populations and those already struggling to make ends meet, those who would stand to see the greatest impact from UBI would likely have their potential benefit constrained the most if single-payer health care was not adopted.[34]

Much like UBI, the specifics of the program could take many forms and would need to be designed to be flexible over time. Also like UBI, the key factor for single-payer health care under the hard path is that it must be truly universal. Under this proposal, all individuals living in the United States—including undocumented immigrants—would receive access to quality health care at little to no out-of-pocket cost. There are single-payer models that use nominal copays which do not necessarily work against the hard path.

However, any kind of deductible, patient cost-sharing or balance-billing model would stand outside the goals of this proposal. In this, the proposed single-payer model is aligned with the criteria used by Christopher Cai and colleagues in their 2020 systematic review of economic evaluations of single-payer plans.[35]

In their review of twenty-two different plans, Cai and colleagues determined there was a "high degree of analytic consensus that single-payer financing would result in a favorable outcome for system financial burden: efficiency savings exceeded added costs."[36] The reason that this universal model of health care is likely to result in a decline in overall national health care spending is due to the increases in administrative efficiency provided by a single-payer approach.[37] Thus, when considering the entirety of health care spending in the United States, the majority of studies, but not all, suggest a transition to single-payer would be economically beneficial in the long run.

When it comes to overall health care expenditures, it seems the Congressional Budget Office (CBO) would agree with Cai and colleagues.[38] The CBO evaluated five single-payer plans—although none quite as universal as proposed here—and found that national health expenditures would range from between $0.7 trillion lower to $0.3 trillion higher ten years after adoption. Further, in 2022, the CBO concluded that the move to a single-payer model would result in significant economic benefits to individuals.[39] Benefits would include higher wages from the removal of premiums, decreased out-of-pocket costs, increases in economy-wide productivity, improvements in longevity and population health, and the ability to work fewer hours and focus on tasks not associated with income.[40] Given that the United States health care system is the most expensive in the world and that our higher levels of spending are not associated with better population health than our peer nations, any proposal that increases health care access while cutting overall costs and improving the well-being of individuals is worthy of pursuit.

When it comes to the balance sheet of the federal government specifically, opinions vary on net cost (e.g., the balance between health expenditures and financing) due to the many assumptions needed for such an analysis. The adoption of a single-payer model would mean that the majority of health care spending would be transitioned from public and private entities, or state and local governments and employers, to the federal government.[41] Thus, even if total health care spending may decline nationwide under single-payer, we still need to transfer resources to ensure the government can cover the costs for which it is now responsible. The CBO, when comparing five single-payer plans, estimates that annual federal subsidies for health care would be between 4.9 percent ($1.5 trillion) and 9.7 percent of US GDP ($3.0 trillion) ten years after adoption.[42] Relatedly, the Committee for a Responsible Federal Budget estimates that the total increase in expenditures ten years after adoption, when not accounting for financing or cost savings, would be between $25 trillion and $35 trillion.[43] The actual impact on the federal deficit remains unclear because of the many ways we may choose to finance this increase in spending.

Under the single-payer model, increases in federal spending would be balanced by increases in revenue, likely through taxes. Thus, the specific form of these taxes will likely serve as a significant conflict should single-payer health care be pursued. Multiple strategies have been advanced, including payroll taxes, income taxes, value-added taxes, and deficit financing, among others.[44] Aside from taxes, in 2020, researchers at Penn Wharton Budget Model tested the impact of a flat monthly premium paid by all workers regardless of income, with the costs of those unable to pay the premium being absorbed by Medicaid and the Supplemental Nutrition Assistance Program (SNAP).[45] In this model, the move to single-payer would actually increase GDP over time due to cost savings and gains in productivity. Importantly, no matter how we choose to finance the system, it is exceedingly unlikely we could finance single-payer health care solely through taxing high earners and corporations. We will all have to pay our share.[46]

Much like with UBI, the ultimate challenge will be finding a plan enough people can agree on. All told, our current health care system stands as a major barrier to labor mobility in the United States. As a result, it is actively working against the sustainability of rural America and contributing to its decline. Without reforming our system into a single-payer model, the other hard path components would likely fall short. Finally, it must be stressed that the transition to a single-payer model must be sensitive to the disruption it would cause. There are over 500,000 people working in the health insurance industry.[47] Just as we must pay attention and assist those left behind by the green energy transition, we must take care of those whose jobs would be affected by health care reform. As such, single-payer health care would need to be launched in tandem with the implementation of UBI and likely alongside targeted programs to assist these individuals in their transition to new jobs or industries.[48]

Reparations and Tribal Restitution

Although UBI and single-payer health care serve as the primary policy anchors of the hard path, they are unlikely to be enough to sustain and foster a more just rural America. We find ourselves in a country where centuries of marginalization have created unacceptable levels of inequality between ethnic and racial groups. Because of this, the Hard Path for Rural Sustainability would be incomplete without explicit attention to the two most persistently and dramatically marginalized groups in the United States — Black Americans and American Indians. Without this explicit attention, UBI would only perpetuate injustice and inequality. Although there are other populations that could certainly benefit from direct policy attention, such as rural Latino communities and poor Americans of all races, here the proposal focuses on the two populations that have endured the most extreme abuse at the hands of the federal government, state governments, and white Americans; continue to have the worst relative outcomes in health and prosperity; and require the most resources to right past wrongs and achieve parity with their white counterparts.

To be clear, these groups represent relatively small yet highly clustered populations in rural America; the rural population is only 7.9 percent Black and 1.8 percent American Indian.[49] Thus, one might be confused by the inclusion of these programs in this proposal. The reason these programs are essential is because the goal is to separate the tether of work and place for *all* Americans by ensuring a base level of economic security. Because American Indian and Black populations, and particularly the rural portions of these groups, continue to face such extreme inequality relative to the rest of the country, UBI and single-payer health care are insufficient for providing economic security for all. Thus, it is essential that we take a path that acknowledges these inequalities and works to set things right. To be clear, a program of just UBI and single-payer health care could likely engender sustainability for many rural areas. The point is that efforts for rural sustainability that do not pay explicit attention to existing inequality, power dynamics, and oppression are socially unjust and have the potential to exacerbate rather than remedy ongoing patterns of marginalization. As such, reparations and tribal restitution are central to the Hard Path for Rural Sustainability.

The case for reparations for Black populations in the United States is strong and was perhaps made most famously by Ta-Nehisi Coates in *The Atlantic* in 2014.[50] While not belaboring the arguments here, the centuries of abuse, theft, murder, and genocide endured by Black Americans that were discussed in chapter 2 warrant formal apology and reparations from the federal government. Through a history of slavery, Jim Crow, redlining, land loss, and labor violations, Black Americans have been prevented from accruing wealth in the same manner as white Americans. As such, a key element of the hard path is the delivery of reparations.

The exact form of these reparations is certainly up for debate, but the structure of reparations proposed here is generally in line with the proposal advanced by William A. Darity and A. Kirsten Mullen in their 2020 book *From Here to Equality: Reparations for Black Americans in the Twenty-First Century*.[51] Darity and Mullen's model is grounded in the notion that reparations must contain three essential components, which they term ARC: acknowledgment, redress, and closure. Acknowledgment in this context requires "recognition and admission of the wrong by the perpetrators or beneficiaries of the injustice."[52] As such, reparations must include not only a formal apology and acknowledgment of wrongdoing and unjust benefit by white Americans but also a commitment to making things right going forward. Redress, the second component, is the portion of reparations discussed most widely. Under the model advanced by Darity and Mullen, redress would take the form of restitution, wherein resources would be provided to eliminate the persistent racial gaps found in the United States related to wealth, health, education, and other aspects of life. The focus would be on reducing wealth gaps as the mechanism for engendering broader equality, the financial cost of which will be discussed shortly. The final essential component for reparations is closure. Here, closure means a dialogue between white and Black Americans, wherein both parties come to terms over past wrongdoings, ensure that redress is full, and unite behind a shared vision for an equal and transformed country.[53]

While acknowledgment and closure are concepts that are more easily conveyed, redress requires more elaboration. To begin, we must understand that reparations will *never* fully cover the damage caused by slavery, Jim Crow, and the vast injustices that continue to be enacted against Black Americans. While no amount of money will ever cover the loss and pain caused by these practices, Darity and Mullen outline several plausible ways that a satisfactory level of redress could occur. While not fully recounting the proposal for reparations they provide, it is valuable to discuss some key points.

To begin, it is vital that reparations be an effort led and conducted by the federal government. As noted by Darity and Mullen, a piecemeal approach by specific actors, local governments, universities, states, or others will not achieve the large-scale redress necessary to achieve racial equality in the future. Further, even though local efforts may help specific populations, they risk distracting from the larger goal of nationwide reparations. For example, if a state feels it has already done what is needed, why would the state support a congressional reparations effort? Additionally, if reparations are pursued, it must be through Congress and not the judiciary or the executive branches. The powers of the president and the courts are insufficient for achieving the large-scale acknowledgment, redress, and closure needed in the United States. It is vital that Congress, which holds the power of the purse in the United States, be responsible for establishing reparations.[54]

Second, we must consider the question of eligibility. Darity and Mullen argue that eligibility for reparations should have two main components: (1) the ability to establish at least one ancestor who was enslaved in the United States after the establishment of the country and (2) self-identifying as Black at least twelve years before the payment of reparations. In their view, these factors would appropriately select those who have been subject to the legacy of injustices stemming from enslavement while ensuring benefit does not go to those who do not deserve it. Although we may agree with the rationale behind these factors, continuing injustices after the Civil War such as Jim Crow, redlining, and police brutality mean that Black Americans whose families immigrated after the abolishment of slavery also faced extreme injustice and arguably deserve reparations. Thus, an essential question for any reparations program will be whether or not the reparations are for the specific practice of slavery or the more long-term practice of disenfranchisement enacted upon Black populations in the United States.

Following eligibility, the third obvious question is the total amount of money required for reparations. Here, the goal is to provide an amount of wealth sufficient to permanently erase the racial wealth gap in the United States. The estimates for this vary widely depending on the basis for such estimates as well as the interest rate applied to that basis. Common ways to determine the basis for reparations include estimates based upon wages slaves should have received, land former slaves were promised and did not get, and the amount of resources required to erase the current racial wealth gap.

The hard path is aligned with Darity and Mullen in that the basis for reparations should be the current gap between Black and white wealth in the United States. As such, the total bill required to raise Black wealth to a level reflective of their population representation would be at least $10.7 trillion spread across 40 million eligible Americans—meaning a cost of $267,000 for each eligible Black American.[55] Similar to UBI and single-payer health care, this immediately raises questions of financing and the potential for inflation. An obvious way to avoid a one-time massive increase in federal expenditures would be to disperse reparations over a period of years. Although cash transfers to eligible Black Americans is a vital leg of any reparations policy, funds could also be used to create institutions focused on supporting the creation of Black wealth. For example, one idea advanced by Darity and Mullen is a set disbursement for eligible Black Americans through trust funds, with the ability to apply for greater amounts of money from said trust funds should there be a need to invest in a new business, property, or other venture.[56]

In terms of financing, reparations could be financed in some of the same ways as discussed for UBI and health care, including higher income taxes and alternative forms of wealth taxation. Further, given their more short-term nature relative to long-term programs like UBI and single-payer health care, reparations could also be financed through pure deficit spending or by drawing on the securities and assets already held by the Federal Reserve.[57] Although a price tag of $10.7 trillion is large and likely to generate sticker shock, it is essential that we do not balk at the cost of righting past wrongs but instead recognize how disastrous it is that we as a society ever let such an unjust and dramatic gap in wealth develop.

Regardless of how the issue is framed, it is clear that all of the options for financing a long-term reparations program could lead to a variety of political and social issues such as inflation, political vitriol, and dramatic changes in consumption, among others. It is for this reason that House Bill 40—which would authorize a Commission to Study and Develop Reparation Proposals for African Americans—has been introduced into Congress every year since 1989. This bill would charge the created commission with studying reparations and developing proposals for a formal apology and reparations program within one year of the commission's establishment.[58] Unfortunately, this bill has never been passed. However, in April 2021, it cleared the committee for the first time in its history, suggesting movement in the political palatability of these efforts. This shift in political support is also evidenced by a number of smaller-scale initiatives and experiments occurring across the United States. Although Darity and Mullen make a convincing argument that reparations must be a national initiative from the federal government and that smaller efforts may ultimately hinder a national movement, these smaller efforts—such as the reparations paid by Evanston, Illinois, to its Black residents and the recent California initiative to establish a task force on reparations—nonetheless suggest that the movement for reparations is stronger than it has ever been.[59]

While the case for reparations for Black Americans has largely focused on the wealth gap, the need to right the wrongs endured by American Indians goes further. As such, the hard path calls for the establishment of a federal program of tribal restitution. While UBI, single-payer health care, and reparations could likely be handled by standalone programs from the federal government, tribal restitution is significantly more complicated. The relationship between tribes and the federal government is complex. Each tribe is distinct and may or may not be federally recognized. If a tribe has a treaty, the contents of that treaty are unique to that specific tribe. Thus, the proposal for tribal restitution is less specific than the other components of the hard path and more reflective of the need to begin a long-term program of restitution, wherein the federal government evaluates the current conditions of all tribes, as well as any existing tribal agreements, to determine how to enact justice and honor commitments in light of a modern context. This program of tribal restitution could likely be carried out through the Bureau of Indian Affairs (BIA). However, given the complex and troubled history of that bureaucratic arm of the federal government, the restitution program would need to be codirected by both the BIA and a board of leaders from a variety of tribal nations who have equal power to the bureau when making decisions. Although the specifics of tribal restitution would be highly variable and tribe-specific, within this vital effort there are three key priorities that appear essential: (1) respecting sovereignty, (2) honoring land claims, and (3) paying reparations.

First, the sovereignty of tribes, long ignored and encroached upon, needs to be respected and restored. Although not relevant to all tribes, from 1778 to 1881, the United States government signed approximately 374 treaties with tribal nations.[60] These treaties varied in their scope but commonly included guarantees of peace; the provision of land boundaries and corresponding hunting and fishing rights; recognition of US authority and protection; and specific promises of federal provision of various services or assistance.[61] Unfortunately, many of these treaties, and the subsequent land claims and rights of sovereignty they guarantee, have long been ignored by both states and the federal government. The hard path requires us to not only recognize this injustice and work to correct it but also to redress the attacks on sovereignty faced by recognized and unrecognized tribes without treaties as well.

Even though treaties between the federal government and tribes established clear sovereignty on the part of tribal nations, this sovereignty has been eroded over time by judicial and legislative activities. While it is likely that the federal government of the United States will always hold a power advantage over native nations, tribal sovereignty must be respected and preserved to the maximum extent possible. Although the United States officially entered the "era of tribal self-determination" in 1975 with the Indian Self-Determination and Educational Assistance Act, many contemporary tribal members would argue the true era of self-determination has still not arrived. Nick Estes, scholar-activist and citizen of the Lower Brule Sioux Tribe, wrote in 2019 that "racist and colonial legal doctrines—such as doctrine of discovery, the domestic dependent nation status, and plenary power—and oversight by the Bureau of Indian Affairs reveal that Indigenous-US relations are colonial to the core and centered on the acquisition of the land."[62] He later went on to say that "Indigenous peoples and lands today, however, are no more 'self-determined,' but remain under federal control."[63] As Estes makes clear, true self-determination remains out of reach for tribes because of the lack of respect the paternalistic federal government shows for their sovereignty.

This lack of true self-rule is further illustrated by the persistent antagonism shown to native nations by their neighboring states and the corresponding bureaucratic structures that make it difficult for tribes to resist this antagonism. Examples of this persistent encroachment can be found in both the determination of water rights and the regulation of pollution. In the case of water rights, the courts have established clear precedent in the Winters Doctrine that tribal nations have what are called reserved water rights.[64] In brief, these water rights supersede other claims made by settler-colonists and provide special provisions to tribes when it comes to the usage and strength of water rights. Unfortunately, states have a long history of trying to subvert, ignore, or steal these rights for the benefit of settlers and the state government—often with the help of elected or appointed federal officials. For example, the McCarran Amendment of 1952 allowed federal water rights to be tried in state courts, significantly weakening the standing of tribal reserved water rights and leading many tribes to quantify their right through negotiation with states rather than through the courts because state courts have often favored state governments over tribal nations.[65]

Evidence for state-level antagonism related to water can also be found in the regulation of pollution under the Clean Water Act. Under the act, tribes can petition to be "treated as state" (TAS) so that they may develop their own plan for wastewater regulation. While many tribes have successfully gained this status, others have been stymied. A prime example came in 2006, when Senator Jim Inhofe of Oklahoma placed a midnight rider on an unrelated transportation bill to prevent tribes in Oklahoma from obtaining TAS status under the Clean Water Act unless the state of Oklahoma consents. Unsurprisingly, Oklahoma has not consented. Thus, even though Oklahoma has some of the largest, wealthiest, and most well-positioned native nations to obtain this status in the United States, no Oklahoma tribes have active TAS Water Quality Standards Programs under the Clean Water Act. Both of these water-related legislative actions represent a clear and direct encroachment on tribal sovereignty from the federal government. As such, the proposed program of restitution would seek to remove this kind of legislation, and others like it, while also limiting the ability for motivated elected and appointed officials to single-handedly negate the sovereignty of native nations within their state's borders.

While respecting tribal sovereignty is a complex endeavor and the specific details will likely have to vary from tribe to tribe, establishing a revised model of sovereignty that is deemed appropriate by a majority of tribal nations appears essential. As shown by the *McGirt v. Oklahoma* (2020) ruling—wherein the Supreme Court ruled that the majority of Oklahoma is, in fact, tribal land, and thus tribal members are subject to tribal or federal courts instead of state courts within those lands—it is clear that the Supreme Court continues to respect tribal sovereignty within the borders of reservations.[66] Although fraught, this respect has a long history, with the 2020 ruling stemming from the landmark case of *Worcester v. Georgia* (1832), wherein the Supreme Court ruled that individual states have no authority on reservation land.[67] That said, it is clear that tribal sovereignty remains curtailed in many significant ways. As such, a key step for any program of tribal restitution must involve a serious reevaluation of the paternalistic "trust relationship" currently enshrined by the Supreme Court. Tribal nations are nations; at a minimum, it is vital that the United States no longer holds them in a secondary status to the states they neighbor.

The second major piece of tribal restitution is the honoring of tribal land claims. More than sovereignty, land claims are likely to vary dramatically on a case-by-case basis and be highly contingent on the existence, or lack thereof, of treaties. As such, a key activity of the restitution program would be the evaluation of all treaties and their land claims, followed by the development of clear and agreed-upon plans for the honoring of historic agreements. In many cases, honoring the exact historic land claims will likely be infeasible because of land theft, the difficulties of eminent domain, and patterns of urbanization. However, restitution for this loss can be pursued in a number of ways.

One popular example is the transfer of public lands in the United States as a means of restitution.[68] Particularly if historic lands are currently held by the public, this form of transfer appears appropriate. In cases where historic lands are no longer held by the government, either the transfer of alternative public lands or the payment of financial compensation plus interest would be possible means of redress. In addressing land claims and historic theft, it is also vital that we review the mechanisms of past land loss to determine if restitution is possible. For example, the 2020 Land-Grab University project from *High Country News* shed light on the massive amounts of tribal land expropriation that occurred during the establishment of land grant universities in the Morrill Act of 1862.[69] Under the act, over 10.6 million acres of land were transferred from tribal nations to universities to establish operations and seed endowments. These transfers occurred by treaty or seizure and, once adjusted for inflation, are worth over half a billion dollars. Although much of these lands were ultimately sold, landholdings do remain, and the federal government should direct public universities still holding these lands to return them to their historic native residents.

Although the hard path calls for a restitution program that oversees the honoring of land claims and the righting of past wrongs, it is vital that we also learn from past mistakes. Although often forgotten, there was an effort in the 1940s to "settle ancient Indian claims for all time."[70] This effort was conducted through the Indian Claims Commission Act of 1946, which created the Indian Claims Commission (ICC) and charged it with addressing tribal claims to land and resolving them with compensation. The ICC was intended to be cooperative and was given jurisdiction over not just legal claims but also moral claims—that is, claims based on dealings that were not recognized by law. In theory, this meant that the ICC could adjudicate claims that were not ratified by treaty and were based on informal agreements. The inclusion of moral claims, as well as the cooperative model, gave many hope that the ICC could provide restorative justice while also tailoring compensation and redress to the needs of specific tribes.[71]

Unfortunately, the ICC was a failure. Because the ICC adopted an adversarial approach instead of the intended cooperative one, relied on an overly narrow reading of its powers that limited rulings to monetary compensation only, and failed to fulfill other key elements of the law, justice was not achieved and no lands were redistributed. The failure of the ICC illustrates the importance of not only the direct inclusion of tribes in the decision-making process when designing a program of tribal restitution, but also their involvement in the administration of that effort. Absent genuine and meaningful involvement of tribes, any restitution effort enacted by the United States government risks repeating past failures.

Finally, much like reparations are needed for Black Americans to address centuries of injustice, similar reparations are needed for members of tribes who have endured incredible amounts of hardship and land loss at the hands of settler-colonists from the onset of colonization to the present day.[72] Although respecting sovereignty and restoring land claims will likely benefit recognized tribes with treaties more than nontreaty tribes or unrecognized tribes, when it comes to reparations, it is essential that redress is provided to *all* tribes. Although there are around 374 treaties between the federal government and tribal nations, there are a total of 574 recognized tribes and some 400 more that are not recognized by the federal government.[73] These Indigenous populations, while having less formal means of fighting for restitution than native nations with treaties, have still suffered prolonged abuse by the federal government. As this abuse has fundamentally affected the well-being of these tribes in both rural and urban America, a vital task of the proposed restitution program would be to determine how to best redress these historic abuses. In doing so, this would serve as an appropriate time for the federal government to reevaluate its lack of recognition for these groups. As envisioned here, these reparations would be distributed to all enrolled tribal members in the United States and would be at a level determined by those designing the restitution program. There are many complicating factors and histories for each specific tribe. As such, it is likely that the necessary level of reparations would vary across native communities.

Conclusion

All told, we land at the following anchors for the Hard Path for Rural Sustainability: UBI, single-payer health care, reparations to Black Americans, and tribal restitution. Importantly, there is no reason that the components of the soft path should not be incorporated into the hard path. The transition to remote work is already occurring, and remote work will only encourage the movement of labor following the adoption of UBI. Further, student loan forgiveness would allow UBI to go further and decrease the amount of UBI needed to ensure economic security. When considering infrastructure, investment is still needed if we want people to actually choose to live in rural places. Finally, although individual incentives may not be needed, if a rural area has a need for in-demand skill sets such as doctors, lawyers, or therapists, these initiatives would likely still be valuable.

It is clear that the hard path most completely solves the issues facing a sustainable rural America. So, what are the downsides? Well, like the other paths, it reflects a utopian vision. Given that it is a positive utopia, it would certainly be prone to difficult realities. As stated previously, this does not mean utopian thinking is valueless or even foolish. Utopian thinking serves as a bedrock method with sociology and allows us to imagine and fight for a better future.[74] If we do not do the work of imagining and thinking through radical futures, we are doomed to stay put or proceed without vision. As described by Philippe Van Parijs in a 2013 *Politics and Society* article, the problem with Marx was "not too much utopian thinking but not enough utopian thinking."[75] That said, the biggest hurdle to the utopian hard path is that this path is very likely completely unpalatable to capital. As the reader is hopefully aware, capital very much has hold of the reins of the United States. Thus, the only way any elements of the hard path would be adopted is through massive political pressure at all levels. Given the way capital has captured the political apparatus of the United States through campaign finance and lobbying, this seems an increasingly uphill battle.

Beyond the disinterest of capital, it is also important to remember that there are many Americans who would likely be politically opposed to the platform of shared equality and security advanced by the hard path. There remain many in the United States for whom socialism is a dirty word, and social justice is not only not a priority but something to be avoided. This conflict between the hard path and culture could be particularly strong in rural areas where occupational identity, self-reliance, and individuality are driving values. Even in rural areas that vote for Democrats, the radical nature of the hard path could prove a step too far. That said, it is designed to support true freedom, which is a bedrock American value, and elements of the plan would likely be attractive to many rural and urban Americans. Unfortunately, because of disinformation and the political structure of the United States, many popular and valuable policy proposals are voted down even when they are publicly supported. Thus, on-the-ground success would likely come down to a contest of political messaging between those for and against.

Setting the political realities aside, are there other downsides? When taking stock, there is one clear weakness with the Hard Path for Rural Sustainability that is worth noting—the path still depends on people actually wanting to live in rural places. Although many people say they would prefer to live in a more rural setting, it remains unclear how many people would actually choose true rural living once the false freedom of labor mobility is resolved.[76] As noted in previous chapters, the loss of rural America does not mean the loss of pastoral lands. There are many quasi-rural spaces with more reasonable access to metropolitan amenities. It is possible people would choose to compromise and instead live in one of these quasi-rural spaces. Given this, success would be at least partially dependent on the elements of the soft path that would make rural living more desirable, such as infrastructural improvements and incentive programs.

Brittany Packnett Cunningham once noted that "patriarchy is a smog we all breathe in."[77] Capitalism, too, is a force that pulls on us all. Capitalism positions future wealth—despite how improbable it may be—as a realistic goal achievable through hard work. We are still very far away from the myth of meritocracy falling by the wayside in the United States. Even under the hard path, it may be that people feel pressured to continue moving to what they view as high-reward locations because of their desire to achieve greater status and wealth—although if the large-scale transition to remote work is significant enough, then "high-reward locations" may become a thing of the past.

Ultimately, even with the hard path, there is a chance we may still see the continued bifurcation of rural America. At a minimum, there is likely no future where *every* rural area is sustained in the long term. However, even if this is the case, this path would allow people who are currently living in rural America to continue doing so without fear of economic hardship. As a result, even absent an immediate large-scale re-sorting of our population, we would still preserve many of our existing rural cultures that we stand to lose while supporting greater economic security and freedom for rural and urban America. Further, a UBI would address chronic out-migration by allowing young people and others who so wish to remain in rural areas, which would likely work to ameliorate the risk of further political polarization posed by a path that would preserve the status quo.

Conclusion

We have now seen the full case for rural America. As a recap, the broad argument is as follows: Rural areas in the United States, defined by their low population density and remote nature, are full of a diversity of people, cultures, and history. However, we are losing rural America because of the persistent out-migration and depopulation of rural areas, as well as both the direct urbanization of rural communities and the annexation of rural places by metropolitan areas. The reason for these trends, fundamentally, is the false freedom labor faces under capitalism. That is, labor is free to move, but only where capital deems it valuable. Historically, this false freedom was held in check by the need for internal peripheries in the United States supporting rural employment. However, in our era of mass globalization, these peripheries are no longer required. The outcome is that rural America as we know it is destined to go away unless we sever the link between where we live and how we earn our income.

The disappearance of rural America has significant cultural, political, and social implications that outweigh any benefit we may see from its continued transformation. Thus, we should invest in saving rural America. However, we must do so in a manner that is sensitive to historical injustice while also avoiding utilitarian concerns. The only way to do this is the Hard Path for Rural Sustainability, characterized by the establishment of universal basic income (UBI), the adoption of single-payer health care, the payment of reparations to Black Americans, and the development and implementation of a program of tribal restitution. Further, true success would also need to include elements of the Soft Path for Rural Sustainability: increasing remote work, incentivizing key professions, improving rural infrastructure, and forgiving student debt.

The radical approach of the hard path is unique in that it would free *all* workers from the false freedom they face, thus acknowledging the linked fates of rural and urban Americans. Any policy big enough to make a real difference in rural America is unlikely to succeed, politically and with sustained support, unless it also applies to urban America. And for good reason. There is no a priori reason we should focus more resources per capita on rural America than urban America. Just as there is hardship in rural places, there is hardship in urban places. Just as we risk a loss of culture when we lose a small rural town, we risk a loss of culture when we let an urban neighborhood become gentrified. Further, many of the problems rural Americans face are the same problems urban Americans face. Labor is weak relative to capital nationwide, families struggle to make ends meet across the board, and neither urban nor rural Americans are able to live where and how they wish without sacrificing economic security. Finally, to save rural America, urban Americans must be able to return to places they once called home. This means that the best path for rural America must include urban America as well.

The linked fates of rural and urban America also illustrate why the Soft Path for Rural Sustainability falls short. The anchors of the soft path are not universal. Although a push for more remote work would act across the rural-urban spectrum, it ultimately favors elites and certain industries. Moreover, focusing on infrastructure and incentive programs directs resources to rural areas without freeing urban labor from their own false freedom. However, while the soft path is insufficient, as I have noted, pursuing the anchors of the soft path is vital for a more successful implementation of the hard path. If we want newly freed urban labor to choose rural living and rural youth to choose to stay, then increasing remote work options, improving infrastructure, and incentivizing the in-migration of needed skills will be necessary.

Taking in all the value of rural America, as well as the importance of righting past wrongs, we simply should not support the other two paths discussed: the Status Quo Path and the Accelerated Path of Rural Destruction. Sticking to the status quo — tragically, the most likely outcome — amounts to political, social, and economic negligence. Rural areas are already left behind and struggling. Letting the American brand of contemporary capitalism continue unfettered along its course will lead to a massive loss of rural culture, further bifurcation of our electorate, vast social injustice, and an overall reduction in well-being for many Americans. The Accelerated Path, for its part, is simply unnecessary and politically unpalatable. Although a socially just version of the Accelerated Path could plausibly be designed, the loss of culture and the vitriol inspired by forced migration would be difficult to stomach, and given the wealth of the United States, it simply seems unnecessary. Thus, the Hard Path for Rural Sustainability, supported by the soft path, emerges as the road we should take for the future of rural America.

That said, it must be noted that the Hard Path for Rural Sustainability does not solve all social problems plaguing rural and urban America. As such, it is valuable to briefly consider the hard path alongside two movements focused on improving people's well-being and saving our planet. The first to discuss is the conspicuous absence of labor movements from the framework of the hard path. As it stands, labor organization in the United States is weak. However, there is evidence that support for unionization is growing—with a 2022 Gallup poll showing the highest support of labor unions in the United States since 1965.[1] It cannot be stressed enough that increasing labor power in the United States is essential for raising overall well-being. The reason labor organization is not included as an anchor of either the soft or hard path is because labor organization does not directly solve the issue at hand—that being the decline of rural America as a result of the false freedom of labor under capitalism. However, the hard path does have side benefits for the strength of labor. This is because the presence of UBI under the hard path would permanently give power to labor relative to capital. Because workers can leave an employer without risking complete economic fallout, labor can bargain with real security and from a place of power. Thus, although the hard path does not center labor organization as a key tenet, the approach would ultimately embolden and strengthen labor throughout the country.

The second concept to consider alongside the hard path is degrowth. Degrowth is a relatively recent term that signifies a radical reorganization of our political and economic institutions away from the "growth is good" mindset and to a paradigm focused on a dramatic reduction in resource use and environmental impact.[2] A controversial movement that faces criticism from both the right and the left, the framework adopts a normative view counter to conventional economics and asserts that growth is not universally good and should be constrained. In this, degrowth differs from the hard path in that the hard path proposal is generally agnostic about growth, viewing a focus on growth as misguided but not necessarily arguing that growth should be limited overall. Unlike the broad focus on people and communities found here, degrowth is tethered to global environmental concerns related to climate change. Similar to the hard path, degrowth models are generally utopian—which again is valuable because it can help us imagine a better way forward. However, as climate forecasts become increasingly dire, there is more urgency to consider radical solutions, which makes degrowth and similar actions seem more necessary by the day.

Broadly, a sustainable degrowth society would be characterized by a general downscaling of industry and growth, alongside a targeted upscaling of necessary industries such as renewable energy. Importantly, degrowth recognizes the imbalance in global income, power, and growth and calls for degrowth in high-income countries, with a focus on sustainable development in low- and middle-income nations. Along with this downscaling of US growth would be a reorganization of the political apparatus around direct democracy, wherein degrowth is presented as a "social choice."[3] The economy would be repoliticized—meaning that we directly acknowledge that viewing growth as inherently good is a political decision worthy of real debate.[4] From this, degrowth proponents argue we would see a far more sustainable society and a massive reduction in our carbon footprint. When we consider degrowth alongside the hard path, we can see they are generally complementary. Although the hard path is not a path tied to an overall degrowth of the economy, the implementation of UBI would allow workers to step outside the growth machine, should they so desire, and still retain economic security. Further, if everyone's basic needs were met before work becomes an economic necessity, then activities that are environmentally harmful and generally undesirable, such as long-distance commutes, would likely be reduced. Regardless of whether it is specifically degrowth or some other large-scale environmental platform that is adopted, the future of rural and urban America hinges upon us ensuring our planet remains inhabitable for generations to come.

Final Thoughts

Rural America finds itself in a time of flux and transition. Many of the most thriving rural areas have been reclassified as urban over the past forty years, and many of the 1,956 rural counties that remain are struggling to find direction. Because of chronic out-migration, a lack of economic opportunity, and the long-lasting trends of population aging, we are now seeing the depopulation of many rural areas. In step with an aging population and economic hardship, mortality rates are rising, and the rural-urban mortality disparity is growing. With mass globalization and the mechanization of industry, rural labor is no longer nearly as valuable to capital as it once was, and rural America is now in the position of a service economy dominated by low-quality employment opportunities. From this, we are seeing the bifurcation of rural America into either depopulated zones or urbanity. The only way to prevent further bifurcation and the associated negative cultural, political, social, and economic outcomes is to turn onto the Hard Path for Rural Sustainability.

As we have seen, the hard path, while radical and utopian, does not suggest a complete restructuring of our society. That may well be warranted, but that is beyond the purpose of this book. The purpose here has been to present the case for saving rural America, as well as the best way to do so. In that, the hard path shines because it addresses the fundamental issues while taking into consideration other necessary factors. What it does not do is prevent climate change, fully rein in capitalist exploitation, or decenter the imperialism of the United States. Goals such as these require equally radical solutions, such as degrowth, mass labor organization, and the redesigning of local and federal political systems, which the hard path is well poised to support. As said from the outset, rural America is at a crossroads. Should we continue down the road we are currently on, we risk a dramatic loss of diverse cultures, a rise in social injustice, and a continuation and acceleration of our heightened political polarization and problems of minority rule. It is essential that we turn onto the Hard Path of Rural Sustainability. Doing so will not only improve things for those who call rural America home, but it will foster a newfound freedom for urban Americans as well.

Notes

Introduction

1. Goetz et al., "Economic Status of Rural America"; Johnson and Lichter, "Metropolitan Reclassification."
2. Brooks et al., "County Reclassifications and Rural–Urban Mortality"; Brown and Schafft, *Rural People and Communities*; K. M. Johnson, "Rural America Lost Population"; Monnat, "Trends in US Working-Age"; Peters et al., "The Opioid Hydra."
3. Malin and Petrzelka, "Community Development among Toxic."
4. Office of Management and Budget, *OMB Bulletin No. 23–01*; USDA Economic Research Service, "Rural-Urban Continuum Code"; Puerto Rico is excluded from these statistics because metropolitan status was not assigned to Puerto Rican county equivalents in 1980.
5. Brooks et al., "County Reclassification and Rural–Urban Mortality"; Goetz et al., "Economic Status of Rural America"; Johnson and Lichter, "Metropolitan Reclassification."
6. Data extracted from the decennial censuses of 1980 and 2020. Economic data for 2020 comes from American Community Survey (ACS) five-year estimates from 2018 to 2022, with 2020 being the midyear. These pooled ACS estimates are required for accurate rural statistical estimates.
7. Mortality is as reported by the Centers for Disease Control (CDC).
8. Bureau of Economic Analysis, *National Income and Product Accounts*.

Chapter One

1. Brown and Schafft, *Rural People and Communities*; S. Smith, "Institutional and Intellectual Origins."
2. Marx, *Capital: Volume I*.
3. S. Smith, "Institutional and Intellectual Origins."
4. Isserman, "In the National Interest"; Brown and Schafft, *Rural People and Communities*; Schroeder and Pacas, "Across the Rural-Urban Universe."
5. Cromartie and Bucholtz, "Defining the 'Rural.'"
6. Cromartie and Bucholtz, "Defining the 'Rural.'"
7. Cromartie and Bucholtz, "Defining the 'Rural.'"
8. Cromartie and Bucholtz, "Defining the 'Rural.'"
9. Isserman, "In the National Interest"; Office of Management and Budget, "2010 Standard for Delineating."
10. Office of Management and Budget, *OMB Bulletin No. 23–01*.
11. USDA Economic Research Service, "Rural-Urban Continuum Code."

12. US Census Bureau, "2020 Census Urban Areas."

13. Nelson and Nguyen, "Community Assets and Relative Rurality Index"; USDA Economic Research Service, "Rural-Urban Commuting Area Codes."

14. Mueller and Gasteyer, "Widespread and Unjust Drinking Water."

15. Lobao and Kraybill, "Emerging Roles of County Governments."

16. K. M. Johnson, "Where Is Rural America?"

17. Office of Management and Budget, "Standard for Defining Metropolitan."

18. Brown and Schafft, *Rural People and Communities*; Halfacree, "Rethinking 'Rurality.'"

19. Halfacree, "Locality and Social Representation."

20. Cloke and Milbourne, "Deprivation and Lifestyles"; Halfacree, "Locality and Social Representation."

21. Halfacree, "Locality and Social Representation."

22. Halfacree, "Locality and Social Representation"; Halfacree, "Rethinking 'Rurality.'"

23. Halfacree, "Rethinking 'Rurality'"; Gray, "Common Agricultural Policy."

24. Halfacree, "Rethinking 'Rurality.'"

25. Cloke and Milbourne, "Deprivation and Lifestyles."

26. Shucksmith, "Re-imagining the Rural."

27. Bunker, "Matter, Space, Energy"; Tickamyer, "Space Matters!"; Wallerstein, "Rise and Future Demise"; Wallerstein, "The World-System."

28. Halfacree, "Locality and Social Representation."

29. Weber and Miller, "Poverty in Rural America."

30. Brown and Schafft, *Rural People and Communities*.

31. Billings and Blee, *Road to Poverty*.

32. Urso, "Metropolisation and the Challenge."

33. Brown and Schafft, *Rural People and Communities*; Jones and Woods, "New Localities," 36.

Chapter Two

1. Vidich and Bensman, *Small Town in Mass Society*; Friedland, "End of Rural Society."

2. Kelly and Brown, "Cahokia"; Emerson et al., "Dangers of Diversity."

3. Farrell et al., "Effects of Land Dispossession."

4. Taylor, *Rise of the American Conservative Movement*.

5. US Congress, *Act to Secure Homesteads*.

6. Farrell et al., "Effects of Land Dispossession."

7. Dewees, "Native Nations in a Changing Global Economy."

8. Brown and Schafft, *Rural People and Communities*.

9. Eggers et al., "Community Engaged Cumulative Risk"; Teodoro et al., "US Environmental Policy Implementation."

10. Taylor, *Rise of the American Conservative Movement*.

11. Bloome et al., "Tenancy, Marriage, and the Boll Weevil"; Du Bois, *Souls of Black Folk*; Quisumbing King et al., "Black Agrarianism."

12. Du Bois, "Negro Landholder of Georgia."
13. Gilbert et al., "Loss and Persistence."
14. Newkirk, "Great Land Robbery."
15. Newkirk, "Great Land Robbery."
16. Nesbitt, "Black Land Theft."
17. Newkirk, "Great Land Robbery."
18. M. H. Harvey, "Racial Inequalities and Poverty."
19. Duncan, *Worlds Apart*.
20. M. H. Harvey, "Racial Inequalities and Poverty."
21. Taylor, *Rise of the American Conservative Movement*.
22. M. H. Harvey, "Racial Inequalities and Poverty."
23. Taylor, *Rise of the American Conservative Movement*.
24. Massey and Liang, "Long-Term Consequences."
25. Massey and Gentsch, "Undocumented Migration to the United States."
26. Massey and Gentsch, "Undocumented Migration to the United States"; Massey and Gelatt, "What Happened?"
27. Davidhizar and Bechtel, "Health and Quality of Life."
28. Villa, "Rural Social Work."
29. Wutich et al., "Water Insecurity."
30. Roller et al., *Closing the Water Access Gap*.
31. Takaki, *History of Asian Americans*, 25.
32. Campi, "Eating Bitterness."
33. Carson, "Chinese Sojourn Labor."
34. Campi, "Eating Bitterness."
35. Remele, "Things as They Should Be," 15.
36. Daly, "Agricultural Employment"; Bureau of Economic Affairs, *National Income and Product Accounts*.
37. Bureau of Economic Affairs, *National Income and Product Accounts*.
38. Gallardo and Sauer, "Adoption of Labor-Saving Technologies"; S. L. Wang et al., "Increases in Labor Quality."
39. Brown and Schafft, *Rural People and Communities*.
40. Lewis and Severnini, "Short- and Long-Run."
41. Cain, "Historical Perspective on Infrastructure."
42. Azzam and Schroeter, "Concentration in Beef Packing."
43. Azzam and Schroeter, "Concentration in Beef Packing"; Brown and Schafft, *Rural People and Communities*.
44. Whitt et al., "America's Farms and Ranches," 2.
45. Lobao and Meyer, "Great Agricultural Transition."
46. Giri et al., "Off-Farm Income."
47. Whitt et al. "America's Farms and Ranches."
48. Lobao and Meyer, "The Great Agricultural Transition"; Whitt et al. "America's Farms and Ranches."
49. Whitt et al. "America's Farms and Ranches."
50. Lobao and Meyer, "Great Agricultural Transition."
51. Barnett, "US Farm Financial Crisis."

52. Barnett, "US Farm Financial Crisis."
53. Barnett, "US Farm Financial Crisis."
54. Brasier, "Spatial Analysis of Changes."
55. Barnett, "US Farm Financial Crisis."
56. Barnett, "US Farm Financial Crisis."
57. Thiede and Slack, "Old versus the New," 234.
58. Thiede and Slack, "Old versus the New."
59. Kandel and Parrado, "Restructuring of the US Meat Processing Industry."
60. Thiede and Slack, "Old versus the New."
61. Vias, "Perspectives on US Rural Labor Markets."
62. Humphrey et al., "Theories in the Study."
63. Freudenburg and Gramling, "Natural Resources and Rural Poverty"; Thiede and Slack, "Old versus the New."
64. Bureau of Economic Analysis, *National Income and Product Accounts*.
65. Mueller, "Defining Dependence."
66. Mueller, "Dual Dependency."
67. Mueller, "Dual Dependency."
68. Mueller, "Defining Dependence."
69. Mueller, "Defining Dependence."
70. Bureau of Economic Analysis, *National Income and Product Accounts*.
71. Mueller, "Dual Dependency."
72. Farrell, *Billionaire Wilderness*; Pilgeram, *Pushed Out*; Sherman, *Dividing Paradise*.
73. Deller et al., "Role of Amenities"; Deller et al., "Modeling Regional Economic Growth."
74. Brown and Schafft, *Rural People and Communities*.
75. Bureau of Economic Analysis, *National Income and Product Accounts*.
76. Kalleberg et al., "Bad Jobs in America"; Thiede and Slack, "Old versus the New."
77. Brown and Schafft, *Rural People and Communities*.
78. Brown and Schafft, *Rural People and Communities*.
79. K. M. Johnson, "Population Redistribution Trends."
80. It should be noted that due to decadal changes to the Current Population Survey, these estimates exclude the years of 1995, 2004, 2005, or 2015; US Census Bureau, "Table A-3."
81. Lichter, "Immigration and the New Racial Diversity."
82. Carr et al., "Can Immigration Save Small-Town America?"; Johnson and Lichter, "Diverging Demography."
83. Nelson and Nelson, "The Global Rural."
84. K. M. Johnson, "Rural America Lost Population"; K. M. Johnson, "Natural Decrease in America."
85. Carr and Kefalas, *Hollowing Out the Middle*.
86. Lichter and Johnson, "Urbanization and the Paradox."
87. Lichter and Johnson, "Urbanization and the Paradox."
88. Brooks et al., "County Reclassifications and Rural–Urban Mortality."
89. Jensen et al., "Rural Population Health"; Monnat, "Trends in US Working-Age."
90. Analysis conducted by the author using data from the US Census Bureau.

91. Davis et al., "Rural America at a Glance."

92. Brady, "Rethinking the Sociological Measurement."

93. Pacas and Rothwell, "Why Is Poverty Higher in Rural America?"; Shrider and Creamer, "Poverty in the United States."

94. Mueller et al., "Cost of Living Variation"; Pacas and Rothwell, "Why Is Poverty Higher in Rural America?"

95. Author's calculations using 2018–22 American Community Survey estimates from the US Census Bureau; Manson et al., "IPUMS National Historical Geographic Information System."

96. Dandachi et al., "Treating COVID-19 in Rural America"; Henning-Smith, "Unique Impact of COVID-19"; Peters, "Community Susceptibility and Resiliency."

97. Marema, "Analysis: Rural COVID-19 Deaths"; Sun and Monnat, "Rural-Urban and Within-Rural Differences."

98. Sun and Monnat, "Rural-Urban and Within-Rural Differences."

99. Mueller et al., "Impacts of the COVID-19 Pandemic"; Monnat, "Rural Adult Report Worse COVID-19 Impacts."

100. Brooks et al., "Rural-Urban Differences."

101. Mueller et al., "Elevated Serious Psychological Distress"; Wang et al., "Factors Associated with Psychological Distress."

102. Johanson, "Small Cities and Towns Booming"; Johanson, "The 'Zoom Towns' Luring Remote Workers."

103. Petersen et al., "Changes to Rural Migration."

104. K. M. Johnson, "Population Redistribution Trends."

105. US Census Bureau, *County Population Totals*.

106. Collins, "Intersectionality's Definitional Dilemmas."

Chapter Three

1. McMichael, *Development and Social Change*.

2. McMichael, *Development and Social Change*, 7.

3. Lobao et al., "Poverty and Inequality across Space."

4. McMichael, *Development and Social Change*; Isbister, *Promises Not Kept*.

5. United Nations, "The 17 Goals."

6. Liu et al., "Supply Chain Responsibility"; Malin and Petrzelka, "Community Development among Toxic Tailings."

7. Isbister, *Promises Not Kept*.

8. Rostow, "Stages of Economic Growth."

9. Rostow, "Stages of Economic Growth," 53.

10. McMichael, *Development and Social Change*; Isbister, *Promises Not Kept*.

11. McMichael, *Development and Social Change*; Isbister, *Promises Not Kept*.

12. Muro, *Job Creation on a Budget*.

13. Kolko, "Business Relocation and Homegrown Jobs."

14. Edmiston, "Net Effects."

15. Layser, "Unknown Consequences"; Neumark and Young, "Enterprise Zones, Poverty, and Labor Market Outcomes."

16. Flora et al., *Rural Communities*.

17. Flora et al., *Rural Communities*.

18. Flora et al., *Rural Communities*.

19. WealthWorks, *Wealthworks for Your Region*.

20. Siegel et al., "Regional Economic Diversity."

21. Melo et al., "Meta-Analysis of Estimates."

22. Siegel et al., "Regional Economic Diversity."

23. Azar et al., "Labor Market Concentration"; Mueller et al., "Market Concentration."

24. Decker et al., "Role of Entrepreneurship"; Neumark et al., "Do Small Businesses Create More Jobs?"

25. Radley and Macke, "Entrepreneurial Ecosystem-Building"; Rogers et al., "Promoting Economic Inclusion."

26. Lynch, "Small Businesses Thrive"; Stephens and Partridge, "Do Entrepreneurs Enhance Economic Growth?"; Stephens et al., "Innovation, Entrepreneurship, and Economic Growth."

27. Endeavor Insight, *Rural Entrepreneurship*.

28. Yin et al., "Rural Innovation System."

29. Endeavor Insight, *Rural Entrepreneurship*.

30. Davis and Dumont, "'TRIC' to Fostering Shared Economic Prosperity."

31. Kerlin et al., "Rural Rising."

32. Isbister, *Promises Not Kept*.

33. Mueller, "Dual Dependency."

34. Wallerstein, "Rise and Future Demise."

35. Partridge et al., "Riding the Wave."

36. Isbister, *Promises Not Kept*.

37. Frank, "Development of Underdevelopment."

38. Cardoso, "Dependency and Development."

39. Givens et al., "Ecologically Unequal Exchange."

40. Kvangraven, "Beyond the Stereotype."

41. McMichael, *Development and Social Change*.

42. Jackson and Jabbie, "Import Substitution Industrialization."

43. Marx, *Capital: Volume I*.

44. Isbister, *Promises Not Kept*.

45. Isbister, *Promises Not Kept*.

46. Das, "State Theories."

47. Sklair, "Democracy and the Transnational Capitalist Class."

48. Sklair, "Democracy and the Transnational Capitalist Class," 145.

49. McMichael, *Development and Social Change*.

50. D. Harvey, *Limits to Capital*; N. Smith, *Uneven Development*.

51. De Grandi and Tutin, "Marx and the 'Minsky Moment.'"

52. Minsky, "Financial-Instability Hypothesis"; Palley, "Theory of Minsky Super-Cycles."

53. D. Harvey, *Limits to Capital*.

54. Schoenberger, "Spatial Fix Revisited."

55. N. Smith, *Uneven Development*.

56. Marx, *Capital: Volume III*; N. Smith, *Uneven Development*.

57. N. Smith, *Uneven Development*.

58. Abraham and Kearney, "Explaining the Decline."

59. N. Smith, *Uneven Development*, 152.

Chapter Four

1. Federal Reserve Bank of St. Louis, *Investing in Rural Prosperity*.

2. N. Smith, *Uneven Development*.

3. Pilgeram, *Pushed Out*; Sherman, *Dividing Paradise*.

4. Mueller, "Dual Dependency"; Sherman, *Dividing Paradise*.

5. US Economic Development Association, "About USDA Rural Development."

6. USDA Rural Development, "About RD."

7. USDA Rural Development, "About RD."

8. US Environmental Protection Agency, *Supporting Sustainable Rural Communities*.

9. Flora et al., *Rural Communities*, 5th ed.

10. Harvey, *Limits to Capital*.

11. Marx, *Capital: Volume I*, 272. Pronouns are edited by the author to be gender neutral.

12. Harvey, *Limits to Capital*, 381.

13. Harvey, *Limits to Capital*, 381.

14. Partridge et al., "Dwindling US Internal Migration"; Partridge et al., "When Spatial Equilibrium Fails."

15. Graves, "Spatial Equilibrium"; Partridge, "The Dueling Models."

16. Graves, "Spatial Equilibrium."

17. Diamond, "Determinants and Welfare."

18. Patridge et al., "When Spatial Equilibrium Fails."

19. Althoff et al., "Geography of Remote Work."

20. Kandel and Parrado, "Restructuring of the US Meat Processing Industry."

21. O'Leary, *Frackalachia Update*.

22. Peluso et al., "The Rock, the Beach, and the Tidal Pool."

23. Brown and Schafft, *Rural People and Communities*.

24. Harvey, *Limits to Capital*.

25. Simmons et al., "Oregon's Forest Products Industry."

26. He et al., "Logging Industry."

27. Appalachian Regional Commission, "Coal Production and Employment."

28. US Census Bureau, "Bicentennial Edition: Historical Statistics."

29. O'Leary, *Frackalachia Update*.

30. Gittings and Roach, "Who Benefits from a Resource Boom?"

31. US Energy Information Administration, "Wind Explained."

32. Costa and Veiga, "Local Labor Impact."

33. US Department of Energy, *Wind Vision*.

34. Brown et al., "New Dynamics in Fossil Fuel."

35. USDA Economic Research Service, "Farm Labor."

36. Bureau of Economic Analysis, *Regional Data*.

37. Schmitz and Moss, "Mechanized Agriculture."

38. USDA Economic Research Service, "Farm Labor."

39. Weber and Miller, "Poverty in Rural America."

40. Duncan, *Worlds Apart*.

41. Billings and Blee, *Road to Poverty*; Duncan, *Worlds Apart*; Mueller, "Dual Dependency."

42. Carr and Kefalas, *Hollowing Out the Middle*.

43. K. M. Johnson, "Natural Decrease in America"; K. M. Johnson, "Rural America Lost Population."

Chapter Five

1. The United States is not going to become Coruscant.

2. Pender et al., "Rural Wealth Creation."

3. Halfacree, "Rethinking 'Rurality.'"

4. Halfacree, "Rethinking 'Rurality'"; Shucksmith, "Re-imagining the Rural."

5. Lichter and Brown, "Rural America."

6. Kondo et al., "Protecting the Idyll."

7. Lichter and Brown, "Rural America"; McLaughlin and Coleman-Jensen, "Economic Restructuring and Family."

8. Brown et al., "Continuities in Size."

9. Saad, "Country Living Enjoys Renewed Appeal"; Parker et al., *Americans Are Less Likely*.

10. Davis et al., "Rural America."

11. Barry and Agyeman, "On Belonging and Becoming"; McIvor and Anisman, "Keeping Our Languages Alive."

12. Bureau of Indian Affairs, "Tribal Leaders Directory"; US Government Accountability Office, "Indian Issues."

13. Norris et al., "American Indian and Alaska Native Population"; US Census Bureau, "American Indians and Alaska Natives."

14. Hargrove, "Spatial Dimensions of White"; S. Johnson, "Descendants Fight to Maintain."

15. S. Johnson, "Descendants Fight to Maintain."

16. S. Johnson, "Descendants Fight to Maintain."

17. Vecchio et al., "Indigenous Mental Health."

18. MacDonald et al., "A Necessary Voice."

19. Harvey, "Racial Inequalities and Poverty"; Farrell et al., "Effects of Land Dispossession."

20. Schwartz, "Where Critical Race Theory Is Under Attack."

21. Thiede and Slack, "Old versus the New."

22. Harvey, "Racial Inequalities and Poverty."

23. Coates, "Case for Reparations."

24. Brooks et al., "County Reclassifications and Rural–Urban Mortality"; Johnson and Lichter, "Metropolitan Reclassification."

25. Nelson, "Concentrations of the Elderly."

26. Nelson, "Concentrations of the Elderly."

27. O'Hanlon et al., "Access, Quality, and Financial Performance"; Peters, "Community Susceptibility and Resiliency."

28. Lang and Pearson-Merkowitz, "Partisan Sorting"; Tam Cho et al., "Voter Migration."

29. Brown and Mettler, "Sequential Polarization."

30. Brown and Mettler, "Sequential Polarization."

31. Kotkin and Cox, "It Wasn't Rural 'Hicks'"; Frey, *Biden's Victory Came from the Suburbs*.

32. Iyengar et al., "Origins and Consequences."

33. Perumal and Timmons, "Contextual Density."

34. Jones and Kammen, "Spatial Distribution"; Gill and Moeller, "GHG Emissions."

35. Min et al., "High-Resolution Statistical Model."

36. American Society of Civil Engineers, 2021 *Report Card for America's Infrastructure*.

37. Guo et al., "Targeted Poverty Alleviation."

38. Wilkinson, "Greatest Good," 72.

39. Eggleston, "Act Utilitarianism."

40. D. Miller, "Justice."

Chapter Six

1. Ritzer and Stepnisky, *Sociological Theory*.

2. Weber, "'Objectivity' in Social Science."

3. Shucksmith, "Re-Imagining the Rural."

4. Farrell, *Billionaire Wilderness*; Sherman, *Dividing Paradise*; Stuber, *Aspen and the American Dream*.

5. Pilgeram, *Pushed Out*.

6. Congressional Budget Office, "Approaches to Make Federal Highway Spending More Productive"; Reeder and Bagi, "Federal Funding in Rural America"; US Government Accountability Office, "Farm Bill."

7. Harvey and Hoffman, "New Deal for the Mountain Folk."

8. Olson, "Columbus of the New Deal."

9. Schuyler, "Constitutional Problems Confronting the Resettlement."

10. Guo et al., "Targeted Poverty Alleviation."

11. Guo et al., "Targeted Poverty Alleviation."

12. Brooks et al., "Rural-Urban Differences."

13. Brown and Schafft, *Rural People and Communities*.

14. Farrell et al., "Effects of Land Dispossession."

15. Dando, "'Tied to the Land'"; Nadler and Diamond, "Eminent Domain."

16. Delany, "What Challenges Will Organisations Face?"; Felstead and Henseke, "Assessing the Growth," 195.

17. Barrero et al., "COVID-19 Is a Persistent Reallocation Shock," 5.

18. Althoff et al., "Geography of Remote Work."

19. Brooks, "Countering Depopulation in Kansas."

20. Althoff et al., "Geography of Remote Work."

21. Brown and Schafft, *Rural People and Communities*.

22. Abril, "Future of Work."

23. Ali, "Politics of Good Enough."

24. Ali, "Politics of Good Enough."

25. Montana Department of Commerce, "Come Home Montana Initiative."

26. Markowski et al., "After 50 Years."

27. O'Hanlon et al., "Access, Quality, and Financial Performance."

28. Haverstock and Helhoski, "Student Loan Debt."

29. White, "The Contract State."

30. Perry et al., *Student Loans, the Racial Wealth Divide*.

31. Liptak, "Supreme Court Rejects Biden's Student Loan Forgiveness Plan."

32. Sherman, "Not Allowed to Inherit My Kingdom"; Ulrich-Schad and Qin, "Culture Clash?"

33. K. M. Johnson, "Rural America Lost Population."

34. D. Harvey, *Limits to Capital*.

35. Felstead and Henseke, "Assessing the Growth."

36. Wigert et al., "Future of the Office."

37. Althoff et al., "Geography of Remote Work."

Chapter Seven

1. Bidadanure, "Political Theory of Universal Basic Income," 1.

2. Bidadanure, "Political Theory of Universal Basic Income."

3. Bidadanure, "Political Theory of Universal Basic Income."

4. Ku et al., "Effects of SNAP Work."

5. Bidadanure, "Political Theory of Universal Basic Income."

6. Van Parijs, "Basic Income for All."

7. Bidadanure, "Political Theory of Universal Basic Income."

8. Rogers, "Basic Income in a Just Society."

9. Allas et al., *Experiment to Inform Universal Basic Income*.

10. Banerjee et al., "Effects of a Universal Basic Income."

11. Banerjee et al., "Effects of a Universal Basic Income."

12. Banerjee et al., "Effects of a Universal Basic Income."

13. Berman, "Resource Rents, Universal Basic Income, and Poverty"; Guettabi, *"What Do We Know about the Effects of the Alaska Permanent Fund Dividend?"*; Jones and Marinescu, "Labor Market Impacts"; Ruckert et al., "Reducing Health Inequities."

14. Kozminski and Baek, "Can an Oil-Rich Economy Reduce Its Income Inequality?"; Lerner, "Impacts of the Alaska Permanent Fund Dividend."

15. Ruckert et al., "Reducing Health Inequities."

16. Gibson et al., "Public Health Effects"; Hasdell, *What We Know about Universal Basic Income*.

17. Neuwinger, "The Revolution Will Not Be Randomized."

18. Green Party of England and Whales, "Basic Income."

19. Assistant Secretary for Planning and Evaluation, "Poverty Guidelines."

20. Hoynes and Rothstein, "Universal Basic Income."

21. Jones and Marinescu, "Universal Cash Transfers"; J. Miller, "Universal Basic Income."

22. Cai et al., "Projected Costs of Single-Payer"; Crowley et al., "Envisioning a Better US Health Care System for All."

23. Tolbert et al., *Key Facts about the Uninsured Population*; Office of the Assistant Secretary for Planning and Evaluation, "National Uninsured Rate Reaches an All-Time Low."

24. Tolbert et al., *Key Facts about the Uninsured Population*.

25. Blumenthal et al., "Mirror, Mirror 2024."

26. Buettgens, *What Will Happen?*

27. D. Harvey, *Limits to Capital*, 381.

28. Spiegel and Fronstin, "What Employers Say."

29. Chute and Wunnava, "Is There a Link?"

30. Centers for Medicare and Medicaid Services, "What You Should Know."

31. Cooper et al., "Surprise!"

32. Crowley et al., "Envisioning a Better US Health Care System for All"; Tolbert et al., *Key Facts about the Uninsured Population*.

33. Office of the Assistant Secretary for Planning and Evaluation, "HHS Secretary's Report."

34. Brown, "Racial Stratification, Immigration"; Burton et al., "Inequality, Family Processes"; Singh an Siahpush, "Widening Rural-Urban Disparities."

35. Cai et al., "Projected Costs of Single-Payer."

36. Cai et al., "Projected Costs of Single-Payer," 14.

37. Cai et al., "Projected Costs of Single-Payer"; Congressional Budget Office, "How CBO Analyzes the Costs of Proposals."

38. Congressional Budget Office, "How CBO Analyzes the Costs of Proposals."

39. J. Nelson, "Economic Effects of Five."

40. J. Nelson, "Economic Effects of Five."

41. Crowley et al., "Envisioning a Better US Health Care System for All."

42. Congressional Budget Office, "How CBO Analyzes the Costs of Proposals."

43. Committee for a Responsible Federal Budget, *Choices for Financing Medicare for All*.

44. Committee for a Responsible Federal Budget, *Choices for Financing Medicare for All*.

45. Penn Wharton Budget Model, *Medicare for All*.

46. Committee for a Responsible Federal Budget, *Choices for Financing Medicare for All*.

47. Crowley et al., "Envisioning a Better US Health Care System for All."

48. Crowley et al., "Envisioning a Better US Health Care System for All."

49. Author's calculations using 2018–22 American Community Survey data; Manson et al., "IPUMS National Historical Geographic Information System."

50. Coates, "The Case for Reparations."

51. Darity and Mullen, *From Here to Equality*.

52. Darity and Mullen, *From Here to Equality*, 2.

53. Darity and Mullen, *From Here to Equality*.

54. Darity and Mullen, *From Here to Equality*.

55. Darity and Mullen, *From Here to Equality*.

56. Darity and Mullen, *From Here to Equality*.

57. Darity and Mullen, *From Here to Equality*.

58. Jackson Lee, *Commission to Study*, H.R. 40.

59. Lee, "California Panel Sizes Up Reparations."

60. Smithsonian, "Nation to Nation."

61. Bahr, "After 400 Years."

62. Estes, "Red Deal."

63. Estes, "Red Deal."

64. Christian-Smith et al., *Twenty-First Century US Water Policy*.

65. Blumm et al., "Mirage of Indian Reserved Water Rights."

66. Barnwell, "McGirt v. Oklahoma."

67. Walters, "Review Essay."

68. Hendrix, *Ownership, Authority, and Self-Determination*.

69. Lee et al., "Land-Grab Universities."

70. Newton, "Indian Claims for Reparations."

71. Newton, "Indian Claims for Reparations."

72. Farrell et al, "Effects of Land Dispossession."

73. Bureau of Indian Affairs, "Tribal Leaders Directory"; Dewees, "Native Nations"; US Government Accountability Office, "Indian Issues."

74. Van Parijs, "The Universal Basic Income," 172.

75. Van Parijs, "The Universal Basic Income."

76. Brown et al., "Continuities in Size"; Saad, "Country Living Enjoys Renewed Appeal"; Parker et al., *Americans Are Less Likely*.

77. This quote originally was posted on Twitter, now known as X, by Brittany Packnett Cunningham at the account @MsPackyetti. Following changes in Twitter and its leadership, the tweet was deleted and the account is now dormant. I retain the quote to ensure proper attribution of the concept.

Conclusion

1. Saad, "More in US See Unions Strengthening."

2. Kallis et al., "Research on Degrowth."

3. Schneider et al., "Crisis or Opportunity?"

4. Asara et al., "Socially Sustainable Degrowth."

Bibliography

Articles in Popular Media

Abril, Danielle. "Future of Work: 'The Office as We Know It Is Over,' Airbnb CEO Says." *Washington Post*, May 28, 2022.

Coates, Ta-Nehisi. "The Case for Reparations." *The Atlantic*, June 2014.

Estes, Nick. "A Red Deal." *Jacobin Magazine*, August 6, 2019.

Haverstock, Eliza, and Anna Helholski. "Student Loan Debt: How Much Do Borrowers Owe in 2025." *Nerd Wallet*, January, 2025. https://www.nerdwallet.com/article/loans/student-loans/student-loan-debt.

Johanson, Mark. "The Small Cities and Towns Booming from Remote Work." *BBC Worklife*, January 26, 2022.

———. "The 'Zoom Towns' Luring Remote Workers to Rural Enclaves." *BBC Worklife*, June 8, 2021.

Johnson, Sharon. "Descendants Fight to Maintain Historic Black Communities. Keeping Their Legacy Alive Is Complicated." Associated Press, December 21, 2023.

Kotkin, Joel, and Wendell Cox. "It Wasn't Rural 'Hicks' Who Elected Trump: The Suburbs Were—and Will Remain—the Real Battleground." *Forbes*, November 22, 2016.

Lee, Kurtis. "California Panel Sizes Up Reparations for Black Citizens." *New York Times*, December 1, 2022.

Lee, Robert, Tristan Ahtone, Margaret Pearce, Kalen Goodluck, Geoff McGhee, Cody Leff, Katherine Lanpher, and Taryn Salinas. "Land-Grab Universities: A *High Country News* Investigation." *High Country News*, 2020.

Liptak, Adam. "Supreme Court Rejects Biden's Student Loan Forgiveness Plan." *New York Times*, June 30, 2023.

Lynch, Kevin. "Small Businesses Thrive in Holmes, Wayne County Area—Why These Counties Are Successful." *Wooster Daily Record*, August 22, 2023.

Marema, Tim. "Analysis: Rural COVID-19 Deaths in Four Graphs." *The Daily Yonder*, December 20, 2021.

Newkirk, Vann R., II. "The Great Land Robbery: The Shameful Story of How 1 Million Black Families Have Been Ripped from Their Farms." *The Atlantic*, September 2019.

Rogers, Brishen. "Basic Income in a Just Society." *Boston Review*, May 3, 2017.

Schwartz, Sarah. "Map: Where Critical Race Theory Is Under Attack." *Education Week*, June 13, 2023.

Van Parijs, Philippe. "A Basic Income for All." *Boston Review*, April 16, 2000.

Book Chapters, Policy Briefs, Theses, and Working Papers

Banerjee, Abhijit, Michael Faye, Alan Krueger, Paul Niehaus, and Tavneet Suri. "Effects of a Universal Basic Income during the Pandemic." Innovations for Poverty Action Working Paper, 2020.

———. "Universal Basic Income: Short-Term Results from a Long-Term Experiment in Kenya." Working Paper, 2023.

Barrero, Jose M., Nicholas Bloom, Steven J. Davis, and Brent H. Meyer. "COVID-19 Is a Persistent Reallocation Shock." Federal Reserve Bank Working Paper No. 2021-02, January 2021.

Campi, Alicia J. "'Eating Bitterness': The Impact of Asian-Pacific Migration on US Immigration Policy." Policy Brief, Immigration Policy Center, 2004.

Cardoso, Fernando H. "Dependency and Development in Latin America." In *The Globalization and Development Reader: Perspectives on Development and Global Change*, edited by J. Timmons Roberts, Amy B. Hite, and Nitsan Chorev, 115–25. Malden, MA: Basil Blackwell, 2015. Originally published in 1972.

Dewees, Sarah. "Native Nations in a Changing Global Economy." In *Rural America in a Globalizing World: Problems and Prospects for the 2010s*, edited by Conner Bailey, Leif Jensen, and Elizabeth Ransom, 471–88. Morgantown: West Virginia University Press, 2014.

Eggleston, Ben. "Act Utilitarianism." In *The Cambridge Companion to Utilitarianism*, edited by Ben Eggleston and Dale E. Miller, 125–45. Cambridge: Cambridge University Press, 2014.

Emerson, Thomas E., Kristin M. Hedman, and Ronald K. Faulseit. "The Dangers of Diversity: The Consolidation and Dissolution of Cahokia, Native North America's First Urban Polity." In *Beyond Collapse: Archaeological Perspectives on Resilience, Revitalization, and Transformation in Complex Societies*, edited by Ronald K. Faulseit, 147–75. Carbondale: Southern Illinois University Press, 2016.

Frank, Andre G. "The Development of Underdevelopment." In *The Globalization and Development Reader: Perspectives on Development and Global Change*, edited by J. Timmons Roberts, Amy B. Hite, and Nitsan Chorev, 105–14. Malden, MA: Basil Blackwell, 2015. Originally published in 1969.

Friedland, William H. "The End of Rural Society and the Future of Rural Sociology." Rural Sociological Society Annual Meeting. Guelph, Canada, August 1981.

Graves, Philip E. "Spatial Equilibrium in Labor Markets." In *Handbook of Regional Science*, edited by Manfred M. Fischer and Peter Nijkamp, 539–55. New York: Springer, 2021.

Halfacree, Keith. "Rethinking 'Rurality.'" In *New Forms of Urbanization: Beyond the Urban-Rural Dichotomy*, edited by Tony Champion and Graeme Hugo, 285–304. Milton Park, UK: Routledge, 2004.

Harvey, Gwen Russell, and Alice Hoffman. "A New Deal for the Mountain Folk: Recollections of the Resettlement Administration." In *Blue Ridge Parkway: Proceedings of the Blue Ridge Parkway Golden Anniversary Conference*, 91. Boone, NC: Appalachian Consortium Press, 1986.

Harvey, Mark H. "Racial Inequalities and Poverty in Rural America." In *Rural Poverty in the United States*, edited by Ann R. Tickamyer, Jennifer Sherman, and Jennifer Warlick, 141–67. New York: Columbia University Press, 2017.

Humphrey, Craig R., Gigi Berardi, Matthew S. Carroll, Sally Fairfax, Louise Fortmann, Charles Geisler, Thomas G. Johnson, et al. "Theories in the Study of Natural Resource-Dependent Communities and Persistent Rural Poverty in the United States." In *Persistent Poverty in Rural America*, edited by Gene Summers, 136–72. Milton Park, UK: Routledge, 1993.

Jackson, Emerson Abraham, and Mohamed N. Jabbie. "Import Substitution Industrialization (ISI): An Approach to Global Economic Sustainability." In *Industry, Innovation and Infrastructure*, edited by Walter L. Filho, Anabela M. Azul, Luciana Brandli, Amanda Salvia, and Tony Wall, 506–18. New York: Springer International, 2021.

Johnson, Kenneth M. "Natural Decrease in America: More Coffins than Cradles." *Carsey Research Issue Brief #30*. Carsey Research Institute, University of New Hampshire, 2011.

———. "Rural America Lost Population over the Past Decade for the First Time in History." *Carsey Research National Issue Brief #160*. Carsey Research Institute, University of New Hampshire, 2022.

———. "Where Is Rural America and Who Lives There?" In *Rural Poverty in the United States*, edited by Ann R. Tickamyer, Jennifer Sherman, and Jennifer Warlick, 1–27. New York: Columbia University Press, 2017.

Kelly, John E., and James A. Brown. "Cahokia: The Processes and Principles of the Creation of an Early Mississippian City." In *Making Ancient Cities: Space and Place in Early Urban Societies*, edited by Andrew T. Creekmore III and Kevin D. Fisher, 292–336. Cambridge: Cambridge University Press, 2014.

Lerner, Mattathias. "The Impacts of the Alaska Permanent Fund Dividend on High School Status Completion Rates." arXiv, 2019. arXiv:1910.04083.

McIvor, Onowa, and Adar Anisman. "Keeping Our Languages Alive: Strategies for Indigenous Language Revitalization and Maintenance." In *Handbook of Cultural Security*, edited by Yasushi Watanabe, 90–109. Cheltenham: Edward Elgar Publishing, 2018.

McLaughlin, Diane K., and Alisha Coleman-Jensen. "Economic Restructuring and Family Structure Change, 1980 to 2000: A Focus on Female-Headed Families with Children." In *Economic Restructuring in Rural America*, edited by Kristin E. Smith and Ann R. Tickamyer, 105–23. State College: Penn State University Press, 2011.

Miller, David. "Justice." *Stanford Encyclopedia of Philosophy*, August 2021.

Miller, Joshua. "Universal Basic Income and Inflation: Reviewing Theory and Evidence." UBI Center, June 2021. https://ssrn.com/abstract=3920748.

Minsky, Hyman P. "The Financial-Instability Hypothesis: Capitalist Processes and the Behavior of the Economy." *Hyman P. Minsky Archive* 282 (1982).

Monnat, Shannon M. "Rural Adults Report Worse COVID-19 Impacts than Urban Adults." *Lerner Center for Public Health Promotion Research Brief #67*, Lerner Center, Syracuse University, 2022.

Nelson, Peter B. "Concentrations of the Elderly in Rural America: Patterns, Processes, and Outcomes in a Neoliberal World." In *Rural America in a Globalizing World: Problems and Prospects for the 2010s*, edited by Conner Bailey, Leif Jensen, and Elizabeth Ransom, 347–64. Morgantown: West Virginia University Press, 2014.

Newton, Nell J. "Indian Claims for Reparations, Compensation, and Restitution in the United States Legal System." In *When Sorry Isn't Enough: The Controversy over Apologies and Reparations for Human Injustice*, edited by Roy L. Brooks, 261–69. New York: NYU Press, 1999.

Olson, Katelin E. "Columbus of the New Deal: Rexford G. Tugwell and the Goals, Challenges and Physical Legacies of the Resettlement Administration." Cornell University Master's Thesis, 2009.

Partridge, Mark D., Dan S. Rickman, M. Rose Olfert, and Ying Tan. "When Spatial Equilibrium Fails: Is Place-Based Policy Second Best?" In *Place-Based Economic Development and the New EU Cohesion Policy*, edited by Philip McCann and Attila Varga, 63–85. Milton Park, UK: Routledge, 2018.

Rostow, Walt W. "The Stages of Economic Growth: A Non-Communist Manifesto (1960)." In *The Globalization and Development Reader: Perspectives on Development and Global Change*, 2nd ed., edited by J. Timmons Roberts, Amy B. Hite, and Nitsan Chorev, 52–61. Hoboken, NJ: Wiley-Blackwell, 2015. Originally published in 1960.

Smith, Suzanne. "The Institutional and Intellectual Origins of Rural Sociology." Rural Sociology Society 74th Annual Meeting. Boise, Idaho, July 2011.

Thiede, Brian, and Tim Slack. "The Old versus the New Economies and Their Impacts." In *Rural Poverty in the United States*, edited by Ann R. Tickamyer, Jennifer Sherman, and Jennifer Warlick, 231–49. New York: Columbia University Press, 2017.

Vias, Alexander C. "Perspectives on US Rural Labor Markets in the First Decade of the Twenty-First Century." In *International Handbook of Rural Demography*, 273–291. Dordrecht: Springer Netherlands, 2011.

Villa, Robert. "Rural Social Work on the US–Mexico Border." In *Encyclopedia of Social Work*. Oxford: Oxford University Press, 2020.

Wallerstein, Immanuel. "The Rise and Future Demise of the World Capitalist System: Concepts for Comparative Analysis." In *The Globalization and Development Reader: Perspectives on Development and Global Change*, edited by J. Timmons Roberts, Amy B. Hite, and Nitsan Chorev, 126–46. Malden, MA: Basil Blackwell, 2015. Originally published in 1979.

———. "The World-System: Myths and Historical Shifts." In *The Global Economy: Divergent Perspectives on Economic Change*, edited by Edward Gondolf, Irwin Marcus, and James Dougherty, 15–25. Milton Park, UK: Routledge, 1987.

Weber, Bruce, and Kathleen Miller. "Poverty in Rural America Then and Now." In *Rural Poverty in the United States*, edited by Ann R. Tickamyer, Jennifer Sherman, and Jennifer Warlick, 28–64. New York: Columbia University Press, 2017.

Weber, Max. "'Objectivity' in Social Science and Social Policy." In *The Methodology of the Social Sciences*, edited by Edward A. Shils and Henry A. Finch. Glencoe: Free Press of Glencoe, 1949. Originally published in 1904.

Books

Billings, Dwight B., and Kathleen M. Blee. *The Road to Poverty: The Making of Wealth and Hardship in Appalachia*. Cambridge: Cambridge University Press, 2000.

Brown, David L., and Kai A. Schafft. *Rural People and Communities in the 21st Century: Resilience and Transformation*. 2nd ed. Cambridge: Polity, 2019.

Carr, Patrick J., and Maria J. Kefalas. *Hollowing Out the Middle: The Rural Brain Drain and What It Means for America*. Boston: Beacon Press, 2009.

Christian-Smith, Juliet, Peter H. Gleick, Heather Cooley, Lucy Allen, Amy Vanderwarker, and Kate A. Berry. *A Twenty-First Century US Water Policy*. Oxford: Oxford University Press, 2012.

Darity, William A., Jr., and A. Kirsten Mullen. *From Here to Equality: Reparations for Black Americans in the Twenty-First Century*. Chapel Hill: The University of North Carolina Press, 2020.

Du Bois, W. E. B. *The Souls of Black Folk*. New Haven, CT: Yale University Press, 2015. Originally published in 1903.

Duncan, Cynthia M. *Worlds Apart*, 2nd ed. New Haven, CT: Yale University Press, 2015.

Farrell, Justin. *Billionaire Wilderness: The Ultra-Wealthy and the Remaking of the American West*. Princeton, NJ: Princeton University Press, 2020.

Flora, Cornelia B., Jan L. Flora, and Stephen P. Gasteyer. *Rural Communities: Legacy and Change*. 5th ed. Milton Park, UK: Routledge, 2016.

Flora, Cornelia B., Louis E. Swanson, Jan L. Flora, Jacqueline D. Spears. *Rural Communities: Legacy and Change*. Boulder: Westview Press, 1992.

Harvey, David. *The Limits to Capital*. New York: Verso, 2018. Originally published in 1982.

Hendrix, Burke A. *Ownership, Authority, and Self-Determination: Moral Principles and Indigenous Rights Claims*. State College: Penn State University Press, 2010.

Isbister, John. *Promises Not Kept: Poverty and the Betrayal of Third World Development*. 7th ed. West Hartford, CT: Kumarian Press, 2006.

Marx, Karl. *Capital: Volume I*. New York: Penguin Random House, 1990. Originally published in 1867.

———. *Capital: Volume III*. New York: Penguin Random House, 1981. Originally published in 1894.

McMichael, Paul. *Development and Social Change*. 6th ed. Thousand Oaks, CA: Sage, 2016.

Pilgeram, Ryanne. *Pushed Out: Contested Development and Rural Gentrification in the US West*. Seattle: University of Washington Press, 2021.

Ritzer, George, and Jeffrey Stepnisky. *Sociological Theory*. 10th ed. Thousand Oaks, CA: Sage, 2017.

Sherman, Jennifer. *Dividing Paradise: Rural Inequality and the Diminishing American Dream*. Berkeley: University of California Press, 2021.

Smith, Neil. *Uneven Development*. New York: Basil Blackwell, 1984.

Stuber, Jenny M. *Aspen and the American Dream: How One Town Manages Inequality in the Era of Supergentrification*. Berkeley: University of California Press, 2021.

Takaki, Ronald. *A History of Asian Americans: Strangers from a Different Shore*. Boston: Back Bay Books, 1998.

Taylor, Dorceta E. *The Rise of the American Conservation Movement*. Durham, NC: Duke University Press, 2016.

Vidich, Arthur J., and Joseph Bensman. *Small Town in Mass Society: Class, Power, and Religion in a Rural Community*. Champaign: University of Illinois Press, 1958.

Databases, Tables, and Statistics

Bureau of Economic Analysis. "CAEMP25N Total Full-Time and Part-Time Employment by NAICS Industry, US Nonmetro Portion." *Regional Data: GDP and Personal Income*, 2023.

———. "Table 6.4D Full-Time and Part-Time Employees by Industry." *National Income and Product Accounts*, 2024.

Manson, Steven, Jonathan Schroeder, David Van Riper, Katherine Knowles, Tracy Kugler, Finn Roberts, and Steven Ruggles. "IPUMS National Historical Geographic Information System: Version 18.0 [dataset]." IPUMS, 2023.

US Census Bureau. *County Population Totals and Components of Change: 2020–2022. Vintage 2022*. US Census Bureau, 2023.

Government Bulletins, Bills, and Reports

Appalachian Regional Commission. "Coal Production and Employment in Appalachia." Bureau of Business and Economic Research, West Virginia University. Report commissioned by the Appalachian Regional Commission, 2022.

Brown, Jason. P., Roger Coupal, Claudia Hitaj, Timothy W. Kelsey, Richard S. Krannich, and Irene M. Xiarchos. "New Dynamics in Fossil Fuel and Renewable Energy for Rural America." USDA White Paper, July 2017.

Congressional Budget Office. "Approaches to Make Federal Highway Spending More Productive." *Congressional Budget Office Report*, February 2016.

———. "How CBO Analyzes the Costs of Proposals for Single-Payer Health Care Systems That Are Based on Medicare's Fee-for-Service Program." Working Paper 2020-08, December 2020.

Cromartie, John, and Shawn Bucholtz. "Defining the 'Rural' in Rural America." *Amber Waves* 6, no. 3 (2008): 28–35.

Davis, Daniel P., and Andrew Dumont. "The 'TRIC' to Fostering Shared Economic Prosperity in Rural America." In *Investing in Rural Prosperity*, edited by Andrew Dumont and Daniel Paul Davis. Federal Reserve Bank of St. Louis, 2022.

Davis, James C., John Cromartie, Tracey Farrigan, Brandon Genetin, Austin Sanders, and Justin B. Winikoff. "Rural America at a Glance." USDA Economic Research Service. *Economic Information Bulletin* 261 (2023).

Du Bois, W. E. B. "The Negro Landholder of Georgia." *Bulletin of the United States Bureau of Labor* VI, no. 35 (July 1901): 647–777.

Federal Reserve Bank of St. Louis. *Investing in Rural Prosperity*, edited by Andrew Dumont and Daniel Paul Davis. Federal Reserve Bank of St. Louis, 2022.

Giri, Anil K., Dipak Subedi, Jessica E. Todd, Carrie Litkowski, and Christine Whitt. "Off-Farm Income a Major Component of Total Income for Most Farm Households in 2019." *Amber Waves*, September 7, 2021.

Green Party of England and Wales. "Basic Income: A Detailed Proposal." Consultation Paper, April 2015.

Jackson Lee, Sheila. *Commission to Study and Develop Reparation Proposals for African Americans Act*, H.R. 40, 117th Cong., 2021.

Kolko, Jed. "Business Relocation and Homegrown Jobs, 1992–2006." Public Policy Institute of California, 2010.

Nelson, Jaeger. "Economic Effects of Five Illustrative Single-Payer Health Care Systems." Congressional Budget Office Working Paper 2022-02, February 2022.

Norris, Tina, Paula Vines, and Elizabeth M. Hoeffel. "The American Indian and Alaska Native Population: 2010." *2010 Census Briefs*. US Census Bureau, January 2012.

Office of Management and Budget. "Revised Delineations of Metropolitan Statistical Areas, Micropolitan Statistical Areas, and Combined Statistical Areas, and Guidance on Uses of the Delineations of These Areas." *OMB Bulletin No. 23–01* (2023).

———. "Standard for Defining Metropolitan and Micropolitan Statistical Areas; Notice." Executive Office of the President, Office of Management and Budget, Office of Information and Regulatory Affairs. *Federal Register* 65, no. 249 (2000).

———. "2010 Standard for Delineating Metropolitan and Micropolitan Statistical Areas; Notice." Executive Office of the President, Office of Management and Budget, Office of Information and Regulatory Affairs. *Federal Register* 75, no. 123 (2010).

Office of the Assistant Secretary for Planning and Evaluation. "HHS Secretary's Report on Addressing Surprise Medical Billing." *A Report Required by Executive Order 13877* (2020).

———. "National Uninsured Rate Reaches an All-Time Low in Early 2023 after Close of ACA Open Enrollment." *Issue Brief No. HP-2023-20* (2023).

Radley, Steve, and Don Macke. "Entrepreneurial Ecosystem-Building in Rural America." In *Investing in Rural Prosperity*, edited by Andrew Dumont and Daniel Paul Davis. Federal Reserve Bank of St. Louis, 2021.

Reeder, Richard, and Faqir Bagi. "Federal Funding in Rural America Goes Far beyond Agriculture." *Amber Waves* 7, no. 1 (2009).

Rogers, Elizabeth L., John Scribner, and Leah B. Thibault. "Promoting Economic Inclusion in Maine: Systems Change in Rural Communities, One Business at a Time." In *Investing in Rural Prosperity*, edited by Andrew Dumont and Daniel Paul Davis. Federal Reserve Bank of St. Louis, 2021.

Shrider, E. A., and John Creamer. "Poverty in the United States: 2022." *Current Population Reports*, P60–280. US Census Bureau, September 2023.

Simmons, Eric A., Kate C. Marcille, Gary J. Lettman, Todd A. Morgan, Dorian C. Smith, Luke A. Rymniak, and Glenn A. Christensen. "Oregon's Forest Products Industry and Timber Harvest 2017 with Trends through 2018." General Technical Report PNW-GTR-997, USDA, 2021.

US Census Bureau. "American Indians and Alaska Natives in the United States."
US Census Bureau Map, 2020. https://www2.census.gov/geo/maps/DC2020
/AIANWall2020/2020_AIAN_US.pdf.
————. "Bicentennial Edition: Historical Statistics of the United States, Colonial
Times to 1970." US Census Bureau, 1975.
————. "Table A-3 Inmigration, Outmigration, and Net Migration by Metropolitan
Status: 1986–2022." US Census Bureau, 2023.
————. "2020 Census Urban Areas FAQs." US Census Bureau, 2022.
US Congress. *An Act to Secure Homesteads to Actual Settler on the Public Domain.*
Pub. L. No. 37–64, 12 Stat. 392, 1862.
US Department of Energy. *Wind Vision: A New Era for Wind Power in the United States.*
US Department of Energy Technical Report, 2015.
US Environmental Protection Agency. *Supporting Sustainable Rural Communities.*
Partnership for Sustainable Communities, 2011.
US Government Accountability Office. "Farm Bill: Reducing Crop Insurance Costs
Could Fund Other Priorities." GAO-23-106228, February 2023.
————. "Indian Issues: Federal Funding for Non-Federally Recognized Tribes."
GAO-12-348, April 2012.
Wang, Sun Ling, Robert A. Hoppe, and Thomas Hertz. "Increases in Labor Quality
Contributed to Growth in US Agricultural Output." *Amber Waves*, February 17, 2022.
Whitt, Christine, Katherine Lacy, and Katherine Lim. "America's Farms and Ranches
at a Glance: 2023 Edition." USDA Economic Research Service. *Economic
Information Bulletin* 263 (2023).

Peer-Reviewed Articles

Abraham, Katharine G., and Melissa S. Kearney. "Explaining the Decline in the US
Employment-to-Population Ratio: A Review of the Evidence." *Journal of Economic
Literature* 58, no. 3 (2020): 585–643.
Ali, Christopher. "The Politics of Good Enough: Rural Broadband and Policy Failure
in the United States." *International Journal of Communication* 14 (2020): 5982–6004.
Althoff, Lukas, Fabian Eckert, Sharat Ganapati, and Conor Walsh. "The Geography
of Remote Work." *Regional Science and Urban Economics* 93 (2022): 103770.
Asara, Viviana, Iago Otero, Federico Demaria, and Esteve Corbera. "Socially
Sustainable Degrowth as a Social–Ecological Transformation: Repoliticizing
Sustainability." *Sustainability Science* 10 (2015): 375–84.
Azar, José, Ioana Marinescu, and Marshall Steinbaum. "Labor Market
Concentration." *Journal of Human Resources* 57, no. S (2022): S167–99.
Azzam, Azzeddine M., and John R. Schroeter. "Concentration in Beef Packing: Do
Gains Outweigh Losses?" *Choices* 12, no. 1 (1997): 26–28.
Barnett, Barry J. "The US Farm Financial Crisis of the 1980s." *Agricultural History* 74,
no. 2 (2000): 366–80.
Barnwell, Allison. "McGirt v. Oklahoma." *Public Land & Resources Law Review* 13
(2020): 2.

Barry, Janice, and Julian Agyeman. "On Belonging and Becoming in the Settler-Colonial City: Co-Produced Futurities, Placemaking, and Urban Planning in the United States." *Journal of Race, Ethnicity and the City* 1, no. 1–2 (2020): 22–41.

Berman, Matthew. "Resource Rents, Universal Basic Income, and Poverty among Alaska's Indigenous Peoples." *World Development* 106 (2018): 161–72.

Bidadanure, Juliana Uhuru. "The Political Theory of Universal Basic Income." *Annual Review of Political Science* 22 (2019): 481–501.

Bloome, Deirdre, James Feigenbaum, and Christopher Muller. "Tenancy, Marriage, and the Boll Weevil Infestation, 1892–1930." *Demography* 54, no. 3 (2017): 1029–49.

Blumm, Michael C., David H. Becker, and Joshua D. Smith. "The Mirage of Indian Reserved Water Rights and Western Streamflow Restoration in the McCarran Amendment Era: A Promise Unfulfilled." *Environmental Law* 36 (2006): 1157.

Brady, David. "Rethinking the Sociological Measurement of Poverty." *Social Forces* 81, no. 3 (2003): 715–51.

Brasier, Kathryn J. "Spatial Analysis of Changes in the Number of Farms during the Farm Crisis." *Rural Sociology* 70, no. 4 (2005): 540–60.

Brooks, Matthew M. "Countering Depopulation in Kansas: An Assessment of the Rural Opportunity Zone Program." *Population Research and Policy Review* 40, no. 2 (2021): 137–48.

Brooks, Matthew M., J. Tom Mueller, and Brian C. Thiede. "County Reclassifications and Rural–Urban Mortality Disparities in the United States (1970–2018)." *American Journal of Public Health* 110, no. 12 (2020): 1814–16.

Brooks, Matthew M., J. Tom Mueller, and Brian C. Thiede. "Rural-Urban Differences in the Labor-Force Impacts of COVID-19 in the United States." *Socius* 7 (2021): 10.1177/23780231211022094.

Brown, David L., Glenn V. Fuguitt, Tim B. Heaton, and Saba Waseem. "Continuities in Size of Place Preferences in the United States, 1972–1992." *Rural Sociology* 62, no. 4 (1997): 408–28.

Brown, Trevor E., and Suzanne Mettler. "Sequential Polarization: The Development of the Rural-Urban Political Divide, 1976–2020." *Perspectives on Politics* (2023): 1–29.

Brown, Tyson H. "Racial Stratification, Immigration, and Health Inequality: A Life Course-Intersectional Approach." *Social Forces* 96, no. 4 (2018): 1507–40.

Bunker, Stephen G. "Matter, Space, Energy, and Political Economy: The Amazon in the World-System." *Journal of World-Systems Research* 9, no. 2 (2003): 219–58.

Burton, Linda M., Daniel T. Lichter, Regina S. Baker, and John M. Eason. "Inequality, Family Processes, and Health in the "New" Rural America." *American Behavioral Scientist* 57, no. 8 (2013): 1128–51.

Cai, Christopher, Jackson Runte, Isabel Ostrer, Kacey Berry, Ninez Ponce, Michael Rodriguez, Stefano Bertozzi, Justin S. White, and James G. Kahn. "Projected Costs of Single-Payer Healthcare Financing in the United States: A Systematic Review of Economic Analyses." *PLoS Medicine* 17, no. 1 (2020): e1003013.

Cain, Louis P. "Historical Perspective on Infrastructure and US Economic Development." *Regional Science and Urban Economics* 27, no. 2 (1997): 117–38.

Carr, Patrick J., Daniel T. Lichter, and Maria J. Kefalas. "Can Immigration Save Small-Town America? Hispanic Boomtowns and the Uneasy Path to Renewal." *Annals of the American Academy of Political and Social Science* 641, no. 1 (2012): 38–57.

Carson, Scott Alan. "Chinese Sojourn Labor and the American Transcontinental Railroad." *Journal of Institutional and Theoretical Economics (JITE)/Zeitschrift Für Die Gesamte Staatswissenschaft* (2005): 80–102.

Chute, Benjamin W., and Phanindra V. Wunnava. "Is There a Link between Employer-Provided Health Insurance and Job Mobility? Evidence from NLSY79." *Open Journal of Human Resource Management* 1, no. 1 (2018): 38–52.

Cloke, Paul, and Paul Milbourne. "Deprivation and Lifestyles in Rural Wales—II. Rurality and the Cultural Dimension." *Journal of Rural Studies* 8, no. 4 (1992): 359–71.

Collins, Patricia Hill. "Intersectionality's Definitional Dilemmas." *Annual Review of Sociology* 41 (2015): 1–20.

Cooper, Zack, Fiona Scott Morton, and Nathan Shekita. "Surprise! Out-of-Network Billing for Emergency Care in the United States." *Journal of Political Economy* 128, no. 9 (2020): 3626–77.

Costa, Hélia, and Linda Veiga. "Local Labor Impact of Wind Energy Investment: An Analysis of Portuguese Municipalities." *Energy Economics* 94 (2021): 105055.

Crowley, Ryan, Hilary Daniel, Thomas G. Cooney, and Lee S. Engel. "Envisioning a Better US Health Care System for All: Coverage and Cost of Care." *Annals of Internal Medicine* 172, no. 2 (2020): S7–32.

Daly, Patricia A. "Agricultural Employment: Has the Decline Ended?" *Monthly Labor Review* 104 (1981): 11.

Dandachi, Dima, Rebecca Reece, Elizabeth W. Wang, Taylor Nelson, Christian Rojas-Moreno, and D. Matthew Shoemaker. "Treating COVID-19 in Rural America." *Journal of Rural Health* 37, no. 1 (2021): 205.

Dando, Christina E. ""Tied to the Land": Pipelines, Plains, and Place Attachment." *Geographical Review* 112, no. 1 (2022): 66–85.

Das, Raju J. "State Theories: A Critical Analysis." *Science & Society* (1996): 27–57.

Davidhizar, Ruth, and Gregory A. Bechtel. "Health and Quality of Life within Colonias Settlements along the United States and Mexico Border." *Public Health Nursing* 16, no. 4 (1999): 300–305.

Decker, Ryan, John Haltiwanger, Ron Jarmin, and Javier Miranda. "The Role of Entrepreneurship in US Job Creation and Economic Dynamism." *Journal of Economic Perspectives* 28, no. 3 (2014): 3–24.

De Grandi, Anthony, and Christian Tutin. "Marx and the 'Minsky Moment' Liquidity Crises and Reproduction Crises in Das Kapital." *European Journal of the History of Economic Thought* 27, no. 6 (2020): 853–80.

Delany, Kevin. "What Challenges Will Organisations Face Transitioning for the First Time to the New Normal of Remote Working?" *Human Resource Development International* 25, no. 5 (2022): 642–50.

Deller, Steven C., Tsung-Hsiu Tsai, David W. Marcouiller, and Donald B. K. English. "The Role of Amenities and Quality of Life in Rural Economic Growth." *American Journal of Agricultural Economics* 83, no. 2 (2001): 352–65.

Deller, Steven C., Victor Lledo, and David W. Marcouiller. "Modeling Regional Economic Growth with a Focus on Amenities." *Review of Urban and Regional Development Studies: Journal of the Applied Regional Science Conference* 20, no. 1 (2008): 1–21.

Diamond, Rebecca. "The Determinants and Welfare Implications of US Workers' Diverging Location Choices by Skill: 1980–2000." *American Economic Review* 106, no. 3 (2016): 479–524.

Edmiston, Kelly D. "The Net Effects of Large Plant Locations and Expansions on County Employment." *Journal of Regional Science* 44, no. 2 (2004): 289–320.

Eggers, Margaret J., John T. Doyle, Myra J. Lefthand, Sara L. Young, Anita L. Moore-Nall, Larry Kindness, Roberta Other Medicine et al. "Community Engaged Cumulative Risk Assessment of Exposure to Inorganic Well Water Contaminants, Crow Reservation, Montana." *International Journal of Environmental Research and Public Health* 15, no. 1 (2018): 76.

Farrell, Justin, Paul Berne Burow, Kathryn McConnell, Jude Bayham, Kyle Whyte, and Gal Koss. "Effects of Land Dispossession and Forced Migration on Indigenous Peoples in North America." *Science* 374, no. 6567 (2021): eabe4943.

Felstead, Alan, and Golo Henseke. "Assessing the Growth of Remote Working and Its Consequences for Effort, Well-Being and Work-Life Balance." *New Technology, Work and Employment* 32, no. 3 (2017): 195–212.

Freudenburg, William R., and Robert Gramling. "Natural Resources and Rural Poverty: A Closer Look." *Society & Natural Resources* 7, no. 1 (1994): 5–22.

Gallardo, R. Karina, and Johannes Sauer. "Adoption of Labor-Saving Technologies in Agriculture." *Annual Review of Resource Economics* 10 (2018): 185–206.

Gibson, Marcia, Wendy Hearty, and Peter Craig. "The Public Health Effects of Interventions Similar to Basic Income: A Scoping Review." *The Lancet Public Health* 5, no. 3 (2020): e165–76.

Gilbert, Jess, Gwen Sharp, and M. Sindy Felin. "The Loss and Persistence of Black-Owned Farms and Farmland: A Review of the Research Literature and Its Implications." *Journal of Rural Social Sciences* 18, no. 2 (2002): 1–34.

Gill, Bernhard, and Simon Moeller. "GHG Emissions and the Rural-Urban Divide. A Carbon Footprint Analysis Based on the German Official Income and Expenditure Survey." *Ecological Economics* 145 (2018): 160–69.

Gittings, R. Kaj, and Travis Roach. "Who Benefits from a Resource Boom? Evidence from the Marcellus and Utica Shale Plays." *Energy Economics* 87 (2020): 104489.

Givens, Jennifer E., Xiaorui Huang, and Andrew K. Jorgenson. "Ecologically Unequal Exchange: A Theory of Global Environmental Injustice." *Sociology Compass* 13, no. 5 (2019): e12693.

Goetz, Stephan J., Mark D. Partridge, and Heather M. Stephens. "The Economic Status of Rural America in the President Trump Era and Beyond." *Applied Economic Perspectives and Policy* 40, no. 1 (2018): 97–118.

Gray, John. "The Common Agricultural Policy and the Re-Invention of the Rural in the European Community." *Sociologia Ruralis* 40, no. 1 (2000): 30–52.

Guo, Yuanzhi, Yang Zhou, and Yansui Liu. "Targeted Poverty Alleviation and Its Practices in Rural China: A Case Study of Fuping County, Hebei Province." *Journal of Rural Studies* 93 (2022): 430–40.

Halfacree, Keith. "Locality and Social Representation: Space, Discourse and Alternative Definitions of the Rural." *Journal of Rural Studies* 93 (1993): 23–37.

Hargrove, Melissa D. "The Spatial Dimensions of White Supremacy: Reinventing the Lowcountry Plantation in the Gullah/Geechee Nation." *Transforming Anthropology* 28, no. 2 (2020): 139–55.

He, Mingtao, Mathew Smidt, Wenying Li, and Yaoqi Zhang. "Logging Industry in the United States: Employment and Profitability." *Forests* 12, no. 12 (2021): 1720.

Henning-Smith, C. "The Unique Impact of COVID-19 on Older Adults in Rural Areas." *Journal of Aging & Social Policy* 32, no. 4–5 (2020): 396–402.

Hoynes, Hilary, and Jesse Rothstein. "Universal Basic Income in the United States and Advanced Countries." *Annual Review of Economics* 11 (2019): 929–58.

Isserman, Andrew M. "In the National Interest: Defining Rural and Urban Correctly in Research and Public Policy." *International Regional Science Review* 28, no. 4 (2005): 465–99.

Iyengar, Shanto, Yphtach Lelkes, Matthew Levendusky, Neil Malhotra, and Sean J. Westwood. "The Origins and Consequences of Affective Polarization in the United States." *Annual Review of Political Science* 22 (2019): 129–46.

Jensen, Leif, Shannon M. Monnat, John J. Green, Lori M. Hunter, and Martin J. Sliwinski. "Rural Population Health and Aging: Toward a Multilevel and Multidimensional Research Agenda for the 2020s." *American Journal of Public Health* 110, no. 9 (2020): 1328–31.

Johnson, Kenneth M. "Population Redistribution Trends in Nonmetropolitan America, 2010 to 2021." *Rural Sociology* 88, no. 1 (2023): 193–219.

Johnson, Kenneth M., and Daniel T. Lichter. "Diverging Demography: Hispanic and Non-Hispanic Contributions to US Population Redistribution and Diversity." *Population Research and Policy Review* 35 (2016): 705–25.

———. "Metropolitan Reclassification and the Urbanization of Rural America." *Demography* 57, no. 5 (2020): 1929–50.

Jones, Christopher, and Daniel M. Kammen. "Spatial Distribution of US Household Carbon Footprints Reveals Suburbanization Undermines Greenhouse Gas Benefits of Urban Population Density." *Environmental Science & Technology* 48, no. 2 (2014): 895–902.

Jones, Damon, and Ioana Marinescu. "The Labor Market Impacts of Universal and Permanent Cash Transfers: Evidence from the Alaska Permanent Fund." *American Economic Journal: Economic Policy* 14, no. 2 (2022): 315–40.

———. "Universal Cash Transfers and Inflation." *National Tax Journal* 75, no. 3 (2022): 627–53.

Jones, Martin, and Michael Woods. "New Localities." *Regional Studies* 47, no. 1 (2013): 29–42.

Kalleberg, Arne L., Barbara F. Reskin, and Ken Hudson. "Bad Jobs in America: Standard and Nonstandard Employment Relations and Job Quality in the United States." *American Sociological Review* (2000): 256–78.

Kallis, Giorgos, Vasilis Kostakis, Steffen Lange, Barbara Muraca, Susan Paulson, and Matthias Schmelzer. "Research on Degrowth." *Annual Review of Environment and Resources* 43 (2018): 291–316.

Kandel, William, and Emilio A. Parrado. "Restructuring of the US Meat Processing Industry and New Hispanic Migrant Destinations." *Population and Development Review* 31, no. 3 (2005): 447–71.

Kondo, Michelle C., Rebeca Rivera, and Stan Rullman Jr. "Protecting the Idyll but Not the Environment: Second Homes, Amenity Migration and Rural Exclusion in Washington State." *Landscape and Urban Planning* 106, no. 2 (2012): 174–82.

Kozminski, Kate, and Jungho Baek. "Can an Oil-Rich Economy Reduce Its Income Inequality? Empirical Evidence from Alaska's Permanent Fund Dividend." *Energy Economics* 65 (2017): 98–104.

Ku, Leighton, Erin Brantley, and Drishti Pillai. "The Effects of SNAP Work Requirements in Reducing Participation and Benefits from 2013 to 2017." *American Journal of Public Health* 109, no. 10 (2019): 1446–51.

Kvangraven, Ingrid Harvold. "Beyond the Stereotype: Restating the Relevance of the Dependency Research Programme." *Development and Change* 52, no. 1 (2021): 76–112.

Lang, Corey, and Shanna Pearson-Merkowitz. "Partisan Sorting in the United States, 1972–2012: New Evidence from a Dynamic Analysis." *Political Geography* 48 (2015): 119–29.

Layser, Michelle D. "The Unknown Consequences of Place-Based Tax Incentives." *Loyola of Los Angeles Law Review* 56, no. 4 (2023): 1261–89.

Lewis, Joshua, and Edson Severnini. "Short- and Long-Run Impacts of Rural Electrification: Evidence from the Historical Rollout of the US Power Grid." *Journal of Development Economics* 143 (2020): 102412.

Lichter, Daniel T. "Immigration and the New Racial Diversity in Rural America." *Rural Sociology* 77, no. 1 (2012): 3–35.

Lichter, Daniel T., and David L. Brown. "Rural America in an Urban Society: Changing Spatial and Social Boundaries." *Annual Review of Sociology* 37 (2011): 565–92.

Lichter, Daniel T., and Kenneth M. Johnson. "Urbanization and the Paradox of Rural Population Decline: Racial and Regional Variation." *Socius* 9 (2023): 10.1177/23780231221149896.

Liu, Li, Jim Cavaye, and Anoma Ariyawardana. "Supply Chain Responsibility in Agriculture and Its Integration with Rural Community Development: A Review of Issues and Perspectives." *Journal of Rural Studies* 93 (2022): 134–43.

Lobao, Linda, and David S. Kraybill. "The Emerging Roles of County Governments in Metropolitan and Nonmetropolitan Areas: Findings from a National Survey." *Economic Development Quarterly* 19, no. 3 (2005): 245–59.

Lobao, Linda M., Gregory Hooks, and Ann R. Tickamyer. "Poverty and Inequality across Space: Sociological Reflections on the Missing-Middle Subnational Scale." *Cambridge Journal of Regions, Economy and Society* 1, no. 1 (2008): 89–113.

Lobao, Linda, and Katherine Meyer. "The Great Agricultural Transition: Crisis, Change, and Social Consequences of Twentieth Century US Farming." *Annual Review of Sociology* 27, no. 1 (2001): 103–24.

MacDonald, Joanna Petrasek, Sherilee L. Harper, Ashlee Cunsolo Willox, Victoria L. Edge, and Rigolet Inuit Community Government. "A Necessary Voice: Climate Change and Lived Experiences of Youth in Rigolet, Nunatsiavut, Canada." *Global Environmental Change* 23, no. 1 (2013): 360–71.

Malin, Stephanie A., and Peggy Petrzelka. "Community Development among Toxic Tailings: An Interactional Case Study of Extralocal Institutions and Environmental Health." *Community Development* 43, no. 3 (2012): 379–92.

Markowski, Justin H., Jacob Wallace, and Chima D. Ndumele. "After 50 Years, Health Professional Shortage Areas Had No Significant Impact on Mortality or Physician Density: Study Examines Impact of Health Professional Shortage Areas on Physician Density and Mortality in Rural Texas." *Health Affairs* 42, no. 11 (2023): 1507–16.

Massey, Douglas S., and Julia Gelatt. "What Happened to the Wages of Mexican Immigrants? Trends and Interpretations." *Latino Studies* 8 (2010): 328–54.

Massey, Douglas S., and Kerstin Gentsch. "Undocumented Migration to the United States and the Wages of Mexican Immigrants." *International Migration Review* 48, no. 2 (2014): 482–99.

Massey, Douglas S., and Zai Liang. "The Long-Term Consequences of a Temporary Worker Program: The US Bracero Experience." *Population Research and Policy Review* 8 (1989): 199–226.

Melo, Patricia C., Daniel J. Graham, and Robert B. Noland. "A Meta-Analysis of Estimates of Urban Agglomeration Economies." *Regional Science and Urban Economics* 39, no. 3 (2009): 332–42.

Min, Jihoon, Zeke Hausfather, and Qi Feng Lin. "A High-Resolution Statistical Model of Residential Energy End Use Characteristics for the United States." *Journal of Industrial Ecology* 14, no. 5 (2010): 791–807.

Monnat, Shannon M. "Trends in US Working-Age Non-Hispanic White Mortality: Rural–Urban and Within-Rural Differences." *Population Research and Policy Review* 39, no. 5 (2020): 805–34.

Mueller, J. Tom. "Defining Dependence: The Natural Resource Community Typology." *Rural Sociology* 86, no. 2 (2021): 260–300.

———. "The Dual Dependency of Natural-Resource-Rich Labor Markets in Contemporary Society." *Sociological Theory* 39, no. 2 (2021): 81–102.

———. "Natural Resource Dependence and Rural American Economic Prosperity from 2000 to 2015." *Economic Development Quarterly* 36, no. 3 (2022): 160–76.

Mueller, J. Tom, Jesse E. Shircliff, and Marshall Steinbaum. "Market Concentration and Natural Resource Development in Rural America." *Rural Sociology* 87, no. 1 (2022): 68–93.

Mueller, J. Tom, Kathryn McConnell, Paul Berne Burow, Katie Pofahl, Alexis A. Merdjanoff, and Justin Farrell. "Elevated Serious Psychological Distress, Economic Disruption, and the COVID-19 Pandemic in the Nonmetropolitan American West." *Preventive Medicine* 155 (2022): 106919.

———. "Impacts of the COVID-19 Pandemic on Rural America." *Proceedings of the National Academy of Sciences* 118, no. 1 (2021): 10.1073/pnas.2019378118.

Mueller, J. Tom, Matthew M. Brooks, and José D. Pacas. "Cost of Living Variation, Nonmetropolitan America, and Implications for the Supplemental Poverty Measure." *Population Research and Policy Review* 41, no. 4 (2022): 1501–23.

Mueller, J. Tom, and Stephen Gasteyer. "The Widespread and Unjust Drinking Water and Clean Water Crisis in the United States." *Nature Communications* 12, no. 1 (2021): 3544.

Nadler, Janice, and Shari Seidman Diamond. "Eminent Domain and the Psychology of Property Rights: Proposed Use, Subjective Attachment, and Taker Identity." *Journal of Empirical Legal Studies* 5, no. 4 (2008): 713–49.

Nelson, Katherine S., and Tuan D. Nguyen. "Community Assets and Relative Rurality Index: A Multi-Dimensional Measure of Rurality." *Journal of Rural Studies* 97 (2023): 322–33.

Nelson, Lise, and Peter B. Nelson. "The Global Rural: Gentrification and Linked Migration in the Rural USA." *Progress in Human Geography* 35, no. 4 (2011): 441–59.

Neumark, David, Brandon Wall, and Junfu Zhang. "Do Small Businesses Create More Jobs? New Evidence for the United States from the National Establishment Time Series." *Review of Economics and Statistics* 93, no. 1 (2011): 16–29.

Neumark, David, and Timothy Young. "Enterprise Zones, Poverty, and Labor Market Outcomes: Resolving Conflicting Evidence." *Regional Science and Urban Economics* 78 (2019): 103462.

Neuwinger, Malte. "The Revolution Will Not Be Randomized: Universal Basic Income, Randomized Controlled Trials, and 'Evidence-Based' Social Policy." *Global Social Policy* 22, no. 1 (2022): 27–45.

O'Hanlon, Claire E., Ashley M. Kranz, Maria DeYoreo, Ammarah Mahmud, Cheryl L. Damberg, and Justin Timbie. "Access, Quality, and Financial Performance of Rural Hospitals Following Health System Affiliation." *Health Affairs* 38, no. 12 (2019): 2095–104.

Pacas, José D., and David W. Rothwell. "Why Is Poverty Higher in Rural America according to the Supplemental Poverty Measure? An Investigation of the Geographic Adjustment." *Population Research and Policy Review* 39, no. 5 (2020): 941–75.

Palley, Thomas I. "A Theory of Minsky Super-Cycles and Financial Crises." *Contributions to Political Economy* 30, no. 1 (2011): 31–46.

Partridge, Mark D. "The Duelling Models: NEG vs Amenity Migration in Explaining US Engines of Growth." *Papers in Regional Science* 89, no. 3 (2010): 513–36.

Partridge, Mark D., Ray D. Bollman, M. Rose Olfert, and Alessandro Alasia. "Riding the Wave of Urban Growth in the Countryside: Spread, Backwash, or Stagnation?" *Land Economics* 83, no. 2 (2007): 128–52.

Partridge, Mark D., Dan S. Rickman, M. Rose Olfert, and Kamar Ali. "Dwindling US Internal Migration: Evidence of Spatial Equilibrium or Structural Shifts in Local Labor Markets?" *Regional Science and Urban Economics* 42, no. 1–2 (2012): 375–88.

Peluso, Nancy Lee, Craig R. Humphrey, and Louise P. Fortmann. "The Rock, the Beach, and the Tidal Pool: People and Poverty in Natural Resource-Dependent Areas." *Society & Natural Resources* 7, no. 1 (1994): 23–38.

Pender, John, Alexander Marré, and Richard Reeder. "Rural Wealth Creation: Concepts, Measures, and Strategies." *American Journal of Agricultural Economics* 94, no. 2 (2012): 535–41.

Perumal, Andrew, and David Timmons. "Contextual Density and US Automotive CO2 Emissions across the Rural–Urban Continuum." *International Regional Science Review* 40, no. 6 (2017): 590–615.

Peters, David J. "Community Susceptibility and Resiliency to COVID-19 across the Rural-Urban Continuum in the United States." *Journal of Rural Health* 36, no. 3 (2020): 446–56.

Peters, David J., Shannon M. Monnat, Andrew L. Hochstetler, and Mark T. Berg. "The Opioid Hydra: Understanding Overdose Mortality Epidemics and Syndemics across the Rural-Urban Continuum." *Rural Sociology* 85, no. 3 (2020): 589–622.

Petersen, Julia K., Richelle L. Winkler, and Miranda H. Mockrin. "Changes to Rural Migration in the COVID-19 Pandemic." *Rural Sociology* 89, no. 1 (2024): 130–55.

Quisumbing King, Katrina, Spencer D. Wood, Jess Gilbert, and Marilyn Sinkewicz. "Black Agrarianism: The Significance of African American Landownership in the Rural South." *Rural Sociology* 83, no. 3 (2018): 677–99.

Remele, Larry. "'Things as They Should Be': Jeffersonian Idealism and Rural Rebellion in Minnesota and North Dakota, 1910–1920." *Minnesota History* 51, no. 1 (1988): 15–22.

Ruckert, Arne, Chau Huynh, and Ronald Labonté. "Reducing Health Inequities: Is Universal Basic Income the Way Forward?" *Journal of Public Health* 40, no. 1 (2018): 3–7.

Schmitz, Andrew, and Charles B. Moss. "Mechanized Agriculture: Machine Adoption, Farm Size, and Labor Displacement." *AgBioForum* 18, no. 3 (2015).

Schneider, François, Giorgos Kallis, and Joan Martinez-Alier. "Crisis or Opportunity? Economic Degrowth for Social Equity and Ecological Sustainability. Introduction to This Special Issue." *Journal of Cleaner Production* 18, no. 6 (2010): 511–18.

Schoenberger, Erica. "The Spatial Fix Revisited." *Antipode* 36, no. 3 (2004): 427–33.

Schroeder, Jonathan P., and José D. Pacas. "Across the Rural-Urban Universe: Two Continuous Indices of Urbanization for US Census Microdata." *Spatial Demography* 9 (2021): 131–54.

Schuyler, D. M. "Constitutional Problems Confronting the Resettlement Administration." *Journal of Land & Public Utility Economics* 12, no. 3 (1936): 304–6.

Sherman, Jennifer. ""Not Allowed to Inherit My Kingdom": Amenity Development and Social Inequality in the Rural West." *Rural Sociology* 83, no. 1 (2018): 174–207.

Shucksmith, Mark. "Re-Imagining the Rural: From Rural Idyll to Good Countryside." *Journal of Rural Studies* 59 (2018): 163–72.

Siegel, Paul B., Thomas G. Johnson, and Jeffrey Alwang. "Regional Economic Diversity and Diversification." *Growth and Change* 26, no. 2 (1995): 261–84.

Singh, Gopal K., and Mohammad Siahpush. "Widening Rural-Urban Disparities in All-Cause Mortality and Mortality from Major Causes of Death in the USA, 1969–2009." *Journal of Urban Health* 91 (2014): 272–92.

Sklair, Leslie. "Democracy and the Transnational Capitalist Class." *Annals of the American Academy of Political and Social Science* 581, no. 1 (2002): 144–57.

Stephens, Heather M., and Mark D. Partridge. "Do Entrepreneurs Enhance Economic Growth in Lagging Regions?" *Growth and Change* 42, no. 4 (2011): 431–65.

Stephens, Heather M., Mark D. Partridge, and Alessandra Faggian. "Innovation, Entrepreneurship and Economic Growth in Lagging Regions." *Journal of Regional Science* 53, no. 5 (2013): 778–812.

Sun, Yue, and Shannon M. Monnat. "Rural-Urban and Within-Rural Differences in COVID-19 Vaccination Rates." *Journal of Rural Health* 38, no. 4 (2022): 916–22.

Tam Cho, Wendy K., James G. Gimpel, and Iris S. Hui. "Voter Migration and the Geographic Sorting of the American Electorate." *Annals of the Association of American Geographers* 103, no. 4 (2013): 856–70.

Teodoro, Manuel P., Mellie Haider, and David Switzer. "US Environmental Policy Implementation on Tribal Lands: Trust, Neglect, and Justice." *Policy Studies Journal* 46, no. 1 (2018): 37–59.

Tickamyer, Ann R. "Space Matters! Spatial Inequality in Future Sociology." *Contemporary Sociology* 29, no. 6 (2000): 805–13.

Ulrich-Schad, Jessica D., and Hua Qin. "Culture Clash? Predictors of Views on Amenity-Led Development and Community Involvement in Rural Recreation Counties." *Rural Sociology* 83, no. 1 (2018): 81–108.

Urso, Giulia. "Metropolisation and the Challenge of Rural-Urban Dichotomies." *Urban Geography* 42, no. 1 (2021): 37–57.

Van Parijs, Philippe. "The Universal Basic Income: Why Utopian Thinking Matters, and How Sociologists Can Contribute to It." *Politics and Society* 41, no. 2 (2013): 171–82.

Vecchio, Emily Ann, Michelle Dickson, and Ying Zhang. "Indigenous Mental Health and Climate Change: A Systematic Literature Review." *Journal of Climate Change and Health* 6 (2022): 100–121.

Walters, William. "Review Essay: Preemption, Tribal Sovereignty, and Worcester v. Georgia." *Oregon Law Review* 62 (1983): 127.

Wang, Yeli, Monica Palanichamy Kala, and Tazeen H. Jafar. "Factors Associated with Psychological Distress during the Coronavirus Disease 2019 (COVID-19) Pandemic on the Predominantly General Population: A Systematic Review and Meta-Analysis." *PloS One* 15, no. 12 (2020): e0244630.

White, Alan "The Contract State, Program Failure, and Congressional Intent: The Case of the Public Service Loan Forgiveness Program." *UC Irvine Law Review* 11, no. 255 (2020).

Wilkinson, Charles. "The Greatest Good of the Greatest Number in the Long Run: TR, Pinchot, and the Origins of Sustainability in America." *Colorado Natural Resources Energy and Environmental Law Review* 26 (2015): 69.

Wutich, Amber, Wendy Jepson, Carmen Velasco, Anais Roque, Zhining Gu, Michael Hanemann, Mohammed Jobayer Hossain, et al. "Water Insecurity in the Global North: A Review of Experiences in US Colonias Communities along the Mexico Border." *Wiley Interdisciplinary Reviews: Water* 9, no. 4 (2022): e1595.

Yin, Ximing, Jin Chen, and Jizhen Li. "Rural Innovation System: Revitalize the Countryside for a Sustainable Development." *Journal of Rural Studies* 93 (2022): 471–78.

Reports from Nongovernmental Agencies

Allas, Tera, Jukka Maksimainen, James Manyika, and Navjot Singh. *An Experiment to Inform Universal Basic Income*. McKinsey & Company, 2020.

American Society of Civil Engineers. *2021 Report Card for America's Infrastructure*. American Society for Civil Engineers, 2022.

Blumenthal, David, Evan D. Gumas, Arnav Shah, Munira Z. Gunja, and Reginald D. Williams II. "Mirror, Mirror 2024: A Portrait of the Failing U.S. Health System." *The Commonwealth Fund*. September 2024. www.commonwealthfund.org /publications/fund-reports/2024/sep/mirror-mirror-2024.

Buettgens, Matthew. *What Will Happen to Health Care Spending If the American Rescue Plan Act Premium Tax Credits Expire? Estimated Impact on Health Care Provider Revenue*. Urban Institute, 2022.

Committee for a Responsible Federal Budget. *Choices for Financing Medicare for All*. Committee for a Responsible Federal Budget, 2020.

Endeavor Insight. *Rural Entrepreneurship in the United States: A Pillar of Economic Development for Rural Communities*. Endeavor Insight, 2021.

Frey, William H. *Biden's Victory Came from the Suburbs*. Brookings Institution, 2020.

Guettabi, Mouhcine. *What Do We Know about the Effects of the Alaska Permanent Fund Dividend?* Report for the Institute of Social and Economic Research, University of Alaska Anchorage, 2019.

Hasdell, Rebecca. *What We Know about Universal Basic Income: A Cross-Synthesis of Reviews*. Stanford, CA: Basic Income Lab, 2020.

Kerlin, Mike, Neil O'Farrell, Rachel Riley, and Rachel Schaff. *Rural Rising: Economic Development Strategies for America's Heartland*. McKinsey & Company, 2022.

Muro, Mark. *Job Creation on a Budget: Regional Cluster Strategies*. Brookings Institute Commentary, 2011.

Nesbitt, Tykeisa. "Black Land Theft and the Racial Wealth Divide." Inequality.org, 2022.

O'Leary, Sean. *Frackalachia Update: Peak Natural Gas and the Economic Implications for Appalachia*. Johnstown, PA: Ohio River Valley Institute, 2023.

Parker, K., Juliana Menasce Horowitz, and Rachel Minkin. *Americans Are Less Likely than before COVID-19 to Want to Live in Cities, More Likely to Prefer Suburbs*. Pew Research Center Report, 2021.

Penn Wharton Budget Model. *Medicare for All: Comparison of Financing Options*. Penn Wharton Budget Model, 2020.

Perry, Andre M., Marshall Steinbaum, and Carl Romer. *Student Loans, the Racial Wealth Divide, and Why We Need Full Student Debt Cancellation*. Brookings Institution, 2021.

Roller, Zoë, Stephen Gasteyer, Nora Nelson, WenHua Lai, and Marie Carmen Shingne. *Closing the Water Access Gap in the United States: A National Action Plan*. Washington, DC: Dig Deep and US Water Alliance, 2019.

Saad, Lydia. "Country Living Enjoys Renewed Appeal in US." *Gallup Politics* (2021).
———. "More in US See Unions Strengthening and Want It That Way." *Gallup Politics* (2023).
Spiegel, Jake, and Paul Fronstin. "What Employers Say about the Future of Employer-Sponsored Health Insurance." *The Commonwealth Fund Issue Briefs*, January 2023.
Tolbert, Jennifer, Patrick Drake, and Anthony Damico. *Key Facts about the Uninsured Population*. Kaiser Family Foundation, 2023.
WealthWorks. *Wealthworks for Your Region: An Introduction*. The Aspen Institute Community Strategies Group, 2022.
Wigert, Ben, Jim Harter, and Sangeeta Agrawal. "The Future of the Office Has Arrived: It's Hybrid." *Gallup Workplace*, October 2023.

Websites

Assistant Secretary for Planning and Evaluation. "Poverty Guidelines," 2024. https://aspe.hhs.gov/topics/poverty-economic-mobility/poverty-guidelines.
Bahr, Jade. "After 400 Years: It Is Time to Honor the Treaties." Montana Budget and Policy Center, 2021. https://montanabudget.org/post/after-400-years-it-is-time-to-honor-the-treaties.
Bureau of Indian Affairs. "Tribal Leaders Directory: A Resource to Help Connect with Indian Country." US Department of the Interior, Indian Affairs, 2022. www.bia.gov/service/tribal-leaders-directory.
Centers for Medicare and Medicaid Services. "What You Should Know about Provider Networks," 2022. www.cms.gov/marketplace/outreach-and-education/what-you-should-know-provider-networks.pdf.
Montana Department of Commerce. "Come Home Montana Initiative," 2024. https://comehomemontana.com.
Smithsonian. "Nation to Nation: Treaties between the United States and American Indian Nations." National Museum of the American Indian, 2016. https://americanindian.si.edu/nationtonation/.
United Nations. "The 17 Goals," 2024. https://sdgs.un.org/goals.
USDA Economic Research Service. "Farm Labor," 2022. www.ers.usda.gov/topics/farm-economy/farm-labor/.
———. "Rural-Urban Commuting Area Codes," 2023. www.ers.usda.gov/data-products/rural-urban-commuting-area-codes/.
———. "Rural-Urban Continuum Code Documentation," 2024. www.ers.usda.gov/data-products/rural-urban-continuum-codes/documentation/.
USDA Rural Development. "About USDA Rural Development," 2024. www.rd.usda.gov/about-rd.
US Economic Development Association. "About EDA," 2024. https://eda.gov/about/.
US Energy Information Administration. "Wind Explained: Electricity Generation from Wind," 2023. www.eia.gov/energyexplained/wind/electricity-generation-from-wind.php.

Index

Accelerated Path of Rural Destruction, 94–98, 128

administrative concept, 15

affective polarization, 86–87, 94

Affordable Care Act (ACA), 113

agglomeration, 51, 54, 61, 93

aging of population, 5, 36–43, 78, 85, 93, 125, 130

agriculture: financing for, 32–33; labor force in, 7, 30–31, 75; large vs. small producers in, 32; mechanization of, 30–31, 33, 72, 73, 75, 76

Agriculture and Food Research Institute, 64–65

Airbnb, 99

air conditioning, 69

Alaska Permanent Fund, 109–10

American Indians, 2, 7, 9, 24–25; cultures of, 82–84; mistreatment of, 44; poverty among, 25, 76; restitution for, 120–24; tribal lands of, 97

annexation, 79, 91, 98, 127, 129

Appalachia, 21–22, 72, 74

Arizona, 29

Asian Americans, 9, 29

Aspen Institute, 51

backwash effects, 56

balance billing, 113, 114

Barrero, Jose, 98

Bensman, Joseph, 24

Bidadanure, Juliana Uhuru, 106

Biden, Joseph, 102

Billings, Dwight, 21–22

birth rate, 36, 38

Black Americans, 5, 7, 9; endangered cultures of, 83; farmers among, 26; mistreatment of, 27, 44; poverty among, 26–27, 76, 84

Blee, Kathleen, 21–22

bourgeoisie, 56, 59

bracero program, 28–29, 84

Brooks, Matthew, 39

Brown, David, 14

Bucholtz, Shawn, 15

built capital, 50

Bureau of Indian Affairs (BIA), 120

business cycle, 61

Butler County, PA, 7, 80; aging population of, 5

Cahokia, IL, 24

Cai, Christopher, 114

Cajun people, 83

California, 29, 119

capital goods, 50

Cardoso, Fernando H., 55, 57

Carr, Patrick, 78

Census Bureau, 16

census tracts, 16; changeability of, 17

Chesky, Brian, 99, 100

childcare, 70, 101

China, 29, 89, 95

Chinese Exclusion Act (1882), 29–30

class conflict, 58

Clean Water Act (1972), 121–22

climate change, 85, 129, 131

Cloke, Paul, 19, 20

Coates, Ta-Nehisi, 116

Coeur d'Alene Tribe headquarters, 25

collective bargaining, 108

colonialism, 48, 56

colonias, 29

Community Capitals Framework (CCF), 10, 49, 50–51, 54, 66–67, 93

linear models of development, 78, 93, 103; and conventional development approaches, 1, 2, 47, 49–54, 63–67; and dependency school and Marxism, 10, 58–60; and early sociologists, 13; subnational application of, 10, 48, 49; weaknesses of, 48–49, 65

livestock, 75

Lobao, Linda, 45

logging, 34, 72, 74

Louisiana, 83

manifest destiny, 30

manufacturing, 33–34, 36, 73

market concentration, 51

Marx, Karl, 10, 13, 58–59, 68

Marxism, 55, 58–61, 70

McCarran Amendment (1952), 121

McGirt v. Oklahoma (2020), 122

McKinsey & Company, 53, 64

McMichael, Philip, 46

means testing, 107–8

meatpacking, 31, 33, 71

mechanization, 7, 35, 77; of coal mining, 74; in food production, 30–31, 33, 72, 73, 75, 76

Medicaid, 112, 115

Medicare, 107, 112

metropolitan vs. nonmetropolitan areas, 4, 15, 23, 39, 82

Mexican-American War (1846–48), 27

Milbourne, Paul, 19, 20

minimum wages, 108

mining, 34, 72, 74

Minsky, Hyman, 61

Mississippi, 27

mobility, 1, 27, 38, 62; of labor, 10, 51, 67–70, 72, 77, 96, 97, 102, 104, 105, 106, 108, 112–13, 115, 126; and health care, 112–13, 115

monetary policy, 32, 33

Montana, 100

Morrill Act (1862), 123

mortality, 36, 38, 39, 40, 43, 85, 130

Mullen, A. Kirsten, 117–18, 119

Native Americans, 2, 7, 9, 24–25; cultures of, 82–84; mistreatment of, 44; poverty among, 25, 76; restitution for, 120–24; tribal lands of, 97

natural capital, 50

natural decrease in population, 38

natural increase in population, 38

natural resource development: core-periphery model of, 55–56, 73; extractive, 34–35; nonextractive, 35

negative income tax, 110

Nelson, Katherine, 16

neoliberalism, 34, 45, 57, 73

New Jersey, 110

New Mexico, 29, 83

Nguyen, Tuan, 16

North Carolina, 110

off-farm income, 31–32

Office of Management and Budget (OMB), 15, 18, 23

Ohio, 72

oil and gas, 34, 72

Oklahoma, 24, 25, 122

oligopsony, 51

opioid crisis, 1, 40

Oregon, 74

organized labor, 12

out-migration, 1, 10, 36–38, 42, 82

pandemic migration, 42–43

paradox of rural population decline, 39–40, 43, 44

Pennsylvania, 72, 110

peripheral nations, 55–56, 58

Petersen, Julia, 42

physical geography, 21

Pinchot, Gifford, 89

Pittsburgh, PA, 5, 6

place-based definitions, 9, 14, 18–23, 79

political capital, 50

pollution, 121

population density, 9, 22, 24; natural resource dependence and, 34–35; poverty and, 21; urbanization vs.

taxes: negative, 110; for reparations, 119; for single- payer health insurance, 115; for Universal Basic Income, 111
tax incentives, 49–50
tenant farming, 26–27
Texas, 27–28, 29
Thiede, Brian, 33
Tönnies, Ferdinand, 13
Torrens Acts, 27
tourism, 8, 35, 64, 75, 78
Trail of Tears, 24
transnational capitalist class (TCC), 60, 63
Tugwell, Rexford G., 95

underdevelopment, 56–57
unemployment insurance, 69
unequal exchange, 56–57
uneven development, 60, 61–62, 65
United Nations Sustainable Development Goals, 46
universal basic income (UBI), 106–11, 113, 124, 126–30
urbanization, 1–3, 10, 11, 45, 49; carbon emissions and, 87–88; direct vs. indirect, 67, 73; internal, 39, 79
Urso, Giulia, 22
US Department of Agriculture (USDA), 64–65, 66

US Department of Housing and Urban Development (HUD), 66
US Department of Transportation (DOT), 66
US Economic Development Administration (EDA), 65–66, 94
utilitarianism, 89–91, 95

Van Parijs, Philippe, 125
variable capital, 68
Vidich, Arthur, 24
virtue ethics, 89
visas, 28

Wallerstein, Immanuel, 55, 57
Walmart, 53
Washington County, UT, 7; low population density in, 14; poverty in, 3, 5
water rights, 121
WealthWorks, 51
Weber, Max, 13, 92
well-being, 43
West Virginia, 72
white supremacy, 2, 76, 84
wind energy, 74–75, 81
Winters Doctrine, 121
Woods, Michael, 22
Worcester v. Georgia (1832), 122
working class, 59

www.ingramcontent.com/pod-product-compliance
Lightning Source LLC
Chambersburg PA
CBHW030847270326
41928CB00007B/1256